Architecture in Natal

Brian Kearney

Architecture in Natal

from 1824 to 1893

A.A. BALKEMA / CAPE TOWN / 1973

CONTENTS

Foreword

by Dr R.B. Lewcock

Where Europeans spread across the seas they took their national and regional differences with them. In America, Asia and Africa colonies grew up with the peculiar stamp of Spain or Portugal, Holland, France or Britain. A detailed study of the architecture of one colony is often a study of a kind of provincial architecture of the mother country, with a brief time-lag introduced. But the discerning eye can also detect another quality, which runs through the architecture of nearly all the colonies tying them together; common forms, materials and type of construction give some meaning to the ubiquitous term "European colonial."

For the first hundred years of European expansion overseas Portugal and Spain had the world to themselves. Command of the seas then passed successively to Holland, France and Britain, with colonies changing hands so often that many of the major outposts came in turn under the hegemony of each of the major powers. No wonder a certain fusion of architectural ideas took place. The British Empire of the nineteenth century was the inheritor of all that had been developed overseas in the preceding centuries, modified by the latest tastes and fashions from the mother country. And among all the British colonies none had a finer architecture than Natal, which therefore serves as an excellent microcosm of conditions and achievements in the whole Victorian empire.

Before considering the architecture of Natal, a brief outline of the topography and history of the colony is important in order to clarify those few influences which are purely local.

If we imagine ourselves looking down on the site of the capital Pietermaritzburg three centuries ago, we see beneath us an elevated plateau, the Natal midlands, which extends to the west, north and south until it reaches higher rising ground. Due west, and not very far away, is the great barrier of the Drakensberg range soaring to a height of 11,000 feet. Due east the land drops quickly in a series of undulating spurs to the sub-tropical coast bordering the Indian ocean. Into this mild and fertile plateau the dark-skinned African races from the north slowly filtered during the seventeenth & eighteenth centuries, displacing the stone-age hunting and food-gathering Bushmen and their pastoral cousins, the Hottentots, the former retreating up into the mountains and the latter moving off to the south and west.

The Africans live at first in small tribes, each with a central compound for the tribal chief, and scattered clusters of dome-shaped huts made of light frame of bent poles covered with woven mats. Around 1818 military conflict produces the amalgamation of the Zulu kingdom of Shaka, which is centred to the north but at this time controls the whole of the midlands and land much further afield as well.

Soon British settlers can be seen on the shores of the little bay of Port Natal, later D'Urban, as a few independent traders and hunters from the Cape Colony make permanent homes for themselves there. Within twenty years émigré Boers from the northern frontiers of the Cape colony appear over the mountains to the west in a great trek of waggons, men, women and children which bring several thousand Dutch-speaking farmers into the Natal midlands, choosing as centre for themselves an idyllic site for a new city — Pietermaritzburg. But almost immediately conflicts break out with the rival claimants for this excellent farming land. First the Zulus massacre the Boer leaders, and no sooner are they punished with the dreadful slaughter of the Battle of the Blood River than the British settlers at Port Natal, at first friendly, become antagonistic, and open warfare results. Backed up by British troops sent from Grahamstown by sea, the British emerge victorious and the most hardened and dissentient of the Boers trek again — out of the midlands to the highlands of the north west.

Now the progress of the Colony follows a relatively untroubled course. Slowly the lands of the African are wrested from them by clever diplomacy. British settlers arrive in their thousands; whitewashed brick or stone farmhouses appear in the valleys around Pietermaritzburg and steadily spread outwards. Towns grow, Pietermaritzburg around its big market square, Richmond, Greytown, Mooi River, and the twin towns of Port Natal, D'Urban and Point.

A railway line (the first in South Africa) starts in the Point and runs to D'Urban, then slowly works its way up the foothills to Pietermaritzburg and the towns beyond. The port at D'Urban (now spelled Durban) is protected with breakwaters and deepened to allow wharf docking. City halls and theatres rise in all the cities and towns, first in Durban, then in Pietermaritzburg and Greytown.

In 1880 the Zulus rebel, and the resulting war of suppression brings economic prosperity to farmers and merchants alike. A similar boom attends and follows the Boer War, in which fighting is restricted to the northwest of the Colony. By the beginning of the century a second mammoth City Hall is being erected in Durban to replace the first, which is relegated for use as a Post Office; the port, now serving the Transvaal, is one of the biggest in Africa. Everywhere man dominates the landscape, only the Drakensberg ranges remaining untouched and empty. Two aspects of the architecture of Natal deserve special attention in a foreword. First, the relationship of Natal buildings to the earlier and contemporary architecture in the rest of Southern Africa, and secondly there is the case for their preservation.

The Portuguese settled in Moçambique in 1510. By the seventeenth century they had developed a special culture along the East African coast which has fused with it a certain amount that was Arabic and Swahili. There was a trading port at Lourenço Marques, just to the north of Natal, and the Portuguese coastal culture spread down from the north to reach there as well. But a region of tropical marshes and an inhospitable coast discouraged it spreading further south, and in the nineteenth century there was virtually no contact at all between the Dutch and English of Natal and their Portuguese neighbours to the north; and therefore, of course, there was no architectural influence.

The Dutch settled first at Cape Town in 1652. By the second half of the eighteenth century they had spread far to the east and north, but zones well settled by African tribes effectively separated them from Natal. The first Dutch architecture in Natal, introduced by the trekkers in the late eighteen-thirties, was already adulterated with British taste.

The traditional Cape house of the Dutch had been a house with a large central entrance — living hall flanked by the main private rooms on either side. Externally it was always symmetrical, the centre generally emphasized by a gable or raised sweep of eaves if the roof were thatched, or by a triangular pediment or stilted vertical "gable" (a "dakkamer") if it were flat-roofed. At the height of the rococo period some of the flat roofed houses were designed with

straight or undulating parapets with only a minor central emphasis. All were plastered and most were whitewashed externally; woodwork in windows and doors was invariably painted green.

The arrival of the British at Cape Town in 1795 was a traumatic experience for the Cape with many turbulent effects on the national culture. One of the results easily observable on many of the old houses was the replacement of the old Dutch fan-light over the front doors by a new fan-light of English design. The fan-light had been one of the main ornaments of the Cape eighteenth century house and by changing it the house's appearance was easily transformed.

In their attempts to keep pace with the new British fashions the Cape citizens were also tempted to alter the Dutch gables, but found them less easy to deal with, as gables had no place at all in late eighteenth century British patternbooks; but even the gables were occasionally given severer lines. At any rate the windows could be altered (and frequently were) from the Dutch vertical double-casements in which only the bottom sash opened, to the recessed, double-sliding-sash type of England. These windows had the characteristic Adam proportioning of late Georgian architecture in Britain — and were just as prone to let the wind whistle into the houses through the loose sashes.

Fortunately not all the effects of the importation of British ideas were detrimental to the old. In the towns a new way of living was introduced, and houses to match it. Well lit rooms with ceilings replaced dark unceiled interiors, elegant fireplaces were built with coal grates where there were few before, lighter furniture was introduced, and central curving staircases of magnificent craftsmanship in polished furniture woods made their appearance. Externally the undulating parapet and *dakkamer* disappeared; facades became simpler and more carefully proportioned; and imported stone (in parapets) or subtle rubbed facebrick replaced plaster. The Regency town house became one of Britain's nobler contributions to South Africa's heritage.

In the following years the Regency houses spread to the country districts, where the box-like, double-storey buildings often replaced the old gable houses, repeating a trend that had started long before during Dutch times.

Meanwhile the 1820 Settlers had transformed the eastern part of the Cape colony, their cob or stone cottages and town houses re-creating rural Britain in Africa. Many of the Settlers were craftsmen, and spread British architectural practice far afield. Others, less fortunate, stayed on the land, often as amateur farmers — and as amateur builders as well. Their first houses fell down or were flooded out, and others had to be built on higher sites and in more permanent materials. They had no cheap labour. Their articles of immigration, at first, forbade it. Later, jobbing Natives infiltrated into the Colony only to find temptations to plunder which led to raids and eventually to the Frontier War of 1835. The damage to the Settlers was immense. Over 450 houses were burned. Their determination to avoid a repetition of such a holocaust led to the appearance of a new building type at the Cape — a fortified house.

Generally, two fort-like towers flanked a single-storey house, which was equipped with heavy iron-bound shutters and an enclosed yard. In times of real emergency all the family and their dependants could take refuge in the towers, light signal beacons on their roof platforms, and easily defend themselves until help arrived. Strangely enough we know of few cases of them ever being used in this way. Courage apparently failed and the families fled.

Eventual security produced the farmhouse that opened up to the land. Repeating the pattern of Lord Charles Somerset's houses, "Newlands" and "Marine Villa", in Cape Town, verandas (soon to be roofed in cheap corrugated iron) encircled the house, ensuring that there was always a cool place somewhere on a hot summer's day. This type, found all over the country, spread quite early into humid Natal, where scarcely a building diverged from it until the 1890's.

The Gothic revival style suddenly blossomed in the 1820's as the various branches of the church competed to be first to bring it to the Cape. Gothic thus made a remarkably early appearance in South Africa. It overwhelmed all opposition — and alas, is still with us. Many pleasant Anglican churches in the style were conceived by Sophia Gray, wife of the Bishop of Cape Town, perhaps the best being St. Peter's, Pietermaritzburg.

Collegiate Gothic was also a great fashion, as exemplified in the Diocesan College, Cape Town, Grey College, Port Elizabeth; and Pietermaritzburg College. But it had to compete with some fine examples in other styles, as, for example, the Egyptian in the South African College, Cape Town and the Paarl Gymnasium; and the Byzantine-Romanesque in Kingswood College, Grahamstown.

The era of Victorian town hall building was inaugurated with the erection of Port Elizabeth's Town Hall in the sixties. Durban's Town Hall (now the Post Office) was built from 1881-1884. It was designed by Phillip Dudgeon, by far the most sensitive architect of the period. Dudgeon also showed later architects how extremely beautiful commercial architecture might become in the right hands. His masterpiece — a bank building as befitted that most capitalistic age — is situated in Pietermaritzburg, and is one of the finest pieces of architecture in South Africa.

Towards the end of the nineteenth century a great spate of building set in, stimulated by the diamond discoveries at Kimberley and the later gold rush to Johannesburg. Most of the building was in the revival styles, with a new fashion for Flemish brickwork taking its place alongside Gothic and Roman. With the Flemish revival came the return of the gable, not directly from the old buildings in the Cape, nor even from Holland and Belgium, but from the fashionable architecture of London.

The simpler buildings of the diamond and gold rush towns were erected with corrugated iron walls as well as roofs. Corrugated iron was mass-produced in Britain, and it was imported in large quantities as the cheapest and most easily transportable building material. Most of the structures erected in it were undesigned, often ugly. But the use of such an industrial material had the enormous advantage that building costs could be reduced to a remarkable extent.

British influence in nineteenth century South Africa reached its culmination in the work of a distinguished professional architect, Sir Herbert Baker. He consolidated the Empire style in buildings at a time when it was already beginning to be an anachronism, but also responded so instinctively to the Africa he had grown to love that his South African architecture far surpassed the rest of his work. And we must never forget it was he who led the campaign for recognition of the beauty of the eighteenth century farmhouses, until then largely neglected. In his own work he attempted to equal in stone and teak the appeal of the Cape materials while evolving an original architectural vocabulary based on his observations in Greece and Rome. Although it is not often recognized, his achievements and the standards he set continue to exert a powerful influence on the whole architecture of South Africa.

In Britain even the most Philistine of town councils will generally show some respect for mediaeval buildings; if they are progressive they may be concerned to preserve Georgian work. But in Natal there are few buildings earlier than 1850, so that Victorian becomes as worthy of consideration as mediaeval in England. Anything earlier seems ancient.

A concern for elegance can usually be detected in this old architecture, even in the case of buildings whose purpose was strictly practical; there is an underlying harmony of proportions, a rhythm, an interplay of line and colour, a natural affinity with site and environment which has always given pleasure — though that increases as the buildings become mellowed with age and rarity. As Lorca put it: "Time makes great architecture'"

For example consider the settler cottages. They are always related to their surroundings so that they become part of the landscape. The materials are largely those of the countryside to which they belong, with an added naturalness due to weathering. Above all they have that quality of suitability, of fitness for the purpose they were built to serve.

As we find our pleasure in the qualities of these old buildings increasing, we become aware of the dangers which threaten them. Decay and disintegration, parasites and mould, heat and damp.

But the most dangerous enemy is man himself — not only the vandal, the iconoclast, the crude "restorer"; the town planner, the engineer, the builder, are all just as much to be feared when they think only in terms of practical efficiency and give in to the mammon-ridden pressures of their age — profit-making, the explosive growth of cities, the chaotic spread of suburbs and industrialized areas.

At all costs a compromise must be found between the heritage of the past and the requirements of the future. We now have the wealth and the required technical means to protect, repair, restore and, if necessary, transfer any monument.

Let us hope that we do not lose the irreplaceable qualities of our old architecture for the sake of a future which will turn out to be correspondingly barren.

Introduction

In 1837 the young Victoria succeeded to the throne of England. In that same year a large number of dissatisfied Dutch colonists, who had left the Cape and trekked through the country to the North of the Colony, crossed over the Drakensberg and entered the well-watered plains of a country on the south-east coast of Africa, already known to sailors and explorers as Natal. This territory was to become the first British Colony to be proclaimed as such by Victoria. After the arrival of thousands of British immigrants it was also to become the most English of the states and colonies in Southern Africa, and can thus be regarded as a truly 'Victorian' colony.

Are there any other characteristics of the period of sixty-five years of Victoria's reign besides the fact that it was Victorian? This was the age of reform, progress and upheaval and the world of 1900 was quite different from that of 1837. With typical nineteenth-century selfconsciousness, Charles Eastlake thought that "... no landmarks exist to indicate the several roads by which we have arrived, or hope to arrive at aesthetic greatness in the reign of Victoria ... Our modern geniuses have struck out new paths for themselves, which here and there cross, indeed, the course of their predecessors, but rarely coincide with it. These are so diverse in their direction that they may be said to have formed a sort of labyrinth which by and by it will be difficult to survey". (I)

In eighteenth century British cultural life, literature, dress, furniture, sculpture, painting, and landscape gardening formed one connected and integrated whole. The dominant characteristics of Georgian architecture were order, restraint and a spirit of neighbourly responsibility. (Fig. a)

Towards the end of the eighteenth century, however, this stability began to be undermined by a growing restlessness which reached its peak by about 1830. Established principles were discarded and their place was taken by a new sense of individualism. The popularity of the romantic novel opened up ways of thought about man's environment which had never before been so widely realised. Men began to criticise their surroundings and artifacts in literary rather than aesthetic terms. These Romantics imitated in their buildings and everyday lives what they read in novels and often resorted to extremely tenuous analogies for the justification of such imitations.

A growing awareness of architectural history, and the widening of architectural opportunities as a direct result of the Industrial Revolution, stimulated a questioning of the fundamentals of architecture. Judgements of architectural design began to be made on a moral basis by those who set out to propagate the reform of the man-made world in their anti-machine dreams. Hence the climate of architectural thought that gave rise to such epithets as 'chaste' and 'correct'.

The most significant architectural movements of the early nineteenth century were the Picturesque and Antiquarianism. Different styles of building were considered more or less appropriate for particular landscapes and, in the attempt to create some kind of congruity between a building and its setting, the silhouette and the arrangement of the forms were carefully composed against the desired background. Thus emerged the 'Picturesque' point of view. The desire for irregularity of space, form and surface prevailed over the earlier ideals of Georgian and Regency architecture with their crisp order and disciplined geometry. Through the experiments of landscape gardeners and architects, physical congruity between the house and the garden appeared in the form of rustic building materials, tentlike roofs, verandas, French casements, trellis's and conservatories. (Fig. b.) Even windows, which already related the interior of a building to its surroundings, were shaped into bows and bays to increase the possibilities of deliberate viewpoints, in addition to their plastic effects. A Bostonian of the late eighteen-eighties has summed up the Picturesque: "It relies upon the variety and vivacity of rapidly changing effects from different points of view, on sharp contrasts, and the piquancy of small detached masses; on quick transitions of form, colour and material. It seldom inspires homage but often compels applause.

It is not a thing before which to be silent, but rather excite the "ohs!" and "ahs!" which denote a pleasing but not too subtle titillation of the senses." (sic) (2)

Some of the early popularity of the revived Gothic style can be attributed to the greater possibilities for irregularity of form and decoration of surface, inherent in the Gothic style. Under the banner of its greatest apostle, Augustus Welby Pugin, however, the Gothic revival was to become theoretically anti-picturesque. Although Gothic had never really been discarded as a building form in certain parts of England, by the middle of the eighteenth century, men of fashion had discovered it to be one of several fabrics suitable for their architectural playthings. When Pugin began to practise as an architect in 1835, Gothic was a popular alternative to Greek for churches mainly because of the the supposedly lower costs. Most of this Gothic, however, was coarse and inaccurate.

Pugin attempted to design in the true spirit of the Gothic style, using archeologically correct form and details. He presented to the world his dream of a revival of Christian architecture, (Fig. c.) a revival which he considered inseparable from a complete revival of medieval life. His ideas on the relationship between medieval church planning and liturgy were continued by the Oxford movement and later by the Ecclesiological Society through their voice, the Ecclesiologist, and together, these two propagated and stimulated a world-wide revival of Gothic architecture. (3)

In England the nationalist cause for the revival was founded on the argument that the style was more indigenous to Northern Europe than the classical style. The use of revived Gothic in Natal, however, and in many other areas in the colonies indicates the fallacious nature of the nationalist argument..However, the persistent striving for a new Victorian architecture, fertilised by the emergence of new building materials and even new building types, was satisfied by Gothic until the style fell into disrepute. This resulted from an unsound formalism which emphasised the external appearances of buildings to the detriment of their internal organization and spatial development.

Only towards the end of the century was there a conscious desire for a Natal style of architecture. Wallace Paton said that: "When the discerning and articulate critic of architecture, who has yet to come, visits us in Natal, his first remark will be that there is no Natal architecture. Occasional efforts interesting, naive, even scholarly, can be found, but they might have been produced anywhere else. Our public buildings, in Pietermaritzburg and Durban, might be the public buildings of Vancouver or Adelaide. The travelled critic of good memory for mediocrity might

remember seeing the elder brothers of our civic prides, the City Halls of Durban and Maritzburg, in the late-Victorian neo-Italian of Belfast, or the mid-Victorian cum Queen Anne, — now happily defunct — of Nottingham", and later: "In any case, the people want verandas, and they will have them; they sit on them in the daytime and they sleep on them at night. The problem our architects have to solve is the problem of the veranda, and its final evolution, as a thing of beauty, not as a flimsy excresence of wooden or cast-iron poles, will mean that we have at last a distinctive national or should it be provincial, style, which we can call our own." (4)

While Gothic (and later Italian Gothic) was the style most favoured for churches, houses and schools, Romantic Classicism in either Greek or Roman was thought to be more appropriate for civic and public architecture. The revived Italian Renaissance Architecture (Fig. d) with its rich plasticity and the wide adaptability of its modular order, was found most suitable for those buildings whose heterogeneous functions could not easily be organized within the straight-jacket perfection of a Greek or Roman temple form. Nineteenth-century eclecticism went so far as to allow various styles to be used together in the same building; thus providing further in the mixed style even easier solutions for the designs of the many new building types. (Fig. 3.)

Towards the end of the nineteenth century, there developed in England a system of architectural design whereby tectonic elements were selected from various sources and assembled into a new and long-sought after style. This attitude allowed such revivals as "Queen Anne", popular in Britain during the 'seventies and 'eighties. (Fig. f.) As in the case of most colonies, however, the communication of new ideas from the mother country was a slow process and the movement was only felt in Natal during the last years of the century.

The most peculiar aspect of Historicism in the nineteenth century was that revivals of several styles took place simultaneously without any particular one being predominant. Stirred on by the indecisiveness of theorists and the controversy-hungry public, the threads of continuity in these styles can only be found in the desire to decorate.

As a reaction to earlier over-ornamentation and in the true traditions of Victorian reform, the Arts and Crafts movement in Britain and the Colonial Revival in America were paralled in Natal by a sudden return to the simplicity of the colonial architecture of the 'forties and 'fifties. At the turn of the century too, there flowered that most enigmatic of styles 'Art Nouveau' whose dynamic influence was felt in Natal outside the period of this study.

It is significant that the major contribution of architecture in Natal before 1893, was in the development of the free-standing veranda-house, for there has been no other period of English history when the home has been such an important element of life than the Victorian era. Unfortunately, this veranda tradition has had little influence on contemporary attitudes to domestic architecture in South Africa since 1925. The contemporary domestic 'box', for example, whether speculative or otherwise, indicates in its organization and use of materials an almost total lack of concern for the most basic element of the environment, climate.

Perhaps this concern for the environment is the most important lesson of the colonial architecture of Natal and it is hoped that the following chapters may lead to a greater realization of the need for an architecture suited to the climate of Natal.

1   HINTS ON HOUSEHOLD TASTE. C. Eastlake.
2   A letter from Boston. AMERICAN ARCHITECT AND BUILDING NEWS.
    XII No 643 21st. April 1888.
3   See Reference 33, Chapter 5.
4   THE PROGRESS OF ARCHITECTURE.
    W. Paton. F.R.I.B.A. A CENTURY OF PROGRESS IN NATAL

AUTHOR'S NOTE

This work was submitted to the University of Natal in 1968 in partial fulfilment for the degree of Master of Architecture. Readers are referred generally to this thesis for further detail as the number of illustrations have been reduced by some 150 for the present publication. Copies of the thesis are to be found in both the Pietermaritzburg and Durban centres of the University of Natal.

Up to this time no documentation of architecture in Natal has been attempted, though certain historians, particularly Professor A.F. Hattersley (refer Bibliography) have, within the wider view of life in nineteenth-century Natal, given great attention to the architecture of the early British settlers.

This study commences with the background of the earliest settlements and continues through seventy years of Natal history up to the establishment of responsible Government in 1893. For various reasons Natal cannot be viewed as a separate architectural region after this date, but rather as an integral part of South Africa, although its political integration only occurred some twenty years later.

SPELLING/ABBREVIATIONS

Original spellings and punctuation have been retained in all quotes. To prevent confusion however the word VERANDA, has been spelt as such throughout, though the spelling VERANDAH was also used during the nineteenth century.

DBN.	Durban.
PMB.	Pietermaritzburg.
L.H.M.	Local History Museum, Durban.
O.H.M.	Old House Museum, Durban.
K.C.M.	Killie Campbell Museum, Durban.
N.MUS.	Natal Museum, Pietermaritzburg.
OGILVIE COLL.	The Ogilvie collection of photographs of early Pietermaritzburg.
DON.LIB.	The Don Library, Municipal Library, Durban.
N.ARC.	The Natal Archives, Pietermaritzburg.

THE ILLUSTRATIONS

These are grouped in the latter part of the book, following page 82, and are referred to in the text within round brackets. The headline of each text page carries a reference to the figure numbers of those illustrations that relate to the double page. Where no source for the illustrations and drawings is indicated, these are the work of the author.

ACKNOWLEDGEMENTS

Dr R.B. Lewcock for his motivation, wisdom and inspiration.

Professor L.T. Croft, School of Architecture, University of Natal. Dr. R.B. Lewcock.

An anonymous donor and the Ernest Oppenheimer Memorial Trust who made it possible for me to see some of the Victorian architecture in Britain and to undertake research in England.

The Town and Regional Planning Commission, Natal Provincial Administration, who provided me with a grant to cover expenses incurred while travelling in Natal.

My wife, Rae for her patient and obliging assistance and her discerning comment.

J. and M. Kearney for their correction of draft.

Mrs. Ogilvie for her loan of the valuable Ogilvie photograph collection of early Pietermaritzburg.

Mrs. D. Strutt and her staff at the Local History Museum, and the Old House Museum in Durban.

The Killie Campbell Museum, Durban. The Don Library, Durban. The Natal Society Library, Pietermaritzburg. The Natal University Library, Pietermaritzburg and Durban. The Natal Archives, Pietermaritzburg. The Royal Commonwealth Society Library, London. The R.I.B.A. Library, London. The Natal Museum, Pietermaritzburg. The National Library of Ireland, Dublin. The City of Bath, Public Library, Bath, England. The Town Clerk's Archives, Durban. The Archdiocesan Archives, Archbishop's House, Durban, for the loan of the Bishop Allard and Bishop Jolivet journals. The City Engineer's Dept. Pietermaritzburg. The Town Engineer's Dept. Estcourt. Peter Newman and Kenneth Henry of the photographic dept. of the School of Architecture. Mr John Clark and Miss Shelagh O'Byrne. Prof. A.F. Hattersley.

P A R T O N E

Chapter 1

Early settlements in Natal

1824 — 1837

"Almighty" he said, "I have never in my life seen such a fine place. I shall never again reside in the Cape colony if the English Government make this a drostdy".[1]
(A remark made by a Cape colonist, Barry, when he first realised the beauty and fertility of the 'Garden Colony' of the future.)

The coast of Natal was discovered by Vasco da Gama on Christmas day, 1497. The only European visitors to Natal between 1497 and 1800 were the crews and passengers of shipwrecked vessels, and no permanent settlements were established.[2] It is quite likely, however, that some shipwrecked seafarers did erect temporary shelters.[3]

Survivors of one such shipwreck described the only inhabitants of Natal as living in "huts made of sticks and rushes, roofed like the haystacks of Holland".[4] The friendliness of the local inhabitants, prompted the Dutch East India Company to send the 'Noord' in January, 1669 to acquire the Port of Natal, but no occupation actually followed.

In 1823, two ex-officers of the British Royal Navy, Farewell and King, in the troopship Salisbury, entered Port Natal. During their stay, King charted the bay. As a result of their visit, Farewell decided to establish a trading post at Port Natal and, finding support in Cape Town from J.R. Thompson and Cr collected together a party of twenty-six who returned to Natal in May 1824.[5]

Their first tasks were directed at erecting a protected camp.[6] "On the following morning the mechanics, assisted by the crew of the vessel, were set to work to cut timber and build a 12 foot square house of wattle and daub" (11 March 1824).[7]

Thereafter Farewell and Fynn received from Shaka a 'cession' of Port Natal and environs and, returning to the Port on the 27th August, Farewell took possession in the name of Great Britain. Before the end of the year, however, twenty of the party had returned to Cape Town.

The little group of traders eventually attracted refugee Zulus escaping the wrath of the Zulu king, Shaka. The members of the party settled around the bay at some distance from each other, each as the chief of a small tribe of the Zulus. (Fig. 1) Farewell's house was a barn of wattle and daub with a thatched roof and a reed door, but without windows. Nathaniel Isaacs, who arrived in 1825, said of this house; "It was not remarkable either for the elegance of its structure or the capacity of its interior".[7A] Cane and Ogle had even more primitive dwellings made of reeds, which as Isaacs said, "resembled a house roof placed on the ground, with one gable-end missing to provide an entrance". [8] Halstead seems to have had no permanent abode at all.[9] (Fig. 2)

"Opposite Mr. Farewell's house was a native hut, in the shape of a beehive, about twenty-one feet in circumference, and six feet high, built of small sticks and supported by a pole in the centre. It was thatched with grass, and had an aperture of about eighteen inches square".[9A]

In 1826, Farewell commenced the building of a fort at the Point. July 1826: "Mr Farewell's fort and house are by this time finished. Within the fort he keeps his cattle, of which he has a good stock. It is of a triangular form sixty feet by twenty, and has six tolerably good rooms..."[10] and "Farewell was at this time building a fort a quarter of a mile nearer the harbour entrance, which was to be a more imposing

1   Sir Andrew Smith. Kirby p106
2   South East Africa, 1488 — 1530. E.Axelson. p37
3   Like the crew of the 'Good Hope', an English ship, which was driven ashore at Port Natal on May 6 1685. They made their home on the Bluff and travelled far inland.
     The cradle days of Natal. H.G. Mackeurtan. Chap IV
4   A history of Natal. E.H. Brookes and C. de B. Webb. p5
5   Diary of Henry Francis Fynn. H.F. Fynn.
6   op cit, Fynn. p60
7   One of the original Farewell settlers was a carpenter.
     The cradle days of Natal. H.G. Mackeurtan. p129
7a   op cit, Mackeurtan. p129
8   Travels and adventures in Eastern Africa. N. Isaacs.
9   Known to the Eastern Cape (1820) settlers as 'hartebeest huts'. Early nineteenth century architecture in South Africa. R.B. Lewcock.
9a   op cit, Mackeurtan. p129
10   Travels (1827). G. Thompson. Appendix No V.

edifice. It was to be triangular and to contain a house and storeroom. It was also to be palisaded and protected by a moat, while three pounder cannonades were to adorn the corners."[11] This fort was never completed. The site was near what is known as Cato's Creek.

There is a long standing tradition that Shaka, as his life was ebbing away, called out to Dingane and Mhlangana; "You kill me, thinking you will rule, but the swallows will do that", meaning the white people, because they built houses of mud.[12] Dingane who succeeded Shaka, sent an impi to the Port to destroy Cane's huts and possessions in 1830. By 1831 Fynn, Ogle and Halstead were the only survivors of the original settlement.

During the 1830's several of the settlers from the Albany district of the Cape Colony made trading expeditions to Natal. Dr Andrew Smith also made an expedition to Natal which reached Dingane's kraal in 1832. He recorded with great interest the presence in the kraal of six rectangular sheds, "consisting of thatched roofs with a single hip supported on poles, in which the assagais and shields of the regiment were stored".[13]

On returning to the Cape he wrote in the Grahamstown Journal of June 15 1832; "Here then it would appear, is a tract of country decidedly superior to any part of the Colony, capable of maintaining thousands of the crowded and suffering population of Great Britain and Ireland, and possessing in Port Natal a sufficient outlet for productions which might be colonised not only without infringement of the rights of Native tribes, but to the benefit of all those who surround it. Notwithstanding all these favourable circumstances, together with the perfect salubrity of the climate..."[14]

In January, 1835 Capt A.F. Gardiner arrived in Natal and established a mission station on an eminence above the bay which he called the Berea.[15]

In his 'Journey to the Zoolu Country in South Africa' he described the settlement at the Port; "With the exception of Mr Collis' house, (Fig. 2) constructed of reeds and mud, there was not a single dwelling of the European fashion in the whole settlement on my first arrival; and to a stranger, unaquainted with the localities, the whole had a most wild and deserted appearance."[16] The reason why the place presented such an appearance was that most of the huts of the residents were carefully concealed in the thicket, presumably for fear of Dingane's impis repeating their attacks of 1830.[17]

On Tuesday June 23 1835 a meeting was held in one of Mr Berkin's huts for the purpose of selecting the site for a town: "being the winter season, it was a sort of reunion of hunters who, tired of chasing sea-cow and buffalo, were now sighing for town houses and domestic cheer".[18] The hunters re-

solved to lay out a town, and to name it D'Urban in honour of the governor of the Cape Colony. Accordingly they selected a site a little farther up the shore of the inlet than the site of the later town. The regulations which they adopted included provision for a church and a hospital and indicate that the little community was intelligent and progressive.[19]

Each of the existing inhabitants was entitled to one building plot, "Every person taking an allotment, does engage to erect a house, conformable to the plan now adopted, within eighteen months from this date; the street front of which is not to be less than twenty-four feet within its walls; the breadth not less than ten feet; and the walls not less than eight feet high".[19]

The settlement was to be named Victoria. No more grass and reed huts were to be permitted except for servants' quarters and funds were set up for clearing the bush and establishing a town and for the erection of a church. A free school was also to be built. Little came of these decisions though Sir Benjamin D'Urban supported them, as the Secretary of State for the Colonies felt himself precluded from offering any encouragement to the project.[20]

In 1834 six men were instructed by the American Board of Commissioners for Foreign Missions to commence work in Africa. Of these, Adams, Champion and Grout were to work among the Zulus. On their arrival at Durban in 1835 they took up their abode in the house built by a Mr Berkin.[21] The house was a structure of wattle and daub, thatched with grass and reeds, and surrounded by a veranda.[22]

Up to this time most of the Europeans living in Natal were traders who lived close to the bay for short intervals of the year and spent long periods on hunting expeditions. There was, however, a Mr Pickman who the missionaries visited on the Umlazi River, some seven miles south of the port. Here he "lived in a reed house overlooking a lagoon, which he had christened Lake Washington, in honor of the hero of America".[23] Pickman was neither a trader nor a hunter but grew corn and vegetables.

Adams established his mission station on the Umlazi River. (Fig. 3) A correspondent to the Grahamstown Journal in 1836 reviewed his efforts thus: "Considering the short time he had been a resident of the country, the improvements made by him were very surprising. His own dwelling house, a very comfortable building furnished with a good library, and several others of a minor character, were finished".[24] Later Dr and Mrs Adams were joined by other missionaries from Mosega. He had ready for them a cottage of two rooms, each room having a small timber shuttered window. The floor was of earth and pronged sticks driven into the floor with cross sticks, and reeds nailed to them formed the

Figure 3 3

bedsteads. The efforts of Adams were probably considerably aided by Hopkins, a carpenter who had accompanied the missionaries to Natal.[25]

Grout and Champion ventured further north into Zululand and built a primitive dwelling of three rooms, each ten feet by eight feet. The floors were made of antheap, pounded hard; the walls were built of mud and stone; the roof was thatched and the ceiling of wagon canvas; the doors and windows were made of reeds and mats. It seems that the building leaked very badly.

By this time some of the 1820 Settlers who had made expeditions to Natal in 1831 and 1832 returned to Port Natal and by 1835 there were about thirty traders residing at the Port. One of them, an Englishman Robert Dunn, had a house on the hills overlooking the Umbilo River and the Bay, which was described at the time as "magnificient", and possessing a "splendid garden". Elizabeth Feilden described it in 1850: "The property is beautifully situated, but the house, a long, low, dark place is choked with trees".[26]

A resident of Port Natal, writing to the Grahamstown journal on the 7th of August 1837, advised would-be immigrants to Natal to rely on their own resources for the comforts and clothing required by their families for at least a year; they were to provide themselves with all tools and equipment and could expect to build their homes with their own hands.[27]

11 Cradle days of Natal. G. Mackeurtan. p129

12 Historic Natal and Zululand. H. Lugg.
13 Andrew Smith. Kirby. p104
14 op cit, p107
As a result of Andrew Smith's descriptions of Natal, one hundred and ninety Cape Town inhabitants petitioned King William IV in favour of a British occupation of Natal. The Secretary of State for the colonies rejected the petition.
15 Gardiner visited Dingane and showed him a view of the Brighton Pavilion. At first he expressed his desire for a similar building but later decided that he would send some of his hut builders to England to build a hut for the King.
Cradle days of Natal. G. Mackeurtan. p178
16 Narrative of a journey to the Zoolu country ... A.F. Gardiner. p84
17 "The other inhabitants resided, like their native vassals, in the more modest beehive-shaped straw huts".
Natal, the land and its story. G. Russell. p150
18 op cit, Gardiner. p84
19 A history of South Africa (1834–1854). Theal. p129
19a op cit, Gardiner. p84
20 Annals of Natal. (Vol.1) Bird. p315
21 A Polish refugee who had accompanied Gardiner to Natal.
op cit, Mackeurtan. p182
22 op cit, Mackeurtan. p306
23 op cit, Mackeurtan. p307
24 op cit, Mackeurtan. p312
25 Natal memories. Buchanan. p44
26 To the shores of Natal. Bulpin. p165
27 Grahamstown journal. August 7 1837

Chapter 2

The Republic of Natalia

1837 – 1842

"In March, 1839, a site for a town was selected, and erven or building allotments were laid out. It was named Pietermaritzburg, after Pieter Retief and Gerit Maritz, and was to be the capital of the republic. The situation was particularly fine, and the founders carried out their ideal of a perfect place of abode for all who were not on farms..."[1]

"Sixteen Boer wagons with forty shots"[1A] had visited Port Natal in 1834, returning to the Cape Colony with a glowing report of the well-watered soil and luxuriant pasturage. Nothing came of this, however, until October 1837 when Piet Retief arrived at Port Natal, to be followed by the Trekkers themselves in November of the same year. They had come to Natal in the belief that this was the paradise they had been searching for, provided that they could obtain the goodwill of Dingane. However, they were to remain living laagered in wagons for many months before a permanent settlement could safely be made.[2]

The first recorded settlement was at Pietermaritzburg.[3] There had been a small laager there on the Bushmansrand in July 1838, but only on the 23rd October was the decision made to establish a town. Piet Greyling received instructions to lay it out. After the Battle of Blood River in December, 1838 the main body of Trekkers occupied the site of the new town.

In February, 1839 the Volksraad decreed that the proprieter of an erf (approximately an acre in extent) should be bound to sow and plant the erf within the term of two months and to surround it with a turf wall or a palisade. All dwelling houses were to be built in front of the erf and in a straight line, as would be regulated by a qualified person to be duly appointed. The layout of the town made

provision for 500 allotments. In June, they resolved that all temporary houses were to be replaced within three years by permanent houses.[4] The fortified laager was retained, however, until Dingane's power had been broken (February, 1840).[5] The only substantial house built in Pietermaritzburg before 1840 seems to have been that of H. Pretorius which stood in Longmarket Street. This may have been built in 1838 before the Battle of Blood River.[6]

The French naturalist Delagorgue, described Pietermaritzburg in 1839 as a mere collection of crude huts made of reeds and plastered with cow dung, infested with rats and barking dogs and harassed at night by leopards. Andries Pretorius wrote of it: "a large pleasant and well-watered town,[7] Pietermaritzburg begins daily to raise its head above the surrounding hillocks; 300 beautiful erven have already been given out, surveyed and partly planted. This town ... has a picturesque site, and combines all the advantages of nature, as well as of local situation, making so fine a prospect that I know nothing similar to it in the colony".[8]

The arrival of the Voortrekkers in November, 1837 introduced a new note of security and prosperity among the settlers at Port Natal, and on the 21st of November the first sale of land ever held at the Port took place. The sites were situated at "Point St Michael's".[9] They each measured a little over an acre and the prices realised caused the settlers to triumphantly report that land had assumed "a value not hitherto thought of".[10] Most of the settlers, however, sailed from Natal on the 'Comet' when they heard that Piet Retief and his comrades had been murdered by Dingane in February, 1838.

Soon after the Battle of Blood River, the Voortrekkers learnt that a detachment of a hundred British soldiers under Major Charters had occupied Port Natal on the 4th December 1838. The first task of Major Charters was to erect a fort. There were standing two stores at the Point; a substantial stone store erected for a Mr Maynard, and a small wooden building close by, belonging to Mr J.O. Smith of Port Elizabeth. These were obtained from their occupants and were converted into a warehouse for provisions and a magazine for arms. The troops occupied tents until wattle-and-daub barracks could be erected. The whole encampment was enclosed with stockades cut from the mangrove swamps and given the name of Fort Victoria.

Captain Jervis, who took over the command from Major Charters early in 1839, recorded the following; "Cutting poles and boating them across the Bay: 25th: Oven finished. 28th: Magazine. 2nd: Bakery. 5th: Guardhouse. 7th: The Well has been lined ... 27th: Soldiers' hut, 54 feet by 16 feet, built with reed walls, 7 feet high ... 10th: Soldiers' hut with walls seven feet high ..."[11A]

The object of the first British Occupation of Natal was to restore peace between the Trekkers and the Zulus. So when the Trekkers entered into a peace treaty with Mpande in October 1839, the small garrison was withdrawn. As their ship sailed, the Voortrekkers fired a salute and hoisted the flag of the Republic of Natalia.

Between 1839 and 1843 the Trekkers set up a Republic based on the old Batavian Republic in the Cape. Weenen and Congella appear to have been settled as villages in 1839, and together with Pietermaritzburg were made the centres of three magisterial and ecclesiastical districts. Every burgher of full age who settled in Natal before 1840 received a free gift of two farms of six thousand acres each and one erf in whichever of the towns he preferred, and everyone who arrived after 1840 received one farm.[12]

Along the coast temporary buildings were erected which followed closely on the pattern laid down by the earliest settlers. The Boers employed first Wahlberg (a Swedish naturalist who arrived with Delegorgue) and then George Christopher Cato to survey and lay out the town of Durban. In June 1840 the second sale of a hundred and twenty-one sites took place. No deeds were tendered. Another sale took place in 1841 with the same results.[13]

In 1839 Charles MacDonald erected a wattle-and-daub structure, its walls strengthened by rough hewn stone, with a thatched roof. A humble beginning for a hotel which was to be described in 1884 as "one of the finest in the colonies".[14]

The dwellings in the nearby village of Congella were also of wattle and daub with narrow verandas and thatched roofs. (Fig. 4) Carl Behrens described them as: 'picturesque and very simple. They have four walls (one door and one window) made of plaited reeds and covered inside and out with clay. The roofs are also made of reeds. The floor in the hut is mother earth".[15] These houses formed a laager-like group and there may have been other such groups south of Durban for; "it was surely handsome to see all the pretty cottages and handsome villages, belonging to the peacable Dutch farmers".[16] One of these may have been on the banks of the Umlazi River for, in 1839 the Rev Erasmus Smit had conducted services there in a temporary church made of reeds.

The only other buildings erected along the coast at this time were those of the American Missionaries who had returned to Natal in 1840. Mr and Mrs Grout founded a station near Empangeni where he built a small house, and planted rye, wheat and barley that he had brought from America. Later he made bricks, burned them and built a comfortable dwelling. This was described as being "as good as a New England barn".[17]

Early in 1840 the Pistorius family arrived in Pietermaritzburg. Friedrich Heinrich Pistorius and his family had come to the Cape from Sachsen – Weimar in 1838. One of his sons, Carl Wilhelm, has recorded that, "I came up almost at once to Pietermaritzburg, which had been laid out very shortly before I came to this country. Philip Nel was one of these who surveyed the erven. As yet no houses had been built. The Dutch farmers were for the most part living in wattle-and-daub huts in the laager, near where the Natal Bank now is; (cnr. Bank and Church Streets) and there were a few scattered huts here and there on the various erven. Houses began to go up at once after my arrival; and I was employed to build some of them, including Mr Burger's house, (Fig. 5) afterwards the first Colonial Office. Though I had never learned the trade, I was handy at work of this kind and took up whatever work offered. A Church was just being put up by the Dutch on the Market Square and I helped with the inside work. A grant was made by the Volksraad to my father of a piece of land at the foot of the Town Hill as a tile-yard. I made a lot of tiles there with my own hands, without machinery of any kind. I supplied a quantity for the camp, then being built at Fort Napier. My brother Carl August, was an architect and builder, and had carried on his business in Cape Town before coming to Natal".[19]

The church which the Dutch were erecting on the Market Square was the fulfilment of the Vow of Danskraal.[20] (Fig. 6) In October, 1839 Sarel Cilliers mentioned in a letter that the people of Natal

1	The progress of South Africa. Theal. p246
1a	Cradle days of Natal. G. Mackeurtan. p169
2	Voortrekkermense (ed. by G. Preller). p220
3	Previously known as Paal Lager (The laager of palisades, so called because of the piles driven into the marshy earth to protect the laager). The Voortrekkers of South Africa. M. Nathan. p265
4	Annals of Natal. (Vol.11). Bird. p530–531
5	More annals of Natal. A.F. Hattersley.
6	The Natalians. A.F. Hattersley.
7	In January, 1839 water from the Dorp Spruit was led down furrows to the settlement.
8	More annals of Natal. A.F. Hattersley.
9	Also known as Point Fynn.
10	The cradle days of Natal. G. Mackeurtan. p211
11	A history of South Africa. (1834–1854). Theal. p154
11a	Shepstone Journal (Natal Archives).
12	The progress of South Africa. Theal. p246
13	See Chapter 11
14	The Royal Hotel. South Africa. J.S. Little.
15	A diary of Congella. Carl Behrens. (Killie Campbell Museum).
16	The cradle days of Natal. G. Mackeurtan. p271
17	op cit, Mackeurtan. p323
18	Drie honderd jaar nasie-bou in Suid Afrika. Malherbe.
19	More annals of Natal. A.F. Hattersley. p114
20	A vow made by the Voortrekkers on December

were preparing bricks and timber for a church.[20A] J.P. Zietsman, who had been Landrost at the time of its erection, affirmed in 1855 that it had been intended only as a temporary building until such time as funds permitted the erection of a larger one. The photograph of it taken later in the century indicates that it probably had a central doorway in the short elevation and a row of windows facing Church Street. Built by William Jurgens and Johannes Pretorius and measuring 50 feet by 30 feet, it had walls two feet thick and a flat wooden roof. While it may have been intended to build the church of brick,[21] local shalestone was actually used. The timber used was yellow-wood, cut in the forests of the Karkloof.

In 1841 the flat roof was replaced by a thatched one and the end wall gables were added. These gables may have been identical to those on the Raadzaal, an observer commenting in 1850 that; "the Court house and Dutch Reformed Church are thatched and built of stone, both on the same model".[21A] The photograph of the church reveals that the window surrounds and recessed frames gave the building a nineteenth century character, though this 'modernity' may be partially attributed to the alterations effected at later stages.

The pulpit, (Fig. 7), which was built of local yellow-wood by Nagel and Heine, was a direct continuation of traditional Cape craftsmanship. It was designed in the restrained style derived from the work of Thibault; a style which probably arrived late in the outlying districts of the Colony. The pulpit was transferred to the second church of the vow in 1861. For this purpose the height was increased by a foot and it was provided with a sounding board.[22]

The meetings of the Volksraad were held in the Raadzaal, (Fig. 8) a building erected in 1841 at the crossing of Kerk and Nel Streets.[23] The building measured forty feet by nineteen feet, and was built with green brick walls on shale foundations and had a thatched roof. The flush window frames gave the building a more traditional eighteenth-century character, in contrast to that of the church on the other side of the Market Square. The interior consisted of a meeting room and two small offices added in 1845. The floor was flagged and the walls inside and out were lime-plastered and limewashed. In 1849 Heine replaced parts of the green brick walls, repaired the gables and placed stone steps before the principal entrance. In 1854 the north-end gable was removed and the roof hipped. A Gaol and Powder Magazine were the only other public buildings in Pietermaritzburg. (See Fig. 88).

By July, 1840, the town consisted of a hundred and fifty huts and about fifteen substantial houses, (Fig. 9) one of which had been built for Delagorgue.[24] Pistorius's brick and tile works facilitated the erection of brick buildings. Shalestone was quarried at Ohrtmann's quarry to the east of the town. The material needs of the small town were provided for by Visagie's Mill which had been erected at the western end of Church Street. The illustration of 1841 (Fig. 9) shows it to be a whitewashed, gabled building with thatched roofs.

The Dutch Reformed Pastorie (Fig. 10,11) was erected for the Rev Daniel Lindley in 1842. Built of shale, and costing £214, it was described as one of the best houses in Pietermaritzburg. The house had a frontage of forty-six feet on Longmarket Street, with a "stoep" six feet broad of flat stones on the street line, while the house ran back forty feet from the street. Lindley described his house as a "clay built cottage with two rooms, one of which was our kitchen, the other was our eating and sitting room. At night we ascended some rough steps to the space above and slept close under the roof".[25] Thus it would seem likely that the rear portion of the house was only added later, the "two rooms" being separated by a hall or "voorkamer" with a small staircase leading up to the attic. Once again a substantial portion of the building was erected by the Pistorius family. The second story was added in 1856 by a Mr Watson, several internal alterations being effected at the same time. (The veranda dates from 1879.)

Shale was also used in building the first double-storeyed house in Pietermaritzburg. (Fig. 12 & 13) but was left unplastered. The roof was originally thatched. Small casement windows were used instead of the sliding sashes as used on the Pastorie. Some doubt surrounds the location of the house belonging to a Mr P.L. Cloete as illustrated by a member of the Cloete family. (Fig. 14 & 15). A certain Cloete had been granted an erf in Pietermaritz Street and the presence of two other houses in the painting, together with the red tiled roof suggest that the house probably stood in Pietermaritzburg. This was a fairly typical Cape house. The front elevation with its central doorway and attic gable, the open stoep and tall flanking windows, and the "pirk"[26] hip and lintel mouldings are examples of the blend of Dutch and English traditions which had taken place in the early part of the century at the Cape.[27]

Another contemporary illustration (Fig. 16) shows the farm of P. Otto at Little Saxony. Otto had come up from the Cape in 1842 and, soon after acquiring land, set about building himself a homestead below the Bluff now known as Otto's Bluff.[28] The "koringhoop" gable suggests that Otto may have come from the Wellington area in the Cape, but this was otherwise a fairly general type of Cape house. The building may have had an L or a T shaped plan but the symmetry of the front elevation of the long arm indicates that the "stoepkamer", with its 'wolwe-ent', and small windows, were later additions. The building faced north.

On her arrival at Durban in 1841, Francis Armstrong found "a few English, German and Dutch people scattered about as far as Congella. The only houses were of wattle and daub, and Mr G.C. Cato gave us shelter under his roof till I put up a house for myself".[29] By May 1842 very few individuals had constructed any habitations for themselves, but several were collecting materials and laying out the plans of their buildings when they were prevented from continuing by another military occupation.[30]

The Second British Occupation of Natal took place on the 4 May 1842, when Captain T.C. Smith and a detachment of 237 men of the 27th Regiment and the Royal Artillery reached Durban. They encamped on the site of the plain to the north of the present town, hauled down the Flag of the Republic of Natalia and hoisted the Union Jack.[31]

Before 1842, buildings in Natal had consisted mainly of temporary shelters of wattle and daub along the coast and small permanent structures of stone and brick inland. Apart from the few missionaries, the settlers came from the Cape and, after long and tragic struggles to find security in this "new paradise", commenced the shaping of their environment. Their first significant statements were to continue the architectural traditions of the Cape Colony.

7 1838 'before the Battle of Blood River in which they vowed to consecrate the day of victory over the Zulus and also to erect a church to the glory of God.
The Voortrekkers of South Africa. M. Nathan. p252
20a op cit, Nathan.
21 op cit, Nathan.
21a More annals of Natal. A.F. Hattersley. p116,117
22 op cit, Nathan
23 The northwest corner of the building was used as the single fixed point for the surveying of the town by Nel and may thus have been commenced early in 1840.
Pietermaritzburg panorama. A.F. Hattersley.
24 A diary of Congella. Carl Behrens. (Killie Campbell Museum).
25 op cit, Nathan.
26 'pirk' or 'jirkin head'; an intermediate form of hipped roof in which the gable wall is carried up for a part of the height, and the roof is then hipped back.
27 See Early nineteenth century architecture in South Africa. R.B. Lewcock.
28 To the North-East of Pietermaritzburg.
29 Natal memories. B. Buchanan. p53
30 The history of old Durban. G. Russell. p59
31 A history of Natal. E.H. Brookes and C. de B. Webb. p38

Chapter 3

Natal in transition

1842 − 1849

"On May 4 1843, Sir George Napier announced to the Legislative Council of the Cape that the Queen would take the inhabitants of Natal under her protection and that a commissioner would be sent to regulate the affairs of the Natal district".[1]

Captain Smith's camp at Durban (Fig. 18) had consisted of tents surrounded by a low earth wall. This camp was besieged by the Boers after the Battle of Congella and was relieved on the 24 June 1842 by a British force consisting of 350 men. Soon after their arrival the men were employed in erecting temporary buildings. Lieut Gibb R.E. described the fort as; "four ranges of wattle and daub buildings placed in the form of a square with flanking redoubts as opposite ends".[2] (Fig. 19)

The sod wall had been increased in height and surrounded by low palisading. In 1845 heavy rains rendered the buildings unfit for the occupation of the troops and more permanent buildings were erected. The magazine was a whitewashed brick building with a slate roof (Fig. 20) while the barracks were contained in a long narrow thatched structure with a continuous veranda giving access to the rooms.[3] (Fig. 21)

On the 31 August 1843, Major Smith led two companies of the 45th Regiment, fifteen engineers and some artillerymen to Pietermaritzburg. They camped on the hill to the west of the town and immediately set about the erection of Fort Napier. Lieut Gibb R.E., writing to Lieut Col Marshall said of it: "we have all been at work making the post defensible, but, I am sorry to say, have had some heavy rains which have delayed us. The barracks I have traced in the form of a square, and have thrown out two small redoubts at opposite angles, each for one gun and musketry. These redoubts will be finished in the course of a few days, and will give protection in case of need. They are riveted with stone, having a command of seven feet six inches parapet, three feet thick, ditches five feet deep and nine feet wide. The soil is very hard, being almost entirely loose stones, and with only about 18 inches of earth at the surface. The ground falls gently on the four sides of the work, forming a natural glacis. When the redoubts are finished, the barracks can be commenced. I have traced them in the form of a square of 240 feet. Stone is close at hand, and roofing materials to be procured in the village. The outer walls being loopholed, and flanked by the redoubts, the post will, I should imagine be defensible".[4] (Fig. 22)

Among the soldiers were many who were skilled in building and plastering and as several of these were employed to build houses for the officials of the town, the barracks were only completed in 1845.[5] (Fig. 23,24)

At that time they were the largest and most substantial buildings in Natal. On the inside of the square the building was surrounded with a veranda. The casement-windows and doors were arranged in regular rows, and where there were no verandas, the tiled roof was clipped short.[6] The stone redoubts at the east and west angles of the fort each mounted three guns on revolving platforms.[7] The deep trench could be quickly filled with water in an emergency. A garrison chapel, St George's was erected, and the first service was held in it on November 14 1846. A theatre was also built in that year. The fort remained in use as the headquarters of the British garrison in Natal until 1914.

By July 1844, 132 houses had been built in Pietermaritzburg.[8] More than half of these were built either of burnt or green brick or shalestone. "Whatever may be said by those whose estates lie contiguous, not one decently good residence is anywhere to be found, nor even a tolerable one, except that belonging to Mr Boshoff and the one recently enlarged and beautified by Her Majesty's Commissioner, the Hon H. Cloete Esq. In the distance these defects and inconveniences are not observed and the group of white-washed houses upon a perfectly denuded plain impress approaching travellers with delusive expectations and hopes".[9] The two houses which this correspondent to the Grahamstown Journal in 1844, found exceptional, had both been built by the Trekkers.

Cloete's house in Commercial Road was a thatched house with gables which he had acquired on his arrival in Natal in 1843.[10] Boshoff's house was a narrow hipped house with a stoep facing Longmarket Street. The tall windows flanking the central door had wide yellow-wood surrounds, small paned sliding sashes and flat arched lintels. (Fig. 25)

This house was rented by Martin West in 1846, for use as Government House until 1849.[11] The uneven spacing of the fenestration, and the wide window-surrounds suggest a continuation of the "voorkamer" plan and also the eighteenth century character of Cape Dutch architecture. On his arrival in Natal in December 1845, Martin West had found it necessary to hire a small house in Church Street for a few months. (Fig. 26) This house had a voorkamer with rooms leading off either side. The geometrical fanlight [12] (Fig. 27) and the eight-panelled door,[13] and the cornice and plinth mouldings suggest that the house was probably designed by Carl Pistorius, as it is known that he and his brothers were the builders.[14]

An interesting feature of both the Boshoff and Martin West house is the emphasis given to the doorways not only by their central position but by the use of a size unequal to that of the flanking windows. Col E.F. Boys of the 45th Regiment, who administered the Government of Natal between the death of Martin West and the arrival of Benjamin Chile Pine, acquired erfs 1 and 2 Burger Street from a P.H. Kritzinger. Professor Hattersley states that "he built the house in which he continued to reside till his final departure from Natal in the early 'fifties".[15] It would seem likely, however, that the gabled house (Fig. 28) had been built by P.H. Kritzinger and that Col Boys effected considerable alterations. The size of this simple gable indicates the small scale of the Dutch houses built in Natal.

Most of the houses in Pietermaritzburg which had been built by the Boers were; "of the single-storey, one room wide type. They stood lengthwise to the street".[16] The Wolhuter house in Longmarket Street and two houses in central Church Street (Fig. 29) were of this type. The latter may have been those referred to by Henry Brooks in 1876; "There are still some few of the original Dutch houses in Pietermaritzburg. These are one-storeyed structures, with regular rows of tall windows, balanced with stiff formality at either side of the central door, and looking out upon a raised platform or stoep, having a seat at each end for the evening lounge and pipe. The rooms are for the most part lofty, with ceilings of planked wood".[17]

The flanking stoep walls of the Church Street houses were to be echoed in many houses erected at the end of the century.[18] At a time when gables were once again becoming fashionable,[19] a watered-down version of the stoep wall was used at the end or ends of the front veranda of the town house.

At the beginning of Martin West's period of office as Lieut Governor, there were nearly four hundred Boer families in Natal, but by 1849 only about sixty families were left.[20] The others had trekked once again, this time over the Drakensberg and into the Transvaal and the Orange Free State.

During the 1840's they had been dispersed over the entire country while about 300 persons remained in Pietermaritzburg. "In some few instances two or three families, influenced by a feeling of insecurity in (their) absolute solitude, built their cottages near the homestead of a friend or relative".[21]

Many were living in dwellings of crude construction. Descriptions of the period all indicate their poverty-stricken conditions. Van Rooyen refers to the 'Kapsteilhuise' which some had erected at Kranskop.[22] (Fig. 30) Some of the Boers continued to use such dwellings as late as 1880.

Others were more fortunate; "On the way to the Dargle (1848) the Fannin family passed two deserted Dutch homesteads, one at Riet Vallei and the other at

1   A history of Natal. E. H. Brookes and C. de B. Webb. p40
2   British Parliamentary papers. XV. May 22 1843
3   B.P.P. 1845, XV Natal p19 Feb. 6 1845
4   B.P.P. 1847–8, XLII, p13–14
5   Reminiscences of early Natal. Thomas Greene. (Killie Campbell Museum).
6   The Pistorius Brick and Tile works supplied tiles for the building. See p285
7   Natal memories. B. Buchanan. p96
8   De Nataller. July 1844
9   Portrait of a city. A.F. Hattersley. p8
10   On March 4 1849, a severe electric storm struck Pietermaritzburg, during which "the electric fluid entered Cloete's drawing room at the gable end".
   The Natal Witness March 9 1849
11   Pioneer days in Natal. B. Buchanan. p104
12   Such fanlights had been popular in Europe in the seventeenth century and had been introduced into the Cape during the eighteenth century.
   Early nineteenth century architecture in South Africa. R.B.Lewcock. p44
13   Eight-panelled doors became popular in the Cape during the first British Occupation.
   op cit, Lewcock. p385
14   Pioneer days in Natal. B. Buchanan.
15   More annals of Natal. A.F. Hattersley. p172
16   Natal memories. B. Buchanan. p71
17   Natal, a history and description of the colony. H. Brooks. p292
18   These are to be found in many South African towns.
19   During the 1880's and 1890's, gables were common in those buildings built in the revived Queen Anne style.
20   Natal 1846–1851 by an old Inhabitant.
21   Natal 1846–1851 op cit.
22   Kultuurskatte uit die Voortrekker tydperk. G.H. van Rooyen. p178–181

Maritzdaal; a fine orchard of trees, a large barn full of sheaves and wheat and a quantity of sawn timber". [23] Several Byrne settlers were to censure such homesteads, as glaring white buildings unrelated to their surroundings, and in 1872 Lady Barker wrote, "Comfort according to our English notions, appears as small an element in the Boer's conception of domestic bliss as enterprise is in his theory of the whole duty of farmers. The farmstead (Riet Spruit) consisted of a low, stone, one-storeyed house, with small windows, and a double door in the centre, a stoep in front, no veranda, and a circular enclosure for cattle on one side". [24]

In 1848 the main body of Trekkers left Natal. Those that remained were settled in Pietermaritzburg, Weenen and the Klip River and Umvoti districts. In the Umvoti district they settled in a village known as Pretoriusdorp. [25] An early photograph of the town (Fig. 31) indicates not only the small thatched cottages as were erected in Pietermaritzburg but also the flat-roofed and whitewashed houses like those one finds in the small towns of the Northern Cape. Such a house with stoepkamers at each end was still standing at Umkomaas in the 'seventies (Fig. 32.) In Ladysmith a Dutch Reformed Church was built which had gables and a thatched roof. (Fig. 33)

In December 1845 the Lieut Governor and the first British officials arrived. Dr William Stanger, the Surveyor General, built a single-storeyed, thatch-roofed cottage of five rooms facing upper Longmarket Street. (Fig. 34) From records of additions and renovations to the building in 1854, [26] it appears that the house had a central corridor with a drawing room and dining room opening off each side and a small staircase leading to the bedrooms in the attic. The building had verandas on the two long sides while the short sides were gabled. In 1850 it was acquired as Government House and G.H. Mason said of it; "I had expected to find a handsome European structure with orderlies, and servants, and all the insignia of royalty, about the residence of the Queen's representative. What however, was my agreeable surprise, at finding Government House to be a quiet, old fashioned straggling building, quite lost in flowering creepers, growing in matted clusters almost over doors and windows... a well furnished drawing room, with low glass doors opening onto a beautiful lawn". [27]

Thomas Phipson, describing Pietermaritzburg in 1849, observed the merits of thatch as a roofing material suitable to the climate. "The town consists of about two hundred houses of various size and structure, but all built more or less in the style of English rural architecture. The walls consist either of brick (burnt or unburnt) or else of stone, which is found in the immediate neighbourhood. With few exceptions they are whitened externally, and the roofs are either thatched or tiled. The former method, though rustic in appearance, has in its favour the classic precedent of ancient Rome, and the more practical advantage of being suited to the variations of the temperature, preserving the interior cooler in summer and warmer in winter than any other available material". [28] Thatch, however, did have its limitations as was found during the severe electric storm of March 1849. Thereafter lightning conductors were hastily erected all over the town.

James Erasmus Methley found that; "nearly all the houses are built in the English style, of stone or brick; many of them are double-storeyed handsome buildings, roofed with tiles and shaded by Seringa trees". [29] Zietsman had built a two-storeyed residence in central Church Street. This evidently had a corniced roof and balustrade. The Methodist Manse, (Fig. 35,36) which had been built in 1848, was also double-storeyed and the largest house in the town. Except for the hood-moulds over the doors and windows this was a typical Cape Georgian house. The character of the building, with the rows of trees set directly between the house and the street, the proportions and the arrangement of the small paned sash windows, is that of the architecture of the Cape after the British occupations. The hoodmouldings, however, are indications of the Early Victorian and for its time and place the house was extraordinarily fashionable.

Two Wesleyan churches were erected in Pietermaritzburg before 1850. (Fig. 36) "A thatched chapel had been opened for service on New Years Eve, 1848". [30] This church with its lancet windows and castellated gable front is the earliest example of the Gothic Revival in Natal, [31] and while the "Gothic" character of the building may have been only superficial, it is significant that this was the first attempt in Natal to reproduce directly the architecture of England. [31A] Its width was certainly in keeping with other buildings in Natal. (Fig. 37) Limitations of roof-span, caused by the difficulty of obtaining long lengths of timber, and the lack of men capable of erecting more complex roofs, reduced buildings to narrow forms. In the case of the Gothic style this restriction could only have been an advantage.

The only other churches erected in Pietermaritzburg before 1850 were St Andrew's Anglican church (1848), a narrow stone church with a chancel articulated from the body of the church, and the Congregational Church erected in 1849. The latter possessed a small organ manufactured and installed locally by a man named Wright. [32]

Pietermaritzburg in 1849 also had a billiard room (erected by Botha in 1846) and the Crown Hotel, which was opened by William Platts in February 1849. (Fig. 38)

The few official buildings were erected either under the supervision of the Commanding officer of the Royal Engineers, stationed at Fort Napier, or the Surveyor General. The latter, Dr William Stanger, was fully occupied on the re-surveying of Durban and Pietermaritzburg and thereafter the survey of farms. The gaol which the Trekkers had built adjacent to the Market Square, was a simple wattle and daub hut which was found to be in a shocking state of disrepair when taken over by the British. (centre of Fig. 88) John Fleming, a local carpenter who inspected its six apartments in February 1846, reported that the beams of the roof were "nearly all gone" and several of the boards were quite rotten. It was decided to add two rooms, using raw bricks, and to re-roof the building with tiles, costing fifteen shillings a hundred.[33] The improvements could not have been very competently effected, for in September, 1849, Harding in his capacity as resident magistrate, insisted that the roof, gables and floors were all rotting.[34]

In 1848 the Government erected a schoolroom (Fig. 39 & 40) which was designed by Stanger or one of his assistants. It was also intended to use the building occasionally as a church. A flat roofed, semi-circular porch was to protect the entrace; this was never built. An entrance lobby gave access to a small room on each side, and all were connected to the school room itself — a rectangular hall approximately seventy by thirty feet. Two small toilets were situated on each side of the building. The walls were of plastered brick and the roof thatched. The contractors were two Irish soldiers, McKeaney and Murphy, who had been members of the garrison at Fort Napier. They experienced difficulties during construction, applying to the Surveyor General on the 28 February 1849, for "an increased amount of rent on the ground that the actual expense of the work has much exceeded their estimate".[35]

When in 1846 the need arose for a temporary military post twenty-seven miles north of Pietermaritzburg, Capt Gibb R.E. decided that the building should be plastered and thatched. Yellow-wood scantlings would be used for the roof and thatch supplied by the natives, while bricks could be made and stone quarried on the spot. Zinc for the ridge though, would have to be procured from Cape Town.

In Durban the men of the 45th Regiment were excused military exercises and were employed on various public works.[36] In addition to stockading the camp and erecting barracks, stores and magazines, they built a mess house and officers quarters to the east of the camp and a block house on Hospital Hill at the Point.[37] (Fig. 41) The latter was a two-storeyed, loopholed building of brick, the lower floor serving as a store and the upper as a guard room, built "to serve as a keep to the position and rallying point to the inhabitants, in case of emergency, and

(to) protect the shipping in the harbour". Capt Gibb R.E., drew up a complete specification for the perusal of his senior officer.[38] The walls were to be burnt brick in lime mortar on foundations of "concrete lime and ironstone gravel" four feet in thickness. The roof was to be constructed with king post trusses, covered with 1 inch deal boarding and duchess slates. The lower floor was to be constructed of concrete and the upper floor of boarding on joists. The entrance was to be protected by a porch and deal sashes fitted to the windows and loopholes with "louvre boarded shutters". The whole building was to be plastered with "rough cast dashing" and whitewashed.[38A]

Mr Archbell, a Wesleyan minister, had accompanied the British forces to Natal and on his arrival; "he erected a wattle-and-daub building with a veranda all round".[39] The mission house built by Archbell was a similar structure. There were only a few brick cottages in Durban when Natal became British; some were said to have "green verandas".[40] Dick King's

23   The Fannin papers. (Killie Campbell Museum).

24   Life at Natal. (V) Lady Barker. The Cape monthly magazine 1872 vol. V. p109

25   Later changed by the Government of Natal to "Greytown" as Andries Pretorius had taken up arms against the British in 1842

26   S.G.O. 111/1/9 161. Sept. 5 1854.

27   Life with the Zulus of Natal. G.H. Mason. p129,130

28   Natal Witness 22 June 1849.

29   The new Colony of Port Natal. J.E. Methley. p12

30   The British settlement of Natal. A.F. Hattersley. p320

31   The other church erected was the 'Kafir Church', a smaller building with a fleche over the entrance gable.

31a   Gothic buildings had also been erected in the Cape Colony after the arrival of the English. Early nineteenth century architecture in South Africa. R.B. Lewcock.

32   Natal memories. B. Buchanan. p110

33   C.S.O. letters received; vol. 37 no. 80.

34   C.S.O. letters received; vol. 27 no. 5 and vol. 49 no. 38.

35   Surveyor General's office, 110/1/4, 1849. The building served as a school, church, concert room, theatre and ballroom, before it became the legislative council chamber.

36   History of old Durban. G. Russell. p70,71

37   Probably called Hospital Hill because it was the site chosen by Gardiner for a hospital in 1834. The situation was not far from the site of the later Addington Hospital.

38   British parliamentary papers XV, 1847 Natal, p167

38a   op cit, B.P.P. XV.

39   Natal memories. B.Buchanan. p88

40   More annals of Natal. A.F.Hattersley. p64

house was described as having windows, far and few between. The Rev W.C. Holden who arrived in 1847 said; "At that time there were a few thatched cottages embowered in the richest herbage. These were made of poles and wattles with clay walls, having verandas to protect them, and, being white-washed, they peeped out prettily among the shrubbery".[41] (Fig. 42)

The only building at Durban which could be described as substantial, was a warehouse, built for the Cape Merchant, Chiappini in 1848. For the purpose, John Dove a bricklayer and Coles a carpenter were engaged by a contractor in Cape Town and sent up to Durban.[42] (Fig. 43) The building was of brick with a slate roof. It was sold to the government in 1850 and the Surveyor General was requested by the Lieut Governor to employ a competent person to examine and report upon the quality of the Customs House; "more particularly as regards the quality of the building and the nature and stability of the foundations".[43] It resembled the type of public building which was erected in the outlying districts of the Cape, a reminder that Natal was, until 1856, one such district.

It is certain that most of the wattle-and-daub buildings in Durban were intended to be only temporary. The fact that many more were built after 1850 and that few were replaced by more permanent buildings until thatched roofs were prohibited in the streets of Durban in 1861, suggests their general acceptance.[44] This may have been for two reasons. The first because they offered a pleasant solution in the sub-tropical climate and the second because there was a general fear that stone or brick walls might crack if built on the sea sand which covered large areas of the town. "Up to that time (1848) no building had been erected stronger than wattles and mud; but we wanted something better. In attempting

to erect a substantial building of brick and stone, as there was nothing but sand on which to lay the foundation, we were afraid that a house so built would fall. But we were resolved to make the experiment..."[45]

When Dove and Coles had completed the warehouse for Mr Chiappini they set about building a house for James and Katharine Saunders at Tongaat. [46] "The homestead was U shaped in plan; it comprised a main portion, the axis of which ran east and west, with two wings which projected from it towards the river, giving the dwelling the appearance of a hollow square. The roof of the homestead was of thatch, and the eaves were extended and brought down low on every side, the rafters being supported by stout poles of mangrove wood, to form deep and shady verandas".[47] (Fig. 44)

The advent of the veranda marks the transition in Natal from the Dutch to the English Colonial tradition. The main Dutch settlement in Natal, Pietermaritzburg, was characterised by building types which had developed in the Cape and dated back to the seventeenth and eighteenth century prototypes brought to South Africa from Northern Europe. Pietermaritzburg was described as a town of whitewashed gables and it would be interesting to speculate as to whether other houses besides the Cloete house (Fig. 14) had central gables. This might well have been so, for the few surviving records indicate the continuation of Dutch traditions; both urban and domestic.

41   History of old Durban. G. Russell. p69
42   Tongaati. Watson p47
43   S.G.O. 217, 111/1/4, Nov 20 1850
44   See chapter 4.
45   Missions in South Africa. Holden p422
46   The Saunders had been sent to Natal to manage a large farm at Tongaat for Mr. Chiappini.
47   Tongaati. Watson. p47

Chapter 4

The British settlers
1849-1856

I

"The Natal Colony, amongst many other advantages, possesses a most salubrious climate, unsurpassed by any other colony, great capabilities for cattle farming and agriculture, as well as for the production of cotton, indigo, coffee, sugar, all of which, it is known may be produced with success, as well as the different varieties of European grain. The passage is less expensive out, and it has a more accessible market for the produce than all the other southern colonies. It is also a settled colony, has its own government and laws, enjoys the advantage of good and sufficient religious provision, and is not a penal colony".[1]

Between 1 January 1849 and 28 June 1852 almost five thousand British immigrants arrived in Natal. Most of the emigration schemes offered steerage passage with twenty acres of land for a payment of £10.

As this kind of settlement was unsuitable in the high grasslands of Natal, many were forced to make their homes in Pietermaritzburg and Durban. Others settled at Richmond, Verulam and Howick but few remained as farmers. Though emigration from Britain in the late 'forties was mainly the result of extreme distress, the Natal settlers of 1849–1852 included in their numbers almost all classes and occupations. Their universal consideration was to become independent landowners.[2]

Attracted by reports like that of J.C. Methley, which advertised Natal as a potential producer of sugar, cotton and other sub-tropical products, the immigrants had been drawn from all parts of Britain. Many came from Lancashire and Yorkshire, two of the counties most affected by the consequences of the Industrial Revolution and the repeal of the corn laws.[3] (1846)

On arrival in Natal their immediate concern was to provide themselves with shelter. Barracks were erected for their temporary accommodation near the landing place at the Point and tents were released from military stocks. The barracks, completed just before the rainy season, consisted of a two-roomed wooden shed with bunks arranged around the walls. [4] Byrne claimed to have sent sixty-eight double tents. He also consigned to his Natal agent, John Moreland; "an iron hotel with a circular roof of fifty-eight feet span".[5] Several parties brought with them covered wagons and tents and one promoter reported that he had despatched an iron house and two cottages.

The first structures which the settlers erected were of the type commonly described as wattle and daub.[6] This form of construction, which is based on the age-old half-timber construction of Northern Europe, consisted of a framework of cross-braced timbers, with a lighter framework of wattles woven across it. The exterior was plastered with clay or a mixture of mud and dung. In some cases the interior was also plastered.[7] Sir John Robinson said of them; "Rougher or humbler abodes could hardly be imagined, and yet to women of gentle nurture they seemed havens of rest and comfort after the ships they had left. Nothing by way of domicile could be more crude. The floors were of mud smoothed over with cow dung".[8]

Russell [9] describes most of the buildings in Durban in 1850 as; "Wattle and daub, thatched with "tambootie" or "tambookie" grass. The Bay supplied mangrove posts for uprights; the Berea bush poles and wattles. Daub was composed of clay or ant-heap, tempered with sand and cow dung, trampled into mud by natives... The doors and windows were made from yellow-wood, at first imported, but afterwards supplied through Pietermaritzburg. Windows were generally hung upon butt hinges; wooden floors were rare, the rule being unburnt bricks, or clay and cowdung; fireplaces and chimneys were only used for kitchens, and were seldom made of burnt bricks, as

1 The new Colony of Port Natal. J.C. Methley. p34
2   Under the Byrne emigration scheme twenty acres of land were to be provided to each settler. Lieutenant Governor Pine increased this to forty-five acres.
3   The British settlement of Natal. A.F. Hattersley. Chapters V and VI.
      Byrne was perhaps the major organizer of immigration schemes to Natal.
4   Ibid. Hattersley. p203
5   This had been on show at Islington before shipment to Natal on the "Globe". Ibid. Hattersley. p203
6   In the Eastern Cape, the 1820 Settlers had also resorted to "wattle and daub" structures on their arrival.
      Early nineteenth century architecture in South Africa. R.B. Lewcock. p141
7   The development of English building construction. C.E. Innocent.
8 A life time in South Africa. Sir John Robinson. p13
9   History of old Durban. G.Russell. p91,92

these were expensive. Roofs were generally "hip-ped",[10] on account of the winds, as well as to allow verandas all round the house, which were utilized for bedrooms, pantry and kitchen, office or workship.[11] The veranda in front was usually supported by sawn timber posts on stumps, or stone blocks, while an ornamental fascia board when decorated with a bright green coat of paint gave a style and finish to the new home".

This method of construction was a standard building solution. At Umhlali a temporary church was erected of coarse grass daubed inside with red mud.[12] (1851) The first Catholic Church in Durban was a similar building with verandas all round.[13] (1853) In 1850 most of the shops in Durban were either part of the houses or built adjacent to them, so that they too were of "wattle and daub". "Some townsmen of a handy turn built themselves frame-houses of yellow-wood, weather boarded, and floored, with thatched roofs; when lined with "bafta", papered with illustrated papers, or cheap wall paper, painted, tarred and whitewashed, they were tolerably comfortable..."[14] (Fig. 45)

Other settlers, especially those in the outlying districts, erected huts which closely followed the Zulu pattern. (Fig. 46 and Fig. A and B) Zulus were also employed to construct such huts. Russell [15] distinguishes between "ordinary huts", which were probably 'beehive' and cost about ten shillings, and "finished huts for Europeans", which cost about thirty or forty shillings each.[16] Charles Barter in 1852 referred to one example of the former as; "a Kaffir hut of sticks and grass, looking like a large and very rough bee-hive".[17] Later he described the farm of an English settler at Spion Kop, which he found remarkable for the peculiar construction of the dwelling house.[18] "It was composed entirely of sticks and grass, like a Kafir hut, but instead of being shaped like a single bee-hive, it was like two divided and put together thus ⊂⊃ and the elevation at a distance gives us ⊂⊃ the idea of half a gigantic melon. The rough and simple materials were put together as neatly as to have quite a finished appearance, and a little porch completed the effect, and made it look not only habitable but really elegant, and certainly much more suited to the country than a staring white house, such as is to be seen on most of the Dutch farms."[18A] Russell also refers to such thatched huts in Durban where the building had been constructed by combining two circular huts into a longer structure, with two central poles and a partition dividing the living from the sleeping area.[19] These had framed doors substi-tuted for the low Zulu entrance and the windows consisted of a "red gin case, cut in two and covered with calico".[20] A group of three such structures constituted the hotel at Camperdown on the road

between Durban and Pietermaritzburg.

The settlers from the villages and small country towns of England and Scotland belonged to the class of cultivating freeholder. Wattle and daub, and cob construction were still in use in some of these villages and towns in the nineteenth century. Good cob construction is a laborious process which consists of laying and treading courses of a carefully blended mixture of mud, lime, straw and ballast. Sometimes the walls were formed between shuttering of wattles and about seven inches apart. They were generally plastered on both sides and limewashed.[21]

In his Encyclopaedia, Loudon reccommenced cob walls, two feet thick, on a foundation of stone for farmhouses.[22] Several cob houses were constructed in the Richmond area but on account of their hasty construction have not survived. In Durban, "some persons, taking example from their country friends, tried houses built of sod, but the sandy soil did not encourage the experiment".[23]

Since the earliest settlements had been estab-lished at Port Natal, one kind of building had been used more than any other. This was the veranda-house. Houses with verandas were built in many parts of the world before the nineteenth century.[24] By the middle of the eighteenth century, a house form had evolved in North America which had verandas all round. In England the architects of the Regency period had found the veranda a useful device in their efforts to link the house and the garden.[25] Veran-das also created special opportunities in attaining the irregularity so much desired by the "Picturesque" point of view, and they became fashionable features there, rather because they suited a Romantic view of architecture than because they were practically use-ful. The first veranda house in South Africa[26] was "Newlands", designed for the Governor of the Cape Colony in 1819. This house, and several other projects carried out by Lord Charles Somerset, led to the increasing popularity of the veranda at the Cape, so that by the eighteen-thirties it had become a characteristic element of South African architecture. [27]

No records exist of veranda-houses built by Boers in the interior of Natal, and there were only a few such erected by the first English settlers in Pieter-maritzburg before 1850.[28] It would be tempting to state that the initial popularity of the veranda-house along the sub-tropical coastlands of Natal, and its apparent absence on the higher grassveld further inland, were due entirely to the differences in climate. There is, however, another factor which is common to most of the early buildings in Natal. This is their essential 'colonialism'. Design and erection were limited not only in a conceptual and physical sense but also by a shortage of building materials and building elements. While roofing materials and "wattles" were easily obtainable along the coast, brick and stone were difficult and expensive to obtain.[29] Exactly the reverse was true of Pieter-maritzburg where stone and brick were relatively freely available and roofing timber expensive. These factors, together with the current fear of building on sea sand, may explain why the wattle-and-daub veranda-houses remained in use for so long in Durban.[30] (Fig. 47,48) Perhaps the influence of the existing Dutch buildings and traditions in Pieter-maritzburg which had little to do with verandas, accounts for their not being used in the town, for verandas were an element of the English colonial tradition.

It is certain that such houses, (Fig. 49 and Fig. B) with their whitewashed walls and French doors leading from the interior onto the veranda, were pleasant architectural solutions in the sub-tropical climate. "Houses in those days were one-storeyed bungalows, often with a veranda all round. Nearly all the houses had French windows, as they were called, a combined window and door; a custom which must have been introduced for motives of economy, as they were not convenient". [31,32] Eliza Feilden described the Mellors house, as having "windows which opened to the ground".[33] These were removed for the occasion of a dance.[34]

One of the essential principles of Regency Architecture was the attempt to adapt the house to the form of the Picturesque landscape. The use of rustic materials together with a profusion of ivy and creepers were two ways of achieving the desired congruity. Bartell stated that thatch was indispensable in rural buildings.[35] (Fig. 50)

J.B. Papworth recommended thatching with reeds; "as the most rural and picturesque covering: the brown tints of its surface oppose the various greens of the foliage by which it is accompanied, and give a neatness of effect that is very prepossessing, which may be improved by the colour given to the walls, should they be built of materials which do not harmonize with them".[36]

The use of rope and wired thatch had developed from the earliest rough brushwood roofs of ancient England, and though its use had been curtailed in London in 1212,[37] many village homes in the drier parts of the south and east of England have used "thack" roofs for centuries. Settlers in the Eastern Cape reading in Loudon's Encyclopaedia would have found thatch suggested for climatic reasons; "our own opinion with respect to thatched roofs, is that in very many cases they are preferable, both for farm

which enclosed the roof and served to protect the ends of the thatch from the wind. After the second British occupation more and more hipped roofs began to appear. Ibid. Lewcock. p203

Gables were difficult to construct in Durban for lack of a cheap and readily available wall material strong enough to be built to a suitable height.

10 Hipped roofs were the normal method of construction in the South of England. Ibid. Lewcock. p79
11 In the Cape most houses were given gables

12 Early days in Natal by William Lister. (Bird Papers, Natal Archives).
13 Trekking for souls. J.E. Brady. p76
14 History of old Durban. G.Russell. p93
15 op cit, Russell. p90
16 The earliest British settlers in North America had also emulated Indian wigwams; "The Lord hath been pleased to turn all the wigwams, huts and hoods the English dwelt in at their first coming into orderly, fair, and well built houses..." (1653)
Architecture, ambition and Americans. W. Andrews. p37
17 The dorp and veld or six months in Natal. C. Barter. p5
18 See chapter one, Fig. 2 and Fig. 281.
18a op cit, Barter p5.
19 op cit, Russell. p129
20 History of old Durban. G. Russell. p89
21 The pattern of English building. Clifton Taylor.
22 Encyclopaedia of cottage farm and villa architecture. Loudon. p417
23 History of old Durban. G. Russell. p91
24 Early nineteenth century architecture in South Africa. R.B. Lewcock. Chapter 7.
25 The Regency style. Donald Pilcher. p47
26 Prior to the first British occupation of the Cape, the Cape Dutch stoep was an unroofed extension of the house, but by the early years of the second occupation it was common for these to be covered with low-pitched boarded or metal roofs. Ibid, Lewcock. p112
27 Ibid, Lewcock. p112
28 As Stanger's house. See p10.
29 See Chapter 12
30 Up until 1861, when they were prohibited within the Borough of Durban by the first Building Byelaw.
31 Acutt Chronicle. (Killie Campbell Museum)
32 Especially during the windy months from August to November.
33 My African home. E.W. Fielden. p169
34 The German Hotel at Pinetown had folding glass doors opening on to the veranda.
Life with the Zulus of Natal. G.H. Mason. p94
35 The Regency style. Donald Pilcher. p25,29
36 Rural residences. J.B. Papworth.
37 "In London, a coating of lime plaster, to reduce combustibility, was made compulsory as early as 1212, when it was at the same time decreed that thatch was not to be used for any new roofs in the capital". Other towns in England gradually followed suit.

buildings and cottages, to roofs of tiles or slates, as these are commonly constructed, even where the latter two are cheaper, because they are less liable to admit through them the influence of every change of temperature".[38] The Kafir wars of 1835 and the pressure of insurance charges for thatched roofs had caused them to pass out of fashion on the Eastern Frontier.[39]

Just as Charles Barter had described the thatched farmhouse at Spion Kop as elegant and better suited to the country than the farmhouses of the Boers,[40] so Lady Barker found the little thatched Catholic Church in Durban to be the nicest building in the town.[41] Eliza Feilden described her new house (Fig. 51) in 1852 as; "standing upon legs, or posts, we can see under it and might possibly creep under if we chose. There are only three rooms at present, parlour and bedroom, with a garret above to have a stair up from the little entrance, and in this our guests when we have any must be content to sleep. A wide veranda surrounds the house, a most important addition in this hot climate. We have papered our sitting room and the vestibule with the pretty white paper we brought from England; they look quite nice and cheerful. But all discomforts we feel trifling in comparison with the purer air and beautiful scenery, while the kitchen under the trees with our dark maiden, the happy ducks and fowls picking about, are quite romantic and picturesque".[42] Though the broad veranda had protected the doors and windows of the house from rain, Eliza Feilden expressed delight when glass at last arrived in the colony in April 1853, as the calico windows darkened the spaces and began to show signs of wear.

An interesting comparison can be made between the first buildings erected by the English in Natal and those of the Voortrekkers. The latter took great pride in re-establishing the traditions of the Cape in Natal. The visible expression of this tradition was an essentially urban environment and one in direct contrast to the rustic conditions so obviously enjoyed by the English. For the latter delighted in their exile from 'home' in such a rough and outlandish place and felt much more like Colonials.[42A]

At Richmond the first settlers built thatched cottages of stone and green brick, surrounded with flower gardens, rose bushes and fruit trees. (Fig. 52) W.J. Irons, the leader of the Methodist settlement at Verulam, set out in some detail a plan of how the village was to be laid out. He was most particular and emphatic about the style of the houses to be erected by the settlers.[43] Houses on town lands were to be built according to certain regulations drawn up by Theophilus Irons and a committee, and were to be placed at a regular distance from the street, which it was felt would secure uniformity of design and prevent the streets being disfigured by shanties and

other shabby dwellings. Until such time as bricks were made, however, wattle-and-daub huts with thatched roofs were erected.[44]

In Pietermaritzburg some British settlers took over houses which had been built by the Dutch. Others erected their own houses, using sun-dried bricks as wattling was not easily obtainable. (Fig. 53, 54,55) Two Cambridge graduates took advantage of "this magnificient landscape, and built our house with its front overlooking it, while behind lay the pretty town, scattered over two square miles, with its groves of fruit trees enclosed by hedgerows of figs and almonds, its snow white buildings and vacant erven". They found excavation for foundations an easy matter "as a solid red clay formed the subsoil of the whole vley, at the depth of eighteen inches below the rich vegetable soil that lay uppermost". The house was to be twenty feet long and fourteen feet wide and "to have built the house entirely of stone, obtained in such a laborious manner, would have taken too much of our time. We therefore determined on completing it with sun-dried bricks, which we could manufacture on our own land, near the building, and thus avoid the trouble of carriage; but as neither of us had ever made a brick in our lives, it was necessary to learn the process before commencing; for which purpose we paid a visit to a brickyard, just opened by some shipwrecked sailors, on the other side of the vley, where we not only learned the art, but also had the offer of moulds, tables and stools, which however we declined, as we had previously made some rough ones for our own use". At the risk of being seen treading the clay for the bricks during the day, they set about doing so late at night, observing that "our first attempt at brick-making was not so remarkable for the number made, as for the peculiarity of their shape". After a week of experimentation they were manufacturing seven hundred green bricks daily and after purchasing "timber and planking for the door frames, window cills, joists, rafters, plates and doors", the shell of the house was completed within a month. "This house, or rather cottage, consisted of two good rooms on the ground floor, twelve feet high in the walls, open to the thatch, with a door and two windows in front; a door at one end, a window at the opposite, together with a third door and fireplace at the back; the whole being surrounded by a thatched veranda, four feet wide, supported on forest poles cut in the town wood, four miles off, and carried home on our shoulders".[45]

Along the coast the wattle-and-daub huts of the settlers gradually began to give way to more permanent and durable forms of building. (Fig. 56,57,58) Bricks were made in several places in 1850 but were expensive, costing about a penny each.[45A] Several settlers found their original houses severely eaten by white ants.[46] Others, more fortunate, had built suspended floors on stumps of salt-grown mangrove, a timber apparently impervious to termites. This kind of construction certainly made housekeeping easier, for the housewife was thereby able to keep out the loose sea sand which covered large areas of Durban at the time. Several settlers expressed the opinion that a floor so built would keep the house cooler in the sub-tropical summer, besides affording protection from the numerous snakes which abounded in the bush. Reed and daub was preferred by some;[46A] "as offering more effectual resistance to the attacks of the white ant".[47]

By 1852 Barter could thus describe Durban: "I had never been in D'Urban since my first arrival, and was able to appreciate the rapid strides it had made in a period of scarcely seven months. Houses had sprung up in all directions. Brick and mortar was in many instances superceding wattle and dab; large warehouses and stores were beginning to give a more substantial and businesslike appearance to this quaintest of cities".[48]

Plans for houses of the period reveal three types. The first appears to be a direct translation of the wattle-and-daub hut into brick. (Fig. 59) These were long narrow buildings sometimes only one room deep,[49] but often consisting of a drawing room or parlour and dining room facing the street with one or more bedrooms behind. Occasionally a small staircase led up from the parlour to an attic which contained other bedrooms. This was not often resorted to, for the only means of lighting and ventilating such attics was by means of dormer windows, felt to be unnecessary complications at that time. These houses had verandas all round or on the two long sides. The main entrance and access between rooms occurred directly off this veranda. A few parlours had fireplaces but these were symbolic rather than useful. Sometimes detached houses were grouped together into one long building. Dacomb advertised such a building as; "three dwellings with twelve rooms; separate cottages under one roof".[50] This particular building had a slate roof, boarded floors and plaster ceilings. (Fig. 60)

Kitchens were built away from the houses and often in the same building as the stables or workshop. Many houses in the Cape had also had detached kitchens.[51] The problems of heat and fire hazards induced many to avoid cooking below thatched roofs. Burchell had observed a frontier boer farmhouse in the Roggeveld Karroo which also had the kitchen separated from the house.[52] Russell says that such kitchens were built at the same time as the more substantial houses. "This state of things was improved as soon as the householder settled down, and had time to look about him, when detached kitchens were built, usually of wood, having brick chimneys and a raised hearth, the discarded hut being utilized for the

accommodation of the native".[53] It seems curious that the settlers should have continued such a practise when living in slate-roofed houses. One reason may have been the constant fear and suspicion of the Zulu cook-boys.[54]

A few people used Yorkshire ovens, which were rather like brick cupboards built at one end of the fireplaces, but only those who had had any previous experience, succeeded.[55] Privies were also located away from the house. In the case of Mr Robert Polybank's house the privy drained into the bay. "The drain from the necessary to be made effectual and to drain the privies into the pond as when the house was first taken".[56]

38 An Encyclopaedia of cottage, farm and villa architecture. Loudon. p417
39 Early nineteenth century architecture in South Africa. R.B. Lewcock. p384
40 The traditional white buildings of the Dutch in Cape Town, also struck the first British visitors to the Cape as unusual. Ibid, Lewcock. p39
41 Life at Natal. Cape monthly magazine 1872 vol. 4 p75. A small chapel, forty by eighteen feet and ten feet high with a thatched roof was opened and consecrated on July 24 1853. Trekking for souls. J.E. Brady. p76
42 My African home. E. Feilden. p25
42a Another interesting comparison can be made between the large windows of the English settlers and small narrow ones of the Dutch.
43 To the shores of Natal. Bulpin. p150
44 History of early Verulam. 1850 60. M. Park. 272
45 Life with Zulus of Natal. G.H. Mason. p169-77.
45a Soon afterwards they began to be cheaper.
46 History of old Durban. G.Russell. p92
46a The reeds of the mangrove swamps were impervious to termite attack.
47 Dorp and Veld. C. Barter. p7
48 op cit, Barter. p236
49 S.G.O. 58. 111/1/9. 12 March 1855
50 S.G.O. 186. 111/11/30. Slates were imported from the Cape and Britain and were generally used as ballast on ships trading with S.A. Ch12.
51 Such kitchens were also used by the first colonists in Australia.
52 Early nineteenth century architecture in South Africa. R.B. Lewcock. p137 and p416
53 History of old Durban. G. Russell. p99
54 Though no encounters between black and white occurred in Natal between those of Dingaan and the Voortrekkers and the Langalibalele affair in 1873, the continuous "kafir" wars on the Eastern Frontier of the Cape colony, and incidents such as the Zulu civil war of Ndondakusuka in 1856, caused tremendous suspicion and insecurity in the towns and even more in the country.
55 Pioneer days in Natal. B. Buchanan. p12
56 S.G.O. 58 111/1/9. (5) 1855
57 S.G.O. 58 111/1/9.
58 My African home. E. Feilden. p12

The second house type was similar to the first, but double-storeyed. Mr Savory's brick house in Pine Terrace (Fig. 61,62) contained two rooms on the ground floor with a staircase at one corner of the larger room, leading upstairs to an arrangement of rooms identical to the lower floor. A narrow balcony extended from this floor and gave some protection to the walls below. A yellow-wood building with a thatched roof was later added to the rear of the house.[57] The windows and doors were carefully proportioned and positioned in the elevations.

The third type was the closest to the house plan which was beginning to prove popular in the detached houses built at the time in England. "The little red brick house I was conducted to was clean and cheerful and looked like rest and comfort. A hall, or, as the ancients called it, "prandenium", ran through from front to back, out of which opened four rooms; a parlour, with bedroom opposite, a servants room and storeroom opposite. Our kitchen was a small building outside".[58] Goodricke's house (Fig. 63,64) was a replacement of two conjoined beehive huts, and boasted folding doors between the parlour and the dining room, while large venetian-shuttered French doors led directly on to a lawn. Such a square house form created roofing problems. There appear to have been two solutions. One was to keep the house small and build up a pyramidal, (Fig. 58) thatched roof, while the other (Fig. 64) was to span the house lengthwise with a pair of hipped roofs joined together at a gutter. This often occurred directly over a continuous wall.

A few "houses for sale" advertisements of 1853 are revealing. "That substantial brick building with good stone foundation, well-slated roof and plastered ceiling, in George's Street; containing two sitting rooms; 12 x 15 feet each with chimneys; 2 bedrooms 10 x 15 feet; passage 4 feet wide; all boarded floors; large kitchen and pantry, with servants room, under back veranda; brick floors". "Red House Farm situate near the little Umhlanga, contains five large apartments (substantial dwellings 57 x 37 feet) and with an excellent and commodius detached kitchen, and having a strong stone built fireplace and chimney; and sundry outhouses".[59]

Several colonists built their homes outside Durban in the early 'fifties. Sydney Peel seems to have been the first to build a house on the Berea. The veranda evidently had to be built without posts, because as soon as an attempt was made to put up posts, wandering elephants knocked them down.[60] Melkhoutkraal, the first substantial house (1849) in the Victoria county was built by the Pietermaritzburg mason John Mullins. He had been employed on the new Houses of Parliament at Westminister before coming to Natal.[61] In 1854, two Hollanders arrived in Natal from Java. van Prehn had "an

attractive house with Javanese servants" on the Umbilo river. Most of the settlers had Zulu servants, [62] though a few brought maids from England, and those from the Cape brought Coloureds.[63]

Buildings similar to the long thatched houses in Durban were built as houses, hotels and stores in all parts of Natal during the early 'fifties. The earliest had no verandas, but rather, very small window openings, such as in the two houses at Umkomaas. (Fig. 65) When there were verandas they very often afforded the only protection from the sun in the vicinity, as there were few trees to be found. (Fig. 66)

They were places for all kinds of activities; (Fig. 67,68) places where gossip of the day could be exchanged amidst the overflow of wares outside country stores and cool, shady places for the waiting queues, as at Ladysmith Magistrate's house. (Fig. 69) Several mission stations found them useful as classrooms when space inside became limited. "It would be impossible, with pen and ink, to do full justice to the varied scenes which are enacted, from morning till night, in this veranda — some of these being highly comic, some very curious, all exceedingly interesting. The veranda itself is worthwhile describing. It runs the whole length of the house, and is much wider than is usual, being twenty-six feet long by fifteen feet wide. It is open at the front and sides, the roof being supported on rough posts, which serve as frames to a succession of exquisite pictures, hills and rocks, wood and water, the beautiful clear sky above, and in the distance the sea, no less clear and beautiful, beneath".[64]

These buildings were the first sensible architectural statements of the new settlers, statements suited to and dictated by the unfamiliar conditions of their new home. They brought with them their age-old building traditions and applied to their immediate environment the stamp of the functional tradition. Limited means led to the development of a "colonial style". One example of this was the restricted sizes of roofing timber and the weight of roof coverings. This tended to produce narrow buildings which in turn afforded excellent opportunity for cross ventilation.

As far as style is concerned, what Prof. Hattersley has said of costume in Natal, would serve just as well for architecture; "long influenced by Cape colonial fashions... In later years, English fashions were, despite the climatic conditions, more in evidence".[65]

59 Natal Mercury. 1853.
60 The house is still known as "The Elephant House". The Acutt Chronicle. (K.C.M.)
61 British settlement of Natal. A.F. Hattersley. p119.
62 To the shores of Natal. Bulpin. p169
63 Pioneer days in Natal. B. Buchanan. p10
64 First impressions of Natal. By A.M. (1853). p26 (Killie Campbell Museum).
65 More annals of Natal. A.F. Hattersley. p111

Chapter 5

The British settlers

1849-1856

II

Besides the iron buildings which emigration agents are said to have despatched to Natal for the purposes of accommodating immigrants, houses roofed with iron were standing in Durban as early as 1849.[1] Barter referred to such as "uncouth buildings of corrugated iron".[2] Others found that the iron roofs contrasted pleasantly with the dark foliage of the shrub-like trees. Mr E.P. Lamport, representing Lamport and Holt, of Liverpool, had a large warehouse and dwelling house of corrugated iron.[3] (Fig. 70) Both these buildings had curved roofs.[4] The walls of the buildings were of flat corrugated sheets of about six feet in length. It seems that the earliest use of corrugated iron in England (c 1838) was also in a curved form.[5] Its major advantage was that a curved sheet could span a greater distance than a flat one.

Loudon foresaw the possibilities of the material for the construction of portable buildings and recommended two ways of overcoming the conduction of heat through the material; "The walls of buildings may be constructed of this iron set on edge, either in single plates, or of double plates with a vacuity between, to lessen the effect of changes in the exterior temperature on the space enclosed... Portable houses might be very readily made of it for exportation, but, wherever such houses were erected, they should be covered with ivy, or some other evergreen creeper, to moderate the effect of changes in the exterior temperature".[6]

Messrs Dickinson used such a store for their ironmongery business. Barter described it as; "an eccentric building — roomy, well ventilated, and much cooler than I could have supposed".[7] Colenso was amused when, "in the middle of the performances of the Durban Philharmonic society, in such an iron store, the ladies were requested to step aside for a few minutes, while part of the roof was taken off to cool the room".[8] An iron villa was also built about this time, but corrugated iron was expensive and used mainly for roofs.

The double-storeyed building of Middleton and Wirsing, (Fig. 71) built in 1850, was described as having a roof of small sheets of iron, fluted at both edges, and known as 'Morewoods' tiles. These tiles are very similar in appearance to zinc-roofing and many buildings which Russell claims to have had such tiles,[9] may have been roofed with zinc. There are two other interesting features of Middleton and Wirsing. The angled corner acknowledged the intersection of Gardiner and Smith streets, and both elevations were carefully fenestrated. The use of projecting eaves was also a sensible device to shade the whitewashed walls.

Another double-storeyed building erected in 1850 was the Royal Hotel. (Fig. 72) An iron archway supporting a square oil lamp gave access to the garden fronting the Hotel, which was set back some distance from the street. A central doorway with flanking windows led into an entrance hall which in turn led into a dining room on the one hand and a drawing room on the other. The drawing room had a painted frieze.[10] A narrow balcony supported on iron brackets provided sun protection for the rooms below. The roof was of shingles. Light wrought-iron posts and railings supported the flat veranda roof. The walls were plastered with incised rustication at the front corners.

Among the immigrants who arrived on the "Ballengeich" in July, 1850 was the architect and

1   The new Colony of Port Natal. J.E. Methley. p4
2   Dorp and Veld. C. Barter. p7
3   The Natalians. A.F. Hattersley. p45
4   Galvanised iron appears to have been first used in Cape Town in 1847.
    The growth and government of Cape Town. Laidler, p310-311, See Chapter 12, p70
5   The architectural magazine and journal vol. V, Feb. 1838. p66 and Encyclopaedia of cottage farm and villa architecture. Loudon. p205,429
6   Ibid. Loudon. p205
7   op cit, Barter. p8
8   Ten weeks in Natal. J.W. Colenso. p29
9   History of old Durban. G. Russell. p94
10   Reminiscences. C.J. Anderson. p13

surveyor, Robert Sellars Upton.[11] According to an agreement between George Pavitt Murdoch of London and Upton of Chelsea,[12] the latter was to proceed to Port Natal as surveyor for the Murdoch emigration scheme. Upton had carried on a practise as an architect and surveyor in Chelsea and had apparently designed a church at East Grenwich.[13] Among his first commissions in Durban were the Congregational church and the first English church, St Paul's.

The Congregational church (Fig. 73) was designed in 1854, the foundation stone being laid on July 11 1855.[14] The building was the earliest example in Natal of the revived Classical style. A prostyle portico of four fluted columns led to a central doorway with tall flanking windows. There were four similar sash windows on the side walls of the church. Lady Barker found the churches to be "the only ambitious edifices of the town... A Congregational chapel, with a Doric portico in front, and on either side windows so square and vast that devotion therein must be fervid at any rate".[15]

It is certain that Upton had had a thorough training in Classical architecture, at any rate a training which took little note of the currently popular Gothic. It was said that, one of his qualities was "a sturdy dislike to anything like sacerdotalism".[16] This may explain why Upton seemed more at home in the classical style and why his Gothic was essentially pre-Puginist.[16A] St Paul's church was designed to be 110 feet long, with transepts and a square tower, (Fig. 74) but a small budget excluded the tower and limited the length to 70 feet.[17] The church consisted of a simple nave with articulated chancel. (Fig. 75,76) The five large windows on either side with their correct geometrical tracery and label mouldings, had curious diamond panes introduced into the upper sections, and a particularly heavy transom occurred at an awkward height. The quality of the detail is remarkable for a structure erected at such an early period in Natal. However the proportion of roof to wall and the essential horizontality of the building (emphasised by the heavy cornice which continued round the entire roof) are not convincing in an otherwise Gothic building. The smooth plastered surfaces, probably resorted to for lack of a suitable stone, are not polychromatic [18] in the contemporary English sense and indicate Upton's so-called anti-sacerdotalism.

Upton advertised for tenders for the erection of the church in January, 1853; "The tenders must be accompanied with samples of the brick and stone the contractors propose using in the erection of the building".[19] These were to be delivered to his office between the hours of ten and four.

On March 3rd, the Natal Mercantile Advertiser announced that the "contract for this structure has been taken by Mr Downs, and the cost will be about £1,000. The design is extremely chaste and beautiful and reflects much credit on Mr Upton". During the ceremony that attended the laying of the foundation stone, Upton led the procession, bearing the plans and a silver trowel. "The church will be in the perpendicular Gothic style of architecture, and in the open position selected for it, will be a beautiful and commanding object, especially when the completed design shall be carried out".[20]

The chosen situation, on an erf adjoining the market square, was the partial fulfilment of Gardiner's proposal of 1834, for his town layout indicated a church in the centre of a large market square.[21]

Together with a donation of bricks and lime, £292.9s. was subscribed and was supplemented by gifts from England and the Cape, "and two impecunious young men each contributed two days labour". Several problems beset Upton during the construction of the church. The original contractor failed to fulfil his contract, and Upton, when asked to take charge of the work, reported that the original contract price would have to be exceeded by £500, owing to the "requirements of the workmen for higher wages, together with the great advances in the price of materials, in some instances to treble that of the original contract prices".[22] At a subsequent meeting he reported that the person who had contracted for the slating of the roof had left the colony, and that his partner repudiated the contract. He also reported that the glass provided by the original contractors was not of the correct size, and asked permission to sell it and procure new glass from England. Eventually calico was fixed to the windows as glass could not be afforded. St Paul's was consecrated on St Peter's Day, 1864.[23] Lady Barker thought that St Paul's was a neat little church, but needed a tower to be complete. (Fig. 76) She found the only other Gothic church in Durban, the Wesleyan chapel, of "the same style, but in worse taste".[24]

St Peter's church in Pietermaritzburg (Fig. 77) is the most 'correct' example of the Gothic Revival built in Natal. In March 1850, erf 17 in Longmarket Street was granted by the Colonial Government to the Church of England.[25] The arrival of the British immigrants created the necessity for the immediate erection of a church, as the schoolroom had become too small for this purpose. Several historians maintain that Sophie Gray, wife of the Bishop of Cape Town was responsible for the original design.[26] Churches in the Cape, such as those at Claremont and Cradock are attributed to her, the Cradock church (1854) having a similar outline and section to St Peter's. Sophie Gray definitely did take more than the usual interest in the design and erection of churches in her husband's diocese. Bishop Gray's biographer states that during childhood, her Governess "taught her to draw with exactness and precision. With this careful training behind her this child was in later life to prove herself an ecclesiastical architect of no inconsiderable achievement. Throughout the length and breadth of the old Cape Colony there stand to this day churches which Mrs Gray designed for God's Glory and honour".[27] In a pastoral letter of December 1849, Bishop Gray spoke of the prospect of twenty-one new churches being built and "already Mrs Gray was working at her plans and drawings as if she were a qualified ecclesiastical architect".

Her design for St Peter's consisted of a small church without chancel and vestry and made no provision for a choir. The foundation stone was laid in November 1851 by Lieutenant Governor Pine. One of the contractors, Jesse Smith, [28] had conveniently discovered a new quarry north of the town so the walls of the church were built of honey-coloured freestone. By 1854 nine hundred pounds had been expended, when a meeting presided over by Bishop Colenso decided to "place the original drawings in the hands of some competent architect in England" in order that "correct designs may be furnished for the proposed additions".[29] It was felt that the original design would not suffice as a cathedral and the committee decided to add a choir and two transepts. No record survives of who the competent architect was. Eventually the transepts were dispensed with and a small vestry was built on the North side of the church. (Fig. 78) The Society for Promoting Christian Knowledge promised £500 on condition that an equal amount was locally subscribed and several other donations helped to pay for the new contract, which included stone and slates to be brought from England.

The building was orientated towards the ecclesiastical "east" and had entrance doors at the west end with an entrance porch and vestry on the north side. William Watson and Gabriel Eaglestone executed the fine stonework.[30] The stepped plinth was of a smooth sand stone while the walls above were of a polychromatic, blue-grey and brown stone of a rougher texture. Eaglestone was also responsible for the carving of the delightful gargoyle (Fig. 79) at the corner of the vestry and chancel and the two corbel stone heads above the door of the vestry. (Fig. 80) The interior of the church (Fig. 81) was extremely simple and consisted of a nave with a timber roof supported on hammer beams, rising from wall posts and corbels. A chancel arch separated the sanctuary from the main body of the church. The three lights of the East window (Fig. 82) which contained stained glass depicting St Matthew, St James and St Simon, were given to Colenso by William Sewell of Radley College.[31] Sewell had been a collector of ecclesias-

tical decorations rescued from monasteries disbanded after the French Revolution, so the glass may originally have been in a church somewhere in France. The whole church was plastered inside and painted white. A Gothic revival building such as St Peter's could only have appealed widely to those who had accepted the Picturesque point of view. The

11   Oliver the spy. A.F. Hattersley. p156
12   Durban Town Clerk's archives, Letters received, H3921.
13   The British settlement of Natal. A.F. Hattersley. p318
14   History of old Durban. G. Russell. p249
15   Life at Natal, Cape monthly magazine, vol. 4. p75
16   Obituary, Natal Mercury, May 7 1883.
16a Goodhart-Rendel in "English architecture since the Regency" suggests that churches of the pre-Puginist Gothic Revival were distinguishable by their well-light interiors, the central steeple at the west end, the greater proportion of wall to roof and the use of smooth building materials. Those which were post-Puginist and 'correct' according to the Ecclesiological Society were built of rough, heavy stonework, with dark interiors and steep roofs rising from low walls. When there was a steeple it was situated 'picturesquely' at the one side and considered to be incomplete without a spire.
17   History of Durban. G. Russell. p260
18   Architectural Polychromy meant the introduction of variegations in the exterior design of facades. It may be taken to include not only variegations of colour but of textures and materials too. Limited means and few materials spared Natal the worst of the dazzling polychromy so popular at the time in England.
19   Natal Mercantile advertiser. January 26 1853
20   Natal Mercantile advertiser. February 17 1853.
21   See Chapter 11
22   History of Durban. G. Russell. p260
23   (Fig. 16). A gallery was added in 1865, and transepts and a new chancel and organ were built in 1880. Unfortunately the building was completely destroyed by fire on 23 March 1906.
24   Life at Natal. Cape monthly magazine. vol.4. p75
25   The Centenary of Bishop Colenso's cathedral. A.F. Hattersley.
26   The British settlement of Natal. A.F. Hattersley. p319 and Englishman's inn. D.F. Shuter.
27   Robert Gray. Audrey Brooke. p7, p49, p65. See Chapter 7
28   Ibid, The British settlement of Natal. p319 Garbutt and Fleming also assisted in the erection of the building.
29   Natal independent. February 23 1854.
30   The British settlement of Natal. A.F. Hattersley. p320
31   Ibid, Hattersley. p320

deliberate irregularity of the side of the building facing Church Street, the articulated chancel and protruding vestry and porch, the plasticity of the whole form and the use of textural and polychromatic materials were the signs of the Picturesque still evident in the mature Gothic revival. (Fig. 83) Charles Barter found the plan to be "chaste and correct". [32] The ecclesiologists, [33] however, might have frowned at the absence of a reredros screen and found fault with the fleche over the centre of the nave roof. Through their periodicals they had spread propaganda prescribing the "correct" method of church building, within which sacramental rites could be "rubrically" performed. In 1862 the East window was re-leaded and storm damages to the West window were repaired. The memorial window in the north wall of the chancel was also fitted at about this time.

In 1863 an English architect, Freeman, prepared designs for the addition of transepts and a steeple. [34] Sophie Gray, however, was also involved in preparing designs for additions in 1864. This can only be accounted for by the schism developing within the church in South Africa.[35] It is likely that Bishop Colenso approached Freeman about the proposed additions, during his four year stay in England (1861–1865) and Dean Green, a close friend of Bishop Gray, took the opportunity afforded by Colenso's absence to request the Bishop's wife for designs.[36]

Mrs Gray first wrote to the Dean in 1864; "You will not forget that I have no plans or measurements of the present church, without which I can do nothing in the way of new plans for the addition".[37] The task of transcribing her husband's journal delayed her working "at any of the plans for churches for Natal". On September 15th she sent drawings to Pietermaritzburg; "for your cathedral, on approbation. I am going next week to Clanwilliam for a month, so that I shall not do any more to it till I hear from you whether it is the sort of thing you wish for – and whether my measurements of the present building are correct. You will see that I could not make up my mind to make your nave and chancel all in one. It would be such a disadvantage in point of appearance, not to have a chancel arch and the saving would not be so much, because you would have fifty feet more of the large roofs and more walling too. Your present chancel must become a chapter house – or chapel for daily service". She found difficulty in understanding the Dean's notes and made lengthy enquiries concerning the corbels supporting the roof, their centres, dimensions and the length of the rafters and the size of the wall post ribs. Towards the close of 1864, Mrs Gray wrote; "I have tried to get your drawings altered ... but other things have come in the way and I have not succeeded. I do not feel that there is any hurry, as you can do nothing in the present state of things".

Neither of the two proposals was carried out, due mainly to a severe economic depression. In 1871 a gallery was built at the West end and in 1907 the South porch was built.[38]

Colenso was also involved in the erection of two other Gothic churches in Natal. He built a small timber church at Bishopstowe shortly before 1860. (Fig. 84) This served as a chapel for his school, "Ekukanyeni" at which he gave education to African boys. As carpentry and building were two of the school subjects, the erection of the building may have been entrusted to the schoolboys. Apart from this the church is only remarkable for the ugliness of the fleche over the nave roof, a form which could only have had its origin in the medieval acolyte's lantern.

St Mary's church (Pietermaritzburg) was also built in 1860.   Mason found the church to be "the most complete in design" in the capital, where the Rev W. Baugh, had a "tolerable congregation of natives, just emerging from barbarism".[39] The original church, which stood on the site of the Legislative Assembly building, had no separate chancel, but the tall pointed fleche and the porch on the south side indicate the attempt to break up the form of the building. (Fig. 86) Buttresses and window reveals were rusticated. The building was pulled down in 1889 and re-erected at the corner of Burger Street and Commercial Road. The tower was changed and a vestry was added during the course of the rebuilding. At the same time the gables were taken up past the roof, the rustication done away with and the porch roof supported on an open, aedicular roof structure. (Fig. 87)

Presbyterians in Pietermaritzburg also chose the Gothic style for their new church. (Fig. 88) Fleming, a local contractor, recorded in his diary on Sat. June 7 1851: "made out at estimate for a proposed Scotch church here, the cost about £700, according to a plan rendered by Mr Baker". Hughbert Baker, who came to Natal in April 1850 on the "Washington", was a surveyor and an acquaintance of Thomas Telford and Isumbard Brunel. Baker left the colony in 1853 before the completion of the building. Work was commenced in 1852, after the Government had donated a site in central Church street, and the municipal commissioners had given certain materials. "The Commissioners of Municipality are thanked for supplying stone and sand free", [40] hope being expressed at the same time that the same would apply to the freestone required. The church had a short square tower at the one end, the walls were of rubble masonry and the roof was of slate. (Fig. 89) Many delays and difficulties were apparently encountered in the process of building and on the first of October, 1854 the still unfinished building was opened for worship. In 1873 alterations were effected and the tower was increased in height for the installation of a clock. (Fig. 90) The front elevation displays a curious, but not uncommon, mixture of Gothic and Classical. [40A] The Gothic tower intersects a broken classical pediment, while tall lancet windows and a pointed arched doorway occur in the spaces between the pilasters and the quoining.

The new Garrison church, built after 1850 to replace the original chapel which had been destroyed by lightning, was described as a "substantial stone edifice". The Catholic church (Fig. 91,92) which was opened on Christmas Day, 1852, was also a small, simple Gothic building, forty feet in length by twenty-five feet broad. Bishop Allard, in a report to his Superior General, Bishop de Mazenod, said that; "our church, built in so short a time and with limited resources, cannot but excite the admiration of all, even the visitors. Anyway it far surpasses any of the edifices erected by protestant sects in the colony. Although it is simple in design the architect has been able to introduce several pleasing features. The sign of our holy religion stands out boldly on the facade, while in the interior, the central and main decoration is the beautiful painting of the Crucifixion by Fiesole, which your Lordship so graciously presented to the mission of Natal before we left".[41]

The church presented some interesting fretwork detailing. "The sign of our holy religion" was intersected with a circle which echoed the arcs of the bargeboards. The introduction of the diamond shaped ventilator which reflected in its lines the slope of the roof indicates a sophistication which may have justified the Bishop's claims, though the porch addition was certainly an improvement over the original curved entrance roof.[41A]

The Anglican church at Richmond was the only other Gothic church built in Natal before 1856. The walls were built of local stone and the roof was tiled. (Fig. 93) By 1853, it was said that, "some of the arches had already been turned and showed careful workmanship on the part of a solitary builder, a native of the valley, who did all the work".[42] The church was originally built without a chancel.

A house built by James Methley in 1854 in the Karkloof, was "a brick and stone building in the Gothic style with a raised garden terrace".[43] Barter described the farm and house, "Here Mr Methley... owns a large farm, and here on a rising ground above a stream, he has built what may be called, par excellence, the country seat of Natal. Indeed it is the only building out of Maritzburg or D'Urban, which pretends to be more than a cottage, and it must have cost a considerable sum. The chief room is a large handsome library, with carved panels to the doors and stained glass in the windows, that give it quite an old-fashioned English appearance. There is a handsome veranda, opening on a terrace, or rather a succession of terraces, communicating with one another by steps, where the garden is to be laid out".[44] The rooms had boarded floors and ceilings and the fireplaces with their fire-grates were said to draw well. Methley quarried the stone for the library himself and built the walls two feet thick, as well as planing 1,000 feet of planking for the flooring and cutting the glass for the windows, "with a bad diamond and an old key".[45]

Colenso's house at Bishopstowe (Fig. 94) was also described as "Gothic" by some, and as a "cottage orné" by others. The steeply pitched roof, the dormer windows, the filigree bargeboards and the bay window were all elements of the Cottage Orné, a house form very much in fashion in England at the time. Though the peculiar use of the extended and enlarged "dormer" roofs would have proved a useful device in the warm climate, the building tends towards an over-elaboration of the parts to the detriment of the whole. The deliberately haphazard,

32 Dorp and Veld. C. Barter. p28

33 The "Ecclesiological Society" was formed in c. 1840 and evolved a pseudo-science of church building. They prescribed a new programme of design which involved the assembly of elements of medieval church architecture into a complex framework suitable to the performance of the liturgy. Their significance lies in their attempt to find architectural solutions suitable to other aspects of the liturgy besides that of the word, around which developed the hall or auditorium church.

34 Ibid, Centenary of Bishop Colenso's cathedral.

35 A history of Natal. E.H. Brookes and C. de B. Webb. p 108,109

36 Bishop and Mrs. Gray sailed for Natal on the 16 April 1864; the day on which the sentence depriving Colenso of his bishopric, became operative.

37 Letters of Sophie Gray to Dean Green. (1864). Anglican Church Archives. (Univ. of Natal. Library. PMB).
    This might indicate that the Dean had assumed that Mrs. Gray would have had drawings of the original church.

38 Ibid, The Centenary of Bishop Colenso's Cathedral.

39 Zululand. Mason. p17

40 The Presbyterian church of Pietermaritzburg 1850—1950. Prof. A. Petrie.

40a Especially found in the churches of Alexander Thompson in Glasgow.

41 Diary of Bishop Allard. O.M.I. (Archdiocesan Archives, Durban).

41a See Fig. 196 Chapter 7.

42 A history of Richmond from 1839 to 1937. S.W.B. Shepstone. p25

43 J. Sheddon Dobie. S.A. Journal. p23

44 Dorp and Veld. C. Barter.

45 Letters from J.E. Methley to J. Methley. Dec. 1854. (Killie Campbell Museum)

or rather picturesque relationships of the roofs and their rich "fretwork and earwig" detail, are quite consistent with this tendency.[45A]

By 1852 Pietermaritzburg had 443 dwelling houses accommodating a white population of 1508. Bird found the town no longer in the very primitive and unusual state that it had been in 1846.[46] Apart from the few wattle-and-daub structures still standing and the green-brick veranda-houses which the settlers had erected on their arrival, many resembled the simple Georgian houses of the Cape Colony or the cottages of the smaller towns and villages in England. (Fig. 95 – 98) The majority were single-storeyed with a loft and whitewashed walls, which Barter disliked for their uniformity, though this was relieved by "verandas, around whose posts were trained beautiful and luxuriant creepers".[47] He also recorded that most of them had tiled or thatched roofs and "some had already been inflicted with the hideous corrugated iron".[48] The first building bye-law in Pietermaritzburg forebade the use of wattle and daub in the streets of the town. Walls were to be nine inches in thickness, whether of burnt of unburnt brick or stone.[49]

Stone was chosen for the alterations to Government House, "to render the house a suitable residence for the Lieut-Governor".[50] Attempts had been made as early as August 1852, to effect the necessary additions. A surviving plan (Fig. 99) indicates that Stanger's cottage [51] may have consisted of the rooms in the upper left-hand corner of the plan, and that the proposed additions were to project at right angles to it and create a U shaped building. A geometrical pattern of gravel walks and driveways led up to the entrance; the entrance hall continued through to the veranda which encircled the entire house. Access between most of the rooms was to occur in this veranda. The drawing also reveals that one of the two principal rooms was to have a large bow window on the shorter wall, and that a few rooms had neither window nor door. Large outhouses with toilets, kitchen and stables were to be situated behind the house and to enclose a separate yard. For some unknown reason this plan was never carried out. On April 19 1854, the Colonial Secretary authorised a rather more modest plan of alteration.[52] This was to include "a fireplace or stove" in the drawing room, the papering of this room together with the dining room and passage, the plastering of most of the walls and the rethatching of the entire roof. Dormer windows were to be inserted in the roof and the verandas were to receive facia-boards and new supports.[53] By April 1855, the roof of the house was again in need of repair. It is likely that the roof was tiled shortly thereafter and that it appeared as at the left of (Fig. 100) without the porte-cochère and the fretwork to the dormer bargeboards.

Dormer windows were yet to be commonly used, a possible reason being that they provided another point of weakness in the thatched roofs. Even without such features, most of the houses in Pietermaritzburg were essentially British in character. (Fig. 101,102,103,104)

The Archbell house (Fig. 105) had a twin chimneyed roof, tall, well-proportioned windows and a little Regency entrance portico. In some cases such houses are now partially hidden behind flamboyant, cast-iron verandas and other additions. No. 121 Loop Street is the kind of house which could easily be found in the Cape. (Fig. 106,107) The house had an entrance hall with a staircase leading to the upper floor and the major rooms were entered off this hall.[54]

Many of the single-storeyed houses of the time were developments of the narrow "colonial" type and took the form of L or U shapes. The shale house at 380 Prince Alfred St (Fig. 108) had small pointed arched windows. This Gothic feature was unusual as most of the buildings of the period are recognisable from their tall, rectangular windows, carefully positioned in relation to the walls and to each other. The two shops (Fig. 109,110) are essentially English in character while that with its narrower windows (Fig. 111) has all the characteristics of the architecture of the Cape after the British occupation. Hotels, mills, and farmbuildings erected throughout Natal during this period all exhibit their English derivations in their fenestration and tightly clipped roofs. (Fig. C) Sometimes in the scale of the window openings this derivation was perhaps indirectly through the Cape. (Fig. 112,113,114,115,116,117)

In 1852 the resident magistrate at Umvoti 'submitted to the Surveyor-General a design for a district courthouse. (Fig. 118,119) The building was to serve as a prison for male and female prisoners and the plan made provision for a Jailer's dwelling. The front portion was to contain a courthouse on two levels and offices for the magistrate and clerk of the peace. The front elevation was to be punctuated with small-paned windows at regular intervals. This kind of plan may well have been a solution to the many small official buildings erected in the centres at which the population had congregated outside of the towns. Dr Stanger himself designed the courthouse at Ladysmith, [55] his original intention being to roof it with corrugated iron. When this proved too expensive, slate was resorted to. The roof below the slates was boarded with ¾" deals, suggesting the kind of problems which beset those who built in areas prone to thunderstorms.

It would appear that Sir George Grey, the Governor of the Cape Colony, at whose instigation the first hospital in Natal was commenced, also designed the building and entrusted the execution thereof to the new Surveyor General of Natal, Dr Sutherland. Work on the site was begun under the latter's supervision towards the close of 1855.[56] The Natal Guardian found that, "The site is ominously convenient to the cemetry". Davis' Almanac described it in 1868; "Grey's Hospital which we desire more expressly to notice, is a building of considerable size; admits of a thorough ventilation of its wards and passages; is well supplied with pure water; and the floors are well raised and dry and have good ventilation underneath ... The destination of the institution is as a retreat for the old and disabled of both sexes; for curing the sick and wounded; for affording assistance to and recovering the strangled, the partially drowned, and the burnt; for the gratuitous delivery of advice and medicines, and for vaccination; and for the care and alleviation of insane people and lunatics, until suitable provision can be made for the latter by the Government". The hospital was built in the pavilion style with dressed stone walls and thatched roof. An entrance hall with a corridor crossing it at right angles, led to small offices and rooms in the centre of the building. There were theatres and wards at each end. Windows were tall sliding sashes, placed at regular horizontal intervals but "floating unhappily" between the thatched eaves and the ground. The building was completed within a shoestring budget by the Colonial Engineer in 1862. (Fig. 121 & 122)

Natal was separated from the Cape by a Charter, promulgated by Letters Patent dated 15 July 1856 and thus created a Colony. The British settlers had at first built according to the traditions of the Cape, or of those parts of England from which they had emigrated, and in some cases under the influence of the revived styles popular in England at the time. Within the new Colony however, they were soon to develop an individuality of their own with only slender links to the other parts of South Africa, across the barriers of the Drakensberg to the north, Kaffraria to the south, and overseas to the mother country and Europe.

45a Bishop Colenso may himself have designed this house in addition to the wooden chapel at Bishopstowe and St. Mary's (Anglican) Church in Pietermaritzburg.
46 Natal by an Old Inhabitant. p27
47 Dorp and Veld. C. Barter. p23
48 op cit, Barter. p178
49 Ordinances, proclamations relating to the Colony of Natal. D. Moodie. Vol. 11.
50 S.G.O. 21 Feb. 1854. 7., 111/1/12.
51 See p10
52 S.G.O. 19 April. and 29 July. 30, 111/1/12.
53 S.G.O. 5. Sept. 161, 111/1/9.
54 The large paned windows were probably added later in the century, though the openings are certainly original.
55 Fleming diary. 20 August 1853. (Killie Campbell Museum).
56 A hospital century. A.F. Hattersley.

Chapter 6

'Days of wider & grander notions' [1]

1856 — 1865

"of late years, indeed, a vast improvement has taken place in our style of living. Town houses are almost invariably furnished and fitted up in English fashion; and in the country, the rude expedient of earlier years, mere shells of houses, comprising little more than four bare walls, and a bare roof, are being superseded by an era of paint, wallpaper, and general upholstery". (Robinson). [2]

By the close of the eighteen fifties the European population of Natal was approaching ten thousand. In their efforts to establish an environment like those they had known in Britain, the colonists reproduced all aspects of life in the mother country. Roads and bridges were built to link the small communities scattered throughout the colony. The systems of local government and jurisdiction necessitated the establishment of representatives of the Queen and of justice in all areas. Communities of different denominations erected churches and chapels for their particular forms of worship, and as visible signs of their religions. Agricultural developments and the growing population injected vitality into the infant economy and, together with the fast developing trade relationships, these factors stimulated domestic commerce. (Fig. 123) Societies, mechanics' institutions and clubs were formed by the colonists, which, though frequently over-ambitious and unrealistic, are a sign of the efforts which were made to recreate the social life of Britain.

The earliest bridges, built to cross the numerous rivers which run down from the highlands of Natal to the Indian Ocean, were structures of local timber. The one across the Alleman's Drift at Howick was carried out by two carpenters, Ellis and Strapp, and consisted of piers of solid masonry supporting sneezewood trusses with a yellow wood, boarded floor. [3]

An iron tension bridge was erected in 1858 to span the Umzindusi, at the entrance to Pietermaritzburg. The "Queens" bridge of wrought iron complete with entrance arches, was built across the Umgeni in 1864. (Fig. 124) Neither of these bridges lasted very long. The first collapsed from severe vibration when a large herd of oxen were driven over it, and the latter, with its seven spans of 100 feet each, supported on cast iron columns, was swept away in the severe floods of 1868.

The first railway in South Africa was a 4ft. $8\frac{1}{2}$" line running from the Point to the centre of Durban. Built in 1860, the termini at both ends were simple sheds of corrugated iron which were to be retained in use until the end of the century, when stations were erected throughout the colony by the Natal Government Railways.

Both Durban and Pietermaritzburg found the erection of new gaols imperative. The resident magistrate in the city recommended that "the Prison be constructed with a view to being enlarged and consider that for the present eight cells, each 11 feet square, for Prisoners and Lunatics and two for hospital paupers ... would be sufficient".[4]

In Durban the Borough Police Force had used the gaol as a police station and in Nov. 1861 the council instructed the Borough Surveyor, Henry Waddington, to prepare a plan for a building to contain "four cells, Sergeant's room and necessary adjuncts".[5] The building was erected on the market square and took the form of a single-storeyed block with a low pitched roof and a veranda on the entrance side which was supported on light cast-iron columns. (Fig. 125) A large roof ventilator was installed at a later date (probably designed by R.S. Upton.) This form of building, which was to become a common one in the commercial streets of Durban, is particularly interesting for its smooth white plastered walls and the emphatic horizontality of the detail.[6]

Robert Sellars Upton chose the classical style for the first hospital in Durban. Built of brick and roofed with iron, it stood close to the Bay but the entrance faced in the other direction towards the north. When it was completed in 1861, it contained two wards. The front elevation consisted of an entrance portico with Tuscan columns in prostyle, supporting a simple pediment. (Fig. 126,127) The lines of the pleasantly proportioned entrance doors and the sash windows were continued in larger windows in the flanking wings, while the ends were terminated with basket arched openings. The horizontality of the building was also emphasised by the continuous cornice and plinth lines. The lowering of the roof at the extremes provided an effective build up towards the entrance portico. The walls were plastered and painted white, their smoothness being more appropriate to the classical style than to Upton's other building, the "Gothic" St Paul's. When it was completed in 1861, the Natal Mercury considered it to be "elegant" and "one of the most considerable buildings in the town". [6A] Though Upton does not appear to have come across the kind of problems which beset him during the erection of St Paul's, it was not long before the Colonial Engineer was called in by the District Surgeon to effect repairs to the hospital.(1865) [7]

Many buildings which were erected to fulfil a public need during this period were of a simple and temporary nature. Such was the market house in Pietermaritzburg, which was constructed of timber and erected in three weeks by Mr George Loveday and Mr Wheeler. Two outlying forts, Fort Buckingham and Fort Cross (Fig. 128) were both erected in 1861 and must also have been regarded as temporary structures for, as they each consisted of a group of large thatched huts, they could find sound defence only in their prominent situations.

By 1863 Durban had changed considerably; the "Natal Mercury and Commercial Advertiser" of October the 2nd suggested that "to those on the spot the change that has passed over the place is great, but to those who have been long absent, it almost amounts to an entire transformation". Noting that the town also offered "immense room for improvement", the newspaper went on to say: "There was a time when the east had very few architectural pretensions, but now it is different. Messrs Blackwood and Couper set an excellent example to the neighbourhood by erecting their handsome two-storeyed establishment, the front of which would do credit to an English street. Mr Jameson's premises are apt to recall pleasant home recollections by the quaint, old fashioned front they have assumed. We should like to see that fragmentary structure, the Natal Bank, (Durban branch) come to maturity, as all the bills inside it do sooner or later. Suppose we protest at that unoccupied corner with its unfinished gable, which is perpetually promising what it apparently never intends to fulfil. Messrs Parker Wood and Co's large store opposite comprises we suppose the largest floor in the colony, being 114 feet by 74 feet. (Fig. 129) When the colonnade round the front is up, this building will furnish the corner of the market square handsomely ... It must be confessed even our friends the recalcitrant auctioneers must allow that the market square is improved. It is useless to deny that the walled in enclosure, with its upper palisadings and its rapidly developing parterres is a pleasanter sight than the "desert" across which you, old friend, and we have so laboriously waded. It has quite changed the aspect of this part of the town, it has made respectable what was once vile, exasperating, and disreputable. When those unoccupied erven on the south side are fenced in and built on, the market

square won't look so bad after all. Messrs Gillespie's arcades we heard likened by a stranger the other day to the quadrant; and when Messrs Acutt and Leslie's handsome premises (Fig. 130) have a worthy vis-a-vis we shall be happy. This last named building, by the by, belongs rather to an anterior age, but it is none the less entitled to all honour, seeing that it holds its own so well in these later days of wider and grander notions. The new Capital Club, (Fig. 131) with its handsome pilastered front, is taken altogether, the finest building in the town. We shall be glad to see more like it arise. It is curious that two-storeyed buildings are not more common than they are, seeing how valuable land has become. That quondam swamp "the valley" is now thickly planted, stores are springing up like mushrooms in this locality. Mr R. Acutt (Fig. 132) has two going up, Mr Cooley's and Mr Henwood's are both near, and in the same style. Then on the other side and farther on we have Messrs Crozier and Louch's large and handsome establishment, (Fig. 133) with its elegant iron roof frame, and its graceful columns in front. Mr Challinor's property, the London and South Africa Bank has, perhaps, the best finished front in the town, when we consider its size and prominent position... As West street advances west, it shows great signs of improvement. Messrs Dickenson and Co's handsome brass and plate glass front is, we should say, as fine a thing in its way as there is in South Africa. Messrs S. and B. Crowder have lately completed a pile of double-storeyed buildings, (Fig. 134) with shops underneath that give one an idea of what the street will look like when it is entirely built up in that way".

Upton is known to have designed the Durban Club (Fig. 131) in 1862 and either he or the few other architect-surveyors in Durban [8] may have been responsible for several of the buildings which the "Natal Mercury" thought worthy of mention. Walls were generally plastered and painted white and sometimes rusticated, though this appears to have been limited to the horizontal coursing only.

The more successful designs presented walls or porticoes only, with the pediments and roofs recessed, while those with projecting eaves reveal a conflict between roof and wall. Crozier and Louch's fine building (Fig. 133) drew attention to itself through the use of a scale larger than those of the adjacent buildings, and the entire portico was set back from

1	Natal Mercury, October 2 1863.
2	Natal. Robinson. p44
3	See Chapter 12
4	S.G.O. 42. 111/1/12.
5	Municipal history of Durban. Henderson.
6	See p27
6a	Natal Mercury. October 2 1863
7	C.S.O. 1956 No.2325 Nov. 29 1865.
8	See Chapter 13, Reference 4

the pavement, contrasting with the projecting verandas of the other buildings in the street. Equal visual emphasis was given in most cases to the horizontal and the vertical. Projecting eaves and the precise classical mouldings of cornices and string courses, with their deep shadow lines, underlined the length of the facades, while the use of tall sash windows and narrow framed, plate glass fronts emphasised the vertical. (Fig. 135)

Such facades, at times independent of and withdrawn from their neighbours or attempting by their very difference to catch the eye, have a refreshing variety and originality of plastic expression. (Fig. 136) Concave and convex walls were used to acknowledge corners (Challinor's Fig. 137 and Leeds House, Fig. 138) and, in the form of flat and basket arches with echoing dripmoulds, this plasticity has an unusual quality. Architects in Britain at the time achieved plasticity not only in the deliberate modulation of surfaces but also in the variegations of texture of the surface material itself. In Durban, plaster was thought essential to protect the brickwork against attack by the marine atmosphere.[9] The exaggerated curves of the building mouldings are reflected in those of the furniture from this period, which was often heavy and obese.

The Natal Bank (1860), which was designed by Joseph Cato (Fig. 140), and Caney's buildings, (Fig. 141) indicate an alternative facade treatment derived from the use of large windows which left little wall surface, leading eventually to a concentration of ornament around door and window openings. The head office of the Natal Bank (Fig. 142) had been erected in Pietermaritzburg in 1858; it also appears to have been the work of Joseph Cato.[10] A good red facebrick, which had become easily available, was used for the bank and other buildings in the city. The corners of the building were quoined and the brackets supporting the hoodmouldings over the door and windows announce the advent of the High Renaissance Revival in Natal. Through Barry and other architects this style had become fashionable for club and commercial architecture in England.

Pietermaritzburg shopkeepers and tradesmen nevertheless were said to have "grander houses, ride better horses, their wives are smarter and they are, in a sense, finer gentlemen than any in the colony".[11] They were also the principal members of the new "gentlemans club" which had been founded in 1859 and they might have frequented the new Theatre Royal,[12] a hall 115 feet long which had an arched and decorated ceiling and is said to have been fitted with opera chairs in the higher priced stalls. Another club, the Athenium, with its library and coffee and reading rooms, was opened in December 1859.

In 1864 Pietermaritzburg looked like "a large garden, thickly dotted with houses. Most of the

public buildings — places of worship being the only pretentious ones — are visible. There is the Wesleyan chapel — a large though not large enough, and not very handsome brick building, but having perhaps the very best material and workmanship employed in its construction, and capable of seating 500 persons. A gallery is being put up in this chapel at the present time...".[13] The large number of Wesleyan immigrants who arrived in Natal in the early eighteen-fifties led to the congregation outgrowing the "little old fashioned structure" which had been erected in 1848. The new church, a simple classical hall without side pavilions, was thought to be curious by some, and ugly by others.[14] (Fig. 143,144) The Ionic columns of the portico were of "enormous blocks of freestone, curiously if not handsomely wrought. The whole appearance of the building was so unusual that it was said to belong to the Roman Dutch order of architecture".[15] (Whiteside) Similar temple models which became increasingly larger in scale and coarser in detail, continued to be popular in England as places of worship for Dissenters up until the 'sixties.[16] So, while their original chapel had been built in the Gothic style, apparently quite acceptable for chapels, "the Grecian style" was thought more appropriate for a metropolitan church.[17] The entrance door and windows with their white surrounds and pediments are certainly original, though the plastered plinth and additions at the rear of the building date from the extensions of 1877 and 1902.

The Wesleyan church was opened for worship in 1859 and would appear to be the earliest and largest public building erected in the light orange brick which was to become so characteristic a wall material in Pietermaritzburg. In most of the larger industrial towns of Britain, wire-cut, red bricks had been used as an economic building material in all types of structures and their low cost in Pietermaritzburg may have been the reason for their use, for they were not liked. J.S. Little in 1884 found the city to have "a Scotch church and a Congregational church, and there is a church built in barberous red brick — in pseudo — Romano — Ionic style, which is really a painful sight to behold".[18]

In Durban the Methodists found satisfaction in plastered Gothic churches; they erected one in West Street in 1857. (Fig. 145) This was designed and supervised by the Rev Calvert Spensley, and was "pretty in appearance, but too light in construction".[19] Churches were also erected on the Berea (1866) (Fig. 146) and at Addington (1865).

Richmond had altered considerably by 1860; "the actual town or village having decreased as to the number of its houses, though it had wonderfully advanced in real prosperity: many excellent buildings and well planted orchards having replaced the temporary huts and garden plots of its earlier days. Close by our rendevous stood the new National School — a substantial building, and about half-a mile further on we found a very comfortable colonial church".[19A] Built in 1860, the Methodist church has all the characteristics of a "chaste" Gothic chapel. (Fig. 147) Sited on a steeply sloping site, it possesses a small differentiated chancel, porch and vestry. Except for its "incorrect" ecclesiastical orientation it could well be an Anglican church, and the blue-grey stonework and steeply pitched roofs suggest that St Peter's Cathedral in Pietermaritzburg might well have been the local inspiration.

It is quite likely that the architect of the Richmond church was also involved in the design of that at "Shafton Grange". James Methley wrote to his father, The Rev J. Methley of Leeds in 1858: "I want to enlist your sympathy for our chapel at Shafton, it is to be built on some land which I have given for the purpose, about a quarter of a mile from the house, a nice situation and we are to have a burying ground attached. We have already got more than the value of £150 subscribed and we intend to present it to the conference free from debt, providing they will send us out zinc for the roof which will cost about £20, also a chapel bible and a large copy of Wesley's. It is to built in the Gothic style and very substantial on the model of an old country church, without the tower and bell which is to be added when our green hills are covered with the fleeces of our sheep". (sic)[20] (Fig. 148,149)

Methley had brought out some stained glass windows with him in 1852 and these were to be incorporated in the building (probably the three lancet windows on the west wall.) The tiny church was also built of local stone and has high pitched roofs with very slightly projecting eaves at the gable ends. The roof covering was originally slate. (Fig. 150) To ensure that the building would have a complete rural character, Methley requested his father for a diagonal battened stable door and iron S neck handles. (Fig. 151) He found that the lowest estimate for locally made windows was £47, compared with the £6 necessary for the same in England. Before the building was completed in 1860, he wrote to his father saying, "people here have subscribed very liberally and we shall have a very handsome and permanent erection, the very antipodes of wattle and daub".[21]

A Scotchman, Adams, is said to have prepared the plans for the Anglican church at Mt Moreland. The building was completed between 1857 and 1860 and consisted of a simple undifferentiated form with high walls of brick and a corrugated iron roof. Anglicans also built churches at Isipingo (1856), Ladysmith (1858), and Addington. St Thomas' church in Durban, (1864) which was provided to serve the inhabitants of the Berea, consisted of a timber frame covered with corrugated iron. In the pseudo-Gothic style, it possessed a tall fleche over the entrance and was sent out in sections from England by Mrs Admiral Harcourt of Swintown Park, Yorkshire. (Fig. 153) Another example of prefabricated Gothic was St Augustine's church in Durban. (Fig. 154)

The Dutch Reformed congregation in Pietermaritzburg partially fulfilled the original vow of Danskraal [22] by the erection of a new church in 1857. It was designed by Edmund Tatham and took the form common to such churches in the Cape, a hall facing lengthwise to the street with the entrance and tower placed centrally on the long elevation. (Fig. 155,156) This was the first public building to acknowledge the market square, [23] in both the axial relationship of its major elevation and the attempt to relate the scale of the spire, though in a square of such dimensions a tower of considerable height would be required.[24]

9   See Chapter 12
10   An early pioneer who was described as a "clever architect". Thomas Greene's reminiscences.
11   Two years in Natal. Fraser's Magazine. Sept. 1875. p312
12   In 1860 Benjamin Moorby, the owner of the Bijou theatre, acquired the Old Vine Inn and erected a larger building of stone and brick which at first was called the new Bijou but later became known as the Theatre Royal.
13   Natal Courier. January 13 1864.
14   History of the Wesleyan church of South Africa. J. Whiteside. p358
15   op cit, Whiteside p364
16   H.R. Hitchcock describes the Great Thornton Street Chapel in Hull (Lockwood and Allom) as the "handsomest church begun in 1841, and putting to shame mose Anglican churches of the period".
     Early Victorian architecture in Britain. H.R. Hitchcock.
17   Perhaps, too, in contra-distinction to the "Gothic", St. Peter's.
18   South Africa. J.S. Little. p250
19   op cit, Whiteside. p365 A Methodist church was built in Verulam in 1864. Cruciform in shape. it was said to combine "elegance with simplicity".
19a Zululand, G.H. Mason. p25
20   Letters; J.E. Methley to the Rev J. Methley. 1858.
21   The building was acquired later in the century by the Anglican church. A baptistry was added on the north side and the slates were replaced by corrugated iron.
22   See p5
23   See Chapter 11
24   Even the present tall needle-spire of the D.R. church in Pietermaritzburg is barely in scale with the square.

It would appear that the original spire was unsatisfactory, for Fleming records that: "The Dutch are finding fault with the spire we have put on the church (and) we have been ordered to make it about 10 feet higher".[25] The building was of red brick with a slate roof and pairs of lancet windows flanked the pointed arched entrance door. The spire was surmounted by a typical rooster and weathervane. It is a strong indication of the almost total Anglicisation of Pietermaritzburg by 1860, that the eventual Voortrekker Church of the Vow should be a Gothic building designed by an English surveyor whose father had been architect to King William 1V.

The Dutch church in Greytown (1861) (Fig. 157) was very similar to that in Pietermaritzburg, but as it lacked a tower, it is closer in character to those erected in the Northern Cape. The parsonage, built in 1859, was a gabled, whitewashed house. Together with the many surviving Cape gabled houses in the area (Fig. 158) this suggests that Greytown was one of the few towns in Natal where the essentials of Cape Dutch architecture were not over-powered by the arrival of the English settlers.

Marked by the rise of Cetywayo as the king of the Zulus, this period saw the establishment of numerous mission stations both in Natal and Zululand. Buildings erected in missions were most often of an extremely functional and simple kind. Verandas were used around the outsides of the houses to protect the interiors from the fury of the summer sun and as pleasant semi-outdoor areas for many different activities. At Hermannsburg, "In the middle of a valley, which does not lie very deep, there is the great dwelling surrounded by a broad veranda, situated in a flower garden, close to which, on one side is a plantation; around it are the farm steadings and workshops... On the right of the valley below, in a little hollow, there is an inconsiderable looking mill..." The Lutheran church at Hermannsburg and the mission church at Kwa Mondi (Fig. 159) are clearly attempts to reproduce the architecture of those areas in Germany and Norway from which the missionaries came.

The first Roman Catholic mission, St Michaels (1859) was "seen from afar by its glowing whiteness. It is surrounded by a portico or veranda, which whilst giving shelter to the natives against the rays of the sun and the rain, helps to strengthen it against the storms".[26] Missions at Kwamagwaza, St Andrew, and Inanda also used verandas.

G.H. Mason described his mission station at Edendale, "The plan of our proposed cottage was extremely simple, consisting merely of a sitting room about ten feet square, a bedroom not quite so large, and a pantry about ten feet by five, with a broad veranda running all round to be planted with fast growing creepers; which with a detached brick kitchen for the caffres, and a summer house for the dining room and study, embraced the full extent of our requirements".[27] (1862)

Besides those who, upon arrival in Natal between 1856 and 1865, erected wattle-and-daub huts as temporary shelters, many had by this time erected permanent buildings of brick. The character of these later buildings is to a large extent a development of the early house forms, though corrugated iron had almost completely replaced thatch as a roofing material. Houses such as the Umhlali parsonage were still constructed only one room wide. It would seem then, that the initial advantages of such a building form in the sub-tropical climate of the coast had been appreciated to the point of becoming a tradition in itself. There can be no doubt, however, that the colonial tradition which was developing was that of the veranda house. Along the coast, where sugar had brought prosperity to many colonists, a kind of "plantation" culture developed, its visible expression being a large, spreading veranda house staffed with many servants, surrounded by lawns and shady trees. (Fig. 160)

Overport House, built in 1860 by a Durban merchant, William Hartley, stood on the ridge of the Berea surveying the entire coast around Durban. (Fig. 161) Sir John Robinson said of the house and its surroundings, "Overport is perhaps the most complete and elaborately finished private residence in the colony ... Passing this road and keeping to a broad carriage way, skirted by a coffee plantation on one side and by a paddock on the other, we come to a spacious and elegant one-storeyed dwelling house, with an irregular roof broken by many gables, flanked by a castellated tower and surrounded by a broad terrace ... (Fig. 162,163) Its two reception rooms are lined by tinted glass ceilings, admitting a soft and mellow light. In the centre of the house is a conservatory with a fountain playing under a glass dome. From this on one side opens out a hall fitted up as a billiard room, while at the further end it terminates in a Gothic Hall. (Fig. 164) All round the house stretch broad terraces adorned with vases of flowering plants, and in front plays a fountain, fed from water tanks enclosed in an ornamental tower. Ascending by a winding stair to the summit of the hall tower, a magnificent view, probably the finest on the Berea, is obtained ... The road leads the traveller to a gate with a gabled lodge near it, and an appearance of cultivated ground beyond, very suggestive altogether of a country residence in some hilly district of old England".[28]

The entrance to the house was up a flight of steps from the carriage way on to the terrace under a porte-cochère. (Fig. 165) Continuing through the reception hall and conservatory, with corridors leading off on either side, one arrived in the Gothic Hall, a tall panelled room with light bow string trusses and a timber ceiling. (Fig. 164) At the end of the room was a Gothic window which Hartley had bought in England. This had been taken from an old English abbey during the reign of Henry VIII and was noted for the beauty and colour of the glass. The deliberate irregularity of the roof, with the Italianate tower and striped awning-like verandas is a peculiar combination of the fashionable English country residence, and the colonial veranda house. "Some people denounced it as a display of arrogance, while others appreciated it as a contribution to the beauty and dignity of the Port, and therefore to the whole colony".[29]

House North at Northdene (1861) had a square plan with a central corridor and a veranda right around the entire house. (Fig. 166) Wide sash windows which opened to the floor might provide access to anyone who wished to duck thereunder and go out onto the wide veranda. (Fig. 167,168,169) A kitchen was built at the rear of the house and was connected with a covered way, constructed of curved sheets of corrugated iron. The roof was covered with corrugated iron tiles. Additions were made to the house later in the century in the form of veranda-rooms at each side, and two separate cottages were also erected close to the original buildings.

Along the coast, houses such as the magistracy at Umzinto, (Fig. 170), and House Anderson at Isipingo, were built with verandas. These were usually incorporated under one roof like most of the thatched veranda-houses, the plans remaining basically the same. Mrs. Anderson herself erected their homestead; "I had a boat and two good native workers, and before long we had the building ready for the carpenter to fix in the doors and windows, and to put on the roof. Then came the plastering and colour washing, and the building of a veranda paved with flagstones which I had found in a particular bend of the river".[30] Lady Barker approved of verandas and visited a veranda-house near Durban; "Their house is barely finished, but one can already see that it will be a large and airy bungalow, with a spacious and spreading veranda. The prevalence of these adjuncts, which takes the place of the Cape "stoep" marks a line of difference, and to my mind a very pleasant one". Lady Barker also remarked that the "prevalent disuse of tall black hats arose from the lowness of the verandas and doorways".[31]

In Pietermaritzburg the veranda was always slightly differentiated from the main roof of the house, a custom which must have been encouraged by the use of tiles as a roofing material and their consequent steep pitch. (Fig. 171) They were also generally narrower and sometimes supported with curved iron brackets. Simple timber balustrading set them apart from the streets onto which they faced. Two plan types were common. One had narrow roofs

in a U or L shape and the other a pyramidal roof with a square plan and central corridor. (Fig. 172,173) Ancillary rooms were often built under lean-to's at the rear of the house.

English traditions were retained and reproduced in the form of tall gables with attic windows and dormers in the roof. (Fig. 174–179) By the end of the 'sixties the availability of building materials and good contractors reduced the necessity for these and double-storeyed houses were often built. A few buildings also exhibited Gothic features either as pointed or leaded light windows. (Fig. 180) A Mr Wathen, who is supposed to have studied architecture in Egypt and published a work on the subject, came to Natal in 1857 and built himself a "Gothic" house near Richmond.

In the main streets of the towns, shopkeepers and others resided on the level above the shops; a certain Madam Vandam had such an apartment in Durban with a balcony on which shuttered windows opened. (Fig. 181) While such devices were not uncommon, the necessity for shutters was largely eliminated by verandas. Those that were used were left in hardwood (often teak) and unpainted. Loudon had recommended this; "What perhaps, increases this dislike is the painting them green and other gaudy colours; instead of keeping them subordinate, by making them the colour of the walls, or of oak".[32]

Joseph Cato designed a cottage and a villa without any form of climatic control. (Fig. 182, 183,184) No record exists of whether they were actually erected, but their strong similarity to catalogue designs of the period lead one to suspect that they may even have been traced from them.

The cottage (Fig. 183) is interesting in that it is a direct forerunner of the typical town house of the 'eighties and 'nineties with its assymmetrical massing of gable and bay-window, and an entrance door immediately to the one side. It is certain that no houses with such a proliferation of ornament were erected during this period, though "Natal being at least, and en permanence, one line of fashion behind the age", [33] this kind of pretension was bound to make its appearance soon.

25   Fleming Diary. 1858.
26   Trekking for souls. J.E. Brady. p99
27   Zululand. G.H. Mason. p20
28   Notes on Natal, Sir J. Robinson.
29   Natal memories. B. Buchanan. p280
30   Reminiscences. Anderson. p44
31   Life at Natal. 1864 (II), Lady Barker. Cape Monthly magazine vol. 4 1872.
32   An Encyclopaedia of cottage, farm and villa architecture. Loudon. (553) p268
33   op cit, Life at Natal. Lady Barker. p69

Chapter 7

'Days of wider & grander notions'

1865 – 1879

II

A severe economic depression gripped Natal in the late 'sixties and there was much unemployment and even some emigration from the colony. The municipal councils found it impossible to collect the rates. Even the street lamps were left unlighted. By 1867 nearly all the banking institutions of Natal had petitioned for winding up orders. Peter Paterson, who had assumed the office of Colonial Engineer in 1860, and was regarded as "the great incumbus of the colony" [1] by those colonists who resented colonial expenditure in periods of such depression, had designed a new government building in Pietermaritzburg in 1864. It was to provide accommodation for the supreme court and the legislative council. Both bodies urgently required new accommodation to replace "the stable", [2] which made no provision for the convenience and comfort of the judiciary and juries.

The foundation stone was laid with much pomp and ceremony on 2 November 1865, the local newspapers commenting on the fine site fronting Commercial Road and expressing the hope that this was to be the beginning of progress and that "the imposing edifice would possess more architectural merit and would lead to further buildings of more commanding aspect".[2A] Paterson chose the Renaissance pavilion style for the new building, the arcaded front acknowledging the severity of the

climate, while alternate bands of plaster and black brick broke up the orange brick wall surfaces. (Fig. 185, 186) A large lantern served to suggest the position within the building of the central hall, though it provided neither sufficient light nor ventilation.

The duplication of functions within the building involved the legislators and the court in much delay, and the great height of the hall resulted in poor acoustics. Paterson also had considerable trouble with the roof, the slates needing repair soon after the completion of the building in 1875. Due to the increased severity of the depression (1866), the Government forbade further work on the building. Although it was recommenced in May of the following year, the colonial budget allowed but one solitary bricklayer to continue work. When it was completed in 1875 a gallery was included for the press and the public which, together with the crimson hangings and morocco covered chairs, made it easier for the colonists "to imitate the forms and trappings of Westminister".[3]

Paterson was also responsible for the court-house in Durban. Early in 1865 the Government decided to proceed with the erection of a Court house and the necessary Government offices, on a site at the eastern corner of the market square, which faced Aliwal street. The Chamber of Commerce thereupon requested the Town council to persuade the Government to change the site to the west end of the market square. A fierce battle between the residents of the east end and the west end followed. The Government eventually decided on Aliwal street, where "the site for the Government offices had been laid prior to the incorporation of the town, and they (the east enders) had been led to purchase land in that part of the town by reason of the advantages which would accrue by having these offices on the Aliwal street site".[4]

The building, which was completed in 1866, consisted of a two-storeyed block containing in the centre a court room with a high lantern, and wings with ancillary offices. (Fig. 187–189) From the coarseness of the design one can only assume that Paterson must have learnt by his mistakes and applied his knowledge to the court-house in Pietermaritzburg. Needless to say he would have attributed the ungainliness of the Durban court-house to the limited budget.

In 1867 Chief Justice Harding complained that the "Court house in Durban is next to useless as it is impossible to hear", [5] and requested that some remedy be applied. On January 29 1868, Paterson forwarded "a plan and estimate of alteration to the present court room".[6] This cannot have been of much effect as the Chief Justice stated in October of the same year that "the defects existing in the Durban court room have only partially been remedied".[7] The Colonial Engineer replied that "plans have been made to erect a gallery to cure the present reverberation". By this stage, the Judge had lost all patience with the Colonial Engineer's department and decried the court room as "next to useless owing to its being almost impossible for the court and jury to distinguish what is said by the witnesses, or for the judge to hear what is said at the bar, or the jury the charge and the objections of the judge..."

To this retort, Paterson presented a fascinating analysis of the acoustic problems and their possible remedies. "The acoustic defects ... are caused chiefly by the emptiness of the room and the perfectly plain and unbroken surface of the walls ... as a result of limited economy. The defects can be remedied by the following; 1; To hang from the roof one or more large frames covered with calico or muslin in imitation of chandeliers, 2; to cover over the space between the entrance doorway and the screen and to fit baze doors to shut out external noise. 3; to provide a canopy over the Judge's dais and to cover the floor thereof with matting. 4; to pierce the coved ceiling with openings to break the reverberations and 5; If necessary to break out windows through the sidewalls and through the end wall behind the Judge".[8] These instructions were to be carried out in their strict order. He explained further how he had already carried out experiments with "calico chandeliers" and that, if none of the other proposals were effective, the last resort would be to construct a gallery around three sides of the room.

Among the few public works which were completed during this period was an eighty-one foot high lighthouse erected on top of the Durban Bluff. (Fig. 190) As early as 1855, the Durban Harbour Authority had requested the Government to represent to the British Government the extreme necessity of providing a new lighthouse for the port. The foundation stone was laid ceremonially on 22 November 1864 and Peter Paterson described the structure: "It is to consist of a cast iron conoidal tower loaded at the base by concrete, surmounted by a cast iron light room on a plinth and a gun-metal lantern glazed by plate glass with a dome roof covered with copper. The total height of the centre of the light above sea level is 281 feet 6 inches and the light will be visible in clear weather for a distance of 28 miles".[8A] Once again the erection of the building was fraught with problems, most of which were derived from the fact that Paterson, who had designed lighthouses in the West Indies, drew up the plans and despatched them to England, the crown agents being thereafter responsible for the manufacture of the iron work and the transport back to Natal. During the course of manufacture Paterson objected strongly to certain alterations which the crown agents themselves had made to the design.[9] The lighthouse was completed

and exhibited to the public on 23 January 1867.[10]

The Colonial Engineer's office was mainly occupied with the construction of roads and bridges throughout the colony, though the occasional magistracy and gaol were also built. Municipalities were concerned, between their bitter controversies, with provisions for law and order in the form of police stations and toll houses. The Durban Town council erected a vagrant house in 1873, corporation stables and a powder magazine in 1875, and a Market hall in 1876. The latter comprised a hall and sixteen stalls which were leased by public auction. The building was designed by R.H. Collins, an engineer of the firm Rolls and Collins. Collins was also responsible for the introduction of tramways in Durban in the early 'eighties.

Richmond and York (Fig. 191) both built public libraries in 1871 and the Natal Society in Pietermaritzburg called for plans for a new library in 1877, a local architect – builder, J. Harding submitted the most successful design. In Durban the Mechanics Institution had outgrown their quarters and in 1879 R.S. Upton designed a modest library and reading room which also served as the institution's meeting place.[11] (Fig. 192) This was the second time that they had called on the services of Upton, for in the 1850's "we made special efforts to raise funds for a new building of our own – a castle in the air, though designed by Mr R.S. Upton".[12]

The growing populations in Durban and Pietermartizburg urgently needed facilities for higher education and, besides the numerous private attempts to establish schools, both towns set up collegiate institutions. In Pietermaritzburg the Government had advertised for architect's plans, specifications and estimates for a new school in 1861. The accommodation was to include offices for a principal and two masters, three class rooms, dormitories for 60 boys, library, dining hall, kitchen with butteries and housekeepers and servants rooms. "The Elizabethan style

1   Portrait of a city. A.F. Hattersley p65
2   The building erected as the first Government schoolroom.
2a The Natal Witness November 4 1865.
3   op cit, Hattersley. p59
4   Fifty years municipal history. W. Henderson. p63
5   C.S.O. Letters received 1857, no. 1115. 18 June 1867.
6   C.S.O. 1868, no. 169. Jan. 29, 1868
7   C.S.O. 1868, no. 89. Oct. 28, 1868
8   C.S.O. Letters dispatched 1858, no. 727, 1868.
8a C.S.O. Letters dispatched 1956 no. 2323, and 2308 Nov. 29 1865.
9   Ibid, C.S.O. 1956, 2323.
10 Demolished in 1941 for military purposes.
11 Times of Natal Jan 20 1877. and Feb. 11 1878.
12 A history of old Durban. G. Russell p308

of architecture is suggested as most suitable".[13] Freestone and burnt bricks on shale stone foundations were to be used and "no external plaster work was desired". The roof was to be of slate and it was "considered desirable to employ iron work for girders etc." Premiums of £75, £20 and £15 were to be awarded for the three best designs. Evidently no suitable designs were forthcoming as Peter Paterson claims to have designed and superintended the erection of the building himself.[14] Several delays ensued and, with a reduced programme of accommodation, the building was commenced in 1864, to be completed in 1866. Many alterations over the years have disguised the original building which has an unusual plastic quality. (Fig. 193,194) The roofs and dormer windows are manipulated in a more successful way than the elements of his two other buildings. The pointed dormer windows with their diamond panes and Gothic geometry, and the unsuccessfully fenestrated gable wall, are tokens of "the Elizabethan style", but the continuous veranda and the complexity of form indicate a marriage between Colonial and Victorian. An interesting feature of the roof was the horizontal patterning of the tiles.[15]

St Mary's Diocesan school in Richmond, erected in 1869, (Fig. 195) also combines dormer windows, gables and verandas, though a limited budget must account for the rectangular window openings and the double roof construction.

Bishop Jolivet recorded in his diary that besides his new house, two new schools were opened in Pietermaritzburg in 1876. The presbytery which stood in Loop street adjacent to St Mary's church was a simple building with regular window openings, a central door and a central dormer window. (Fig. 196, 197) The convent of the Holy Family which stood close by, may have been begun slightly earlier in the 'seventies, but several new buildings were completed in 1875 and 1876.[16] Those facing directly on to Loop street have a particularly fine quality. (Fig. 198) Again a certain playful preoccupation with roof and veranda forms predominates, though the use of a standard sliding sash window gives the building an element of restraint, consistent with their use in the presbytery. St Charles Grammer School, which was opened in 1876, (Fig. 199) exhibited a Gothic tower with a pointed arched doorway in keeping with the angle-arched windows used throughout the rest of the building. A large quadrangle with a continuous veranda indicated an attempt to recreate a medieval scholastic character, in plan as well as in elevation.[17]

Bishop Jolivet himself designed these buildings as well as many others in his diocese which extended over the whole of Natal, the Transvaal and the Orange Free State. Several entries in his diary record his enthusiasm for design; he redrew many plans over and

over again. An engineer and builder, O'Meara, is said to have always been on hand to offer advice.

While in most cases Gothic or "Elizabethan" was thought to be appropriate for schools and institutions, comfortable buildings could be erected more cheaply with less trappings. Regular window openings, usually with sliding sashes, and ground floor verandas override all decoration and give buildings like the Durban Collegiate Institute (1878) (Fig. 200) an unmistakable colonial character. The latter was designed by Moses Holmes in 1877 and consisted of a single block with verandas around three sides. The veranda floors were tiled with mosaics and the roofs were supported on cast-iron columns and brackets.

The Pietermaritzburg Girls Collegiate school was designed by a Canadian architect, F.J. Alexander in 1878.[18] (Fig. 201,202) A more ornate structure, this had pilasters and alternating semi-circular and triangular pediments over the windows, a larger pediment with an awkward semi-circular vent within, and double pilasters occurring over the main entrance. The walls were of orange brick and though the fussy capitals were executed in mortar, all other mouldings were in brick, an indication of how far the brick industry in Natal had progressed by this time. The main portion of the building and two flanking wings enclosed a courtyard.

With few exceptions, buildings erected in the nineteenth century in Natal placed great emphasis on external appearance while accepting straightforward planning arrangements and the simplest kind of interior decoration. One notable exception was St Saviour's, Pietermaritzburg's second cathedral. On the day following the Supreme Court decision, which deprived the Church of the Province of South Africa of the properties for which Colenso had been trustee, the Dean of St Peter's called a meeting of clergy and laity, at which it was resolved "That we do, without delay, erect a temporary church"[19] (January, 1868.) The Dean laid the foundation stone of the building before departing for England and it was said that "a church large enough to hold four hundred and fifty had been erected and fitted out for services and opened for use by Ascension day ... Much was still required however. A ceiling below the tiles to prevent dust seeping in and heat beating down, and also a porch, vestry and a baptistry had still to be added".[19A] The fact that the church was only intended to be temporary, probably explains why relatively more attention was paid to the interior, in the way of fittings and decorations than to the exterior. (Fig. 203) Edmund Byron said that "the other cathedral was a wooden structure, but more pretending in its interior decoration and furniture than St Peter's". The exterior, however, is certainly not plain. (Fig. 204) The large and somewhat overpowering rose window in the west wall; the peculiar combination of a straight label moulding in the pointed style, in close proximity to that around the entrance door; and the popular semi-dormer windows of the nave roof, are all part of the contemporary trend to manipulate simple forms into a plastic complexity.

Built of local brick, relatively unadorned externally and plastered internally, the building has been added to over the years but still retains an overall unity. The interior with its hammer-beam trusses and timber ceilings has good proportions, and mellow and subdued lighting. The floors are of quarry tiles with yellow and brown patterned encaustic tiles along the aisles. When porches were added on the north and south walls, the Baptismal font (Fig. 206) was placed in the north transept directly at the entrance from the porch. "It seemed well to the Dean to give great dignity to the sacrament of Baptism, and constantly reminded people of it".[20] By the sheer size of the font and its open-worked, timber, pyramidal hood it would undoubtedly be a constant reminder to those entering and leaving the Cathedral. The superbly carved pulpit might well have been commissioned by the Dean during his visit to England. (Fig. 205)

On his appointment as the new Bishop of Natal, Dr Macrorie acquired a house in the "Kensington Gardens" area of the town, not far from the Governor's residence. The front portion of the house had been built by Edward Few in 1852 and Macrorie added verandas to the street elevation, erected a double-storeyed addition immediately behind this, and altered the stables and outhouses. In all, seven gables were built of varying pitches, containing doors with black painted mouldings over them, or shuttered windows with pointed arched panels or windows above. (Fig. 208,209) The deliberately haphazard massing and irregularity of the gables and windows are typical of early Victorian. Though the house announces its ecclesiastical associations rather aggressively, those who enter the side door and go through the narrow, dark corridor find some relief in the quiet, shady courtyard.

The earliest Anglican church at Umzinto, a wattle and daub church—cum—school, had been washed away in 1867; when Bishop Macrorie visited the parish in 1872 he found that a substantial little church, St Patrick's had been erected. (Fig. 210) Sophie Gray had mentioned in a letter to Dean Green (1864) that she was working on designs for other churches in Natal besides St Peter's. One was to be for Clairmont (Clermont) and two for Umzinto "and probably a lichgate for Mr Elder".[20A] She and Bishop Gray had stayed with the Barkers at Umzinto during their visit to Natal in 1864, and she may have promised a design for a small church. The building could have been designed by her as the pitch of the

roof, the small entrance porch on the north side and the vestry on the south, together with the roof structure, which is almost identical to that of St Peter's, are all characteristics of her work. (Fig. 211) The plastered walls should perhaps be attributed to the absence of suitable building stone, and the corrugated iron, to its more liberal acceptance by this time for buildings of any description.

An interesting feature of the erection of such country churches as St Patrick's, is that very often the entire building was erected by the local incumbent. In this case the pulpit, altar and reredros were made and carved by the Rev G.E. Pennington. Anglicans also erected new churches at Pinetown (St John's) 1870; Weston, 1872, which was built of yellow-wood from the Karkloof; Isipingo, (St James) 1872 and at Howick where St Luke's (1868) is a small church with an undifferentiated chancel. Built of fine local grey-stone, it has a pleasant entrance porch and triple lancet windows in the east and west walls. (Fig. 212) St Mathias at Estcourt (1872) was a narrow stone building with a thatched roof, a separate chancel and a small belfry over the entrance porch. (Fig. 213)

One of the most unusual chapels in Natal was the Ebenezer chapel in Pietermaritzburg [21] Although built in 1865 it still showed the strong influence of Cape architecture in Natal. While no records exist of what the rest of the building was like, the front elevation consisted of a simple pediment without pilasters, surmounting a wall which contained a central doorway with a semi-circular fanlight and flanking windows capped by semi-circular mouldings. A decorative plaque occupied the space above the doorway and this in turn was surmounted by two garlands draped from a rosette, suggesting in their outline the form of an entrance porch. (Fig. 214,215)

A splinter church of the Pietermaritzburg Presby-

13   Natal Witness, Nov. 1 1861.
14   C.E. Letters received 1186,1889.
      Paterson includes a sketch of his original idea for the building.
16   The window shutters and entrance porch were added in 1892.
17   Quadrangles have proved to be very popular in schools throughout South Africa.
      Those parts of St Charles College now forming the Ansonia Hotel were designed by an American architect, Hulse in 1897.
18   See Chapter 13.
19   Anglicans in Natal. Burnett. p79
19a   op cit, Burnett. p79,80
20   op cit, Burnett. p79
20a   Letters Mrs. Gray to Dean Green, 1864. Natal University, Library. PMB.
21   This was one of the many churches in South Africa designed and built by the Rev. J.Archbell.

terian congregation had found their first home in Colenso's St Mary's church (1870), but after acquiring a site in 1872, commenced the erection of a temporary building, named after St John's church in Glasgow. This was soon replaced by a more permanent structure (1878). The new building (Fig. 216) had an interesting mannered facade. In attempting to integrate the scale of the porch with the building behind, the mouldings of the capitals were continued through the centres of the major pilasters as string courses. The central pilasters appear to have thrust through the cornice mouldings onto the pediment itself. Such mannerisms give the building a rather tense character.

The tradition of plastered Gothic churches was continued in Durban with the erection of the Baptist church in 1874 (Fig. 217) and a new Methodist church in 1877. Rowland Ridgeway, an architect who had married one of Upton's daughters, won the competition for the design of the Methodist church. (Fig. 218) The new church had an almost square plan with a central nave and aisles, each expressed on the front facade. The separating buttresses were employed as useful devices in articulating the different roof pitches of the nave and aisles. Ridgeway was not satisfied with the plain unbroken plastered surfaces which his father-in-law had used, so the front elevation was rusticated and given a cornice frieze. Even though there are pointed—arch openings (with awkward timber louvres) in the clerestoreys, and the buttresses were continued around the sides, the building is essentially "Methodist Gothic".

St Cyprian's Church (Fig. 219) also erected in 1877, had a vast entrance and tower which jutted out through the roof. This presented considerable waterproofing and structural problems and it was soon altered.

This fondness for bold intersecting forms can be seen as a reaction against traditional principles; in Victorian architecture striving towards a new expression, and also as a way of exploiting the rich effects possible in strong sunlight. (Fig. 220) Deep shadows and light surfaces enhance the articulations and strong formal geometry of such buildings.

Pseudo-Gothic was easily attained: all one required was a square tower with castellations, (the Wesleyan church in Greytown had a flat tower) (Fig. 221) a few small pointed windows, a steeply pitched roof and perhaps triple east windows. Analysis of several of the churches erected throughout Natal at this time and after, reveals combinations of some but seldom all, of these features. The only deciding factors were how many could be afforded. Even plastered walls had become acceptable where no suitable stone or face brick could be found. (Fig. 222) Lutheran churches are easily distinguished by their tall spires and towers, occurring at the entrance

to the building. (Fig. 223–225)

St Joseph's Catholic church in Durban was illustrated in 'The Builder' of Sept. 1878; "The church which we illustrate is to be erected for the catholic population of D'Urban in the district of Natal, S. Africa. The design has been made by Mr Goldie, under the instruction of Dr Jolivet and is adapted to the climate and locality. The material is brick partly covered with plaster or rough cast. The clerestory windows are filled with thick glass louvres. The circular openings in the aisles will not be glazed but will have metal fillings. The eaves project with the object of shade. Cast-iron columns are to support the nave arcade, as stone can only be sparingly employed. The nave has, below the roof, a wooden ceiling panelled in each bay. The floor will be in a kind of cement with air channels for ventilation. The leading idea of the design has been to combine simplicity and economy with a certain oriental character, in which the pointed arch remains a distinctive feature".[22] Bishop Jolivet had drawn a rough plan of the church and sent it to Messrs Goldie, Child and Goldie (who were prominent church architects) together with all the details relating to the position, climate and materials to be found on the spot. "A few months after came in from the office of the architect's, drawings of a very peculiar character, which at once took up the fancy of the Bishop and those who saw them".[23] The execution of the proposals would cost £6,000 and the Oblates Provincial Council objected to such a large outlay which was not necessitated by the size of the congregation. Two tenders were therefore called for by O'Meara, who handled the separate contract for the Bishop. Eventually it was decided to accept a tender for the whole which "came to a little over £6,000, exclusive of iron work which was to be imported from England".[24]

Subscriptions were sought in England and France, these being largely aided by donations from colonists and the Empress Eugenie. "The Empress it will be remembered, visited the old church on her sad and touching journey to and from the fatal spot where the Prince Imperial fell, and in gratitude for the spiritual comfort she received there, she gave a handsome donation towards the building of the new church".[25] Difficulties arose during the contract. The contractor was not able to continue work because of the lack of materials. The one who took his place was unsatisfactory. The Natal Mercury said that "The work of erection has not been carried out without trial and difficulty, but these chiefly monetary, though partly professional, have been overcome".[26] A certain architect, P.M. Dudgeon is said to have taken over the supervison of the building and thereafter Bishop Jolivet found that the work was "slow but good".[27] Later he commented that "I am very pleased with our new church which now has a roof. The tower is finished and the height of the exterior gallery makes a good impression".[28] (Fig. 226,227)

The church was certainly found to be adequately ventilated and it is remarkable that a London firm of architects should have concerned themselves so much with the problems of a church building in a sub-tropical climate, to the extent of providing perman-ent louvres at a high level and a ventilating basement under the floor.[29] Indeed the local press was full of praise for the new building; "of the style and convenience of the church we cannot speak too highly. To us it is the "beau ideal" of a church for a hot country: to others it has faults of shape, of height, or arrangement; but we would suggest to these a careful and inquiring study of the reasons which gave rise to its component parts and constructive materials. Briefly speaking, it is of a Gothic design adapted to the materials of modern, as well as colonial, production and to considerations of climatic influences. In counteracting the heat which is the unpleasant concomitant of church attendance in Durban, it is perfect, and to have gained this end, few people will be inclined to quarrel with the architects' free handling of the Gothic style as our fathers knew it. The aim of the wondrous men who elaborated the Gothic was to be natural; to apply to the wants of human life and of imagination, the unsurpassing loveliness and utility of nature. We may be certain that if nature were constructing a grotto for retreat we should find it cool and refreshing. Apparently carrying into execution some such thought as this the architects have planned a building which will form a model for, not only church, but general public buildings erected in Durban and Natal. There has been no copying of a set design or "lumping together" of half a dozen different ones without consideration of the necessities and conditions of the climate, the capabiliities of procuring materials and labour, or even the wants of the colony in those respects; but a careful, strict and effective attention has been paid to all these requirements, and the result is a church which both in point of economy and convenience is remarkable, as it certainly is from an artistic point of view, the man who designed it being in the true sense of the word — an artist. The architectural description of the building is as follows:— The ancient and time consecrated plan of the Christian church has not been departed from in the ground lines. A nave and aisles, the former terminating in a polygonal or "apsidal" chancel, the latter in two chapels with diagonal terminations, give the simplest and most commodious of areas, afford-ing accommodation for about 900 worshippers. At the extremity of the nave is the tower, forming a porch below, and an organ tribune above".(sic)[30]

When Bishop Jolivet was a young curate in Liverpool in the 1850's he commissioned Augustus Welby Pugin to design a new church for the Holy Cross parish. The sanctuary apse of Holy Cross church (1859) must have appealed to the Bishop, (Fig. 228) for his new church in Durban, and the Cathedral which followed it, both contained similar apses. (Fig. 229) The memorial altar of the Cathedral is an exact replica of that in Holy Cross Church.[31]

Durban was very soon to have a religious structure with a real oriental character. In 1878 the Times of Natal announced that "a Mohommedan Temple is about to be erected" to serve the Muslims who had accompanied the Government sponsored indentured Indians to Natal and who had begun to arrive in 1860. Though not entirely Muslims and traders, these so-called "passenger Indians" had come to Natal at their own expense and without recruit-ment. Unfortunately few records survive of their earliest buildings. The Indian labourers, however, had to a large extent assisted the sugar farmers in the establishment of a plantation culture on the Natal coast which was not "unlike the civilisations of the planters of Virginia and South Carolina in the slave days".[32]

The opening of the Kimberley diamond mines in 1871, together with several good agricultural seasons and an expanding trade gave new impetus to com-merical enterprise in the mid-eighteen seventies. This was the heyday of social functions in Pietermaritz-burg. Sir Garnet Wolsey with a salary of £5,000 a year could afford to be lavishly hospitable and many grand gatherings were held at Government House. On one such occasion the ballroom was improvised out of the two largest reception rooms while the avenue

22   The Builder. Sept. 21 1878 p993
23   Journal of St Josephs. Archdiocesan Archives, DBN.
24   op cit, Journal.
25   Father Sabon maintained that the Prince Im-perial had promised a donation on his arrival in Natal en route to the battlefield in Zululand and that when the Empress later heard of this she was eager to fulfil his promise. op cit, Journal.
26   Natal Mercury. November 14 1881.
27   Jolivet diary. 24 Jan. 1880
28   op cit, 23 May 1881.
29   A similar device was used to ventilate the later Emmanuel Cathedral.
30   Natal Mercury. November 14 1881.
31   St Joseph's was pulled down in 1901 and the materials were re-used in the present St Joseph's church (Greyville) while the Em-manual Cathedral was built according to a design by W. Street-Wilson based closely on the original church.
32   A history of Natal. E.H. Brookes and C. de B. Webb. p92

leading up to the porch was illuminated with Chinese lanterns. The house had changed considerably since the 1850's. (Fig. 230) When Governor Keate arrived in 1867 to take up his new post he found the original house unsuitable and he and his family temporarily occupied a house in Pietermaritz Street. A two-storeyed stone addition was erected at the one end of the original house. (Fig. 231) This contained an entrance hall and drawing room with offices for the Governor and his secretary on the ground floor, and additional bedrooms above. A four-hipped porch complete with mounting block was erected at the awkard junction between the two buildings. (Fig. 232) The fine fretwork of the porch and the dormer windows was carried out at this time. An unusual feature of the roofing was the tile patterning in the valleys. According to town gossip, Peter Paterson used materials intended for the new court house to build the additions. By 1878 they were already too small and a further storey was added to the original building. (Fig. 233) Later additions in 1888 and 1890, (Fig. 234) again in different materials and in the new styles make the whole complex a showpiece of colonial architectural history, unfortunately to the detriment of unified architecture. Rider Haggard, who worked as a personal secretary to the Governors during the 1870's, said "Government house is a very pretty building, not nearly so large as the Cape Government house, but far from small. I, who have to look after it find it too large. I have a large bedroom upstairs and my office in the Executive Council Chambers".

Portsdown House in Durban (c 1866), was used by the Governor as his marine residence after 1876. Built by Gillespie, a prosperous Durban merchant, and designed by R.S. Upton, it was described as Italian. (Fig. 235) The ground floor had a large entrance hall, dining room and drawing room with windows facing onto a wide veranda. A broad staircase led to the upper floor which contained five bedrooms and an office. Once again Upton shows his ability as a classicist. The detailing is precise and binds the building together with a severity which probably explains the building's unpopularity. Certainly such restraint was not the order of the day.[33]

The careful emphasis given by spacing to the entrance door of the ground floor and to that on the balcony above, and features such as the brackets under the window pediments, reveal the building's essential Victorian character. One wonders why Upton's capitals have an exaggerated depth. Could this also be the influence of a sun-drenched climate?

The architect of the Greenacre house, 'Caister', (1867) is unknown, but the building might well have been designed in England. (Fig. 236) It is an Italian pavilion house, with arcades conceding the heat of the climate, and it may have been the work of some

lesser-known architect in Britain; one influenced by Sir Charles Barry's earlier houses.

The first 'Manor House' (Fig. 237) and 'Coedmore' (1875) both had castellated towers. The latter had two seemingly Scottish Baronial high gables, and the effect of its true locality is only recognised on the north elevation. (Fig. 238,239) The hard quality of the stone work and the house generally must be attributed to its Scottish derivations. A building such as "Fann's Castle Hotel" (Howick, 1872), with its two ivy-covered towers, was surely a light-hearted commercial gimmick. (Fig. 240) The "Imperial Hotel" in Pietermaritzburg was described as "an inn quite after Ruskins heart". A large rambling old house, which had been added to at various periods to suit the increasing number of visitors, it was thought by Trollope to be the perfection of a Colonial hotel, "where one could sit under the broad veranda or in the cool airy courtyard ... vine leaves trailed over the red-brick wall, and oranges hung within tempting distance".[34] Most of the small inns and hotels in the country were like their commercial counterparts, small, simple, functional buildings. Mills, warehouses and farm buildings were also of an extremely utilitarian nature. (Fig. 241,242)

Lady Barker was justified in writing that Pietermaritzburg was "rather a shabby assemblage of buildings", though "nothing can be prettier, than the effect of the red-tiled roofs and white walls peeping out from among thick clumps of trees".[35] There were, however, a few buildings which would have been obtrusive by their very restraint. (Fig. 243,244) In Durban the newest shops and offices were all double-storeyed buildings, and, while in a sense they are the offspring of the smooth white plastered buildings of the 'sixties, they suggest a restlessness and over-elaboration of detail. (Fig. 245,246)

The common denominator in these buildings was the arch. Sometimes on the lower floor and sometimes on the upper, occasionally on both, arcuated facades were to be found in every street. The only other aspect of these buildings was their general lack of verandas or roof projections of any kind.

Several minor wars in Southern Africa during the decade 1870 – 1880, including the Langalibalele affair in Natal, led to strong fears amongst the Europeans of a "native rising".[36] As a direct result of this affair, the Natal Mounted Police was established. A commission was set up to investigate the defence of the Colony and "the Government moreover, lost no time in carrying out the recommendations of the Commission regarding the construction of armouries and laagers. Prior to the year 1874 there were only two laagers in the colony, one at Greytown and the other at Ladysmith. Both were old fashioned laagers built to take in not only whole families, but also wagons carrying the household goods, and even spans of oxen; and there were many defects in their structure. In 1874 a strong block-house was commenced at Estcourt and was in course of construction at the time the Commission sat in 1875.[37] The block-house was designed by Col Durnford R.E., after whom it is now named. At the time a Captain, he had assumed the office of Colonial Engineer between the retirement of Paterson and the arrival of Capt Hime R.E.

The block-house commanded a considerable area around Estcourt and the Bushman's River, being situated on the summit of a koppie. (Fig. 247,248) The building is a fascinating record of contemporary military practise. Durnford probably consulted his Royal Engineer's handbook; he employed a number of marvellous devices to make the post thoroughly defensible, though no occasion ever arose to test its success. The walls were surrounded by a deep ditch with access across a drawbridge and through a doorway with a massive iron-plated door, into a small vestibule. (Fig. 249,250) Loopholes on either side of the vestibule and another iron-plated door, guarded against the possible penetration of the outer lines of defence, while the staircase at the further end of the entrance passage was constructed of a stone flight with a retractable timber upper-half. A block and pulley was suspended above the stairs to hoist up the heavy cannons onto the first floor. Square towers placed at diagonally opposite corners, provided through their loop holes, excellent defence of the surrounding glacis as well as crossfire to the flanking walls. The large room on the north-west side of the building was originally conceived as a court house to serve the local magistrate, and might also have been used for court-martials. The other rooms on the ground floor were an officer's mess, a strongroom and an armoury. These and the rooms above all had fireplaces, very necessary to warm the large spaces with their bare, stone walls.

The windows were originally specified as cast-iron sashes but were actually fitted with wooden sashes. They were barred and closed with heavy iron shutters which on the upper floor were divided into two sections. The lower part could be opened at the centre, allowing a cannon to point downwards, while the upper section remained closed and afforded protection to the gunners. With the lower part closed, longer ranges could be effected. The shutters were boarded on the exterior, a possible reason being "so that assegais hurled with force would become trans-fixed into the wood and irretrievable to the attack-ers".[38] The original drawings also reveal that it was intended to erect a large basement and feed rain water from the roof down pipes in the walls into a tank, thereby ensuring a water supply of 30,000 gallons. It is interesting to speculate too, on whether or not this water could be released into the ditches,

thereby creating a moat.

The fort was stationed by a detachment of the Mounted Police and in 1876 an "enclosure wall and stables" were added. Two designs were prepared for the stables, one a completely single-storeyed block and the other a single-storeyed block with the addition of piquet rooms at both end. The latter design was built, and, with its square posts at the corner of the enclosure, presented a complete series of defensive positions. (Fig. 251) Altogether, the group was the largest military construction of its day in Natal. Secrecy surrounded the construction but it would seem likely that the buildings were erected by British soldiers under the superintendence of a Royal Engineer.

In 1877 laagers were erected at Newcastle and Stanger and a year later at Dundee, Richmond and Umzinto. Provision was also made for the construction during 1879, of laagers at Harding, Ixopo and Verulam. That at Verulam was erected around the existing court house and may be described as a veranda fort. (Fig. 252) Others such as the ones at Harding and Ixopo were erected as fort—cum—gaol and magistraters office, the prevailing theory being that if the building were difficult to escape from, it would also be difficult to break into.

The "old fashioned" laager at Greytown was repaired, strengthened, and otherwise improved. Tall buttressed walls with ditches and glacis were erected, and the buildings in the corners of the square were given loopholes. (Fig. 253,254) Judging by the masses of correspondence which passed between Greytown and Capt Hime R.E., the Colonial Engineer, concerning this laager, one might be led to believe from the small scale of the operations, that in times of peace the defence of the colony was a longwinded affair. This is certainly in contrast to the erection of forts during the Zulu war. Capt Hime proudly announced during the course of this correspondence that the solution to all problems of defence in Natal would be to cover the approaches to such laagers with a thick growth of "Barbados gooseberry's". Unfortunately these may not have grown in time for the Zulu war which began in January when the British forces entered Zululand at three different points.

After the invasion of Zululand, the line of small stone forts which had been built along the border, including Forts Williamson and Buckingham, were

33   The veranda houses of this period are dealt with in Chapter 8.
34   South Africa. Anthony Trollope.
35   More annals of Natal. A.F. Hattersley. p112
36   A history of Natal. E.H. Brookes and C. de B. Webb. p114
37   British Parliamentary papers, 1880, The Zulu War, Appendix, c2505, p157
38   Background to Estcourt. C.F. Shuter.

abandoned without seeing action. Near the mouth of the Tugela river, Col Pearson built a fort which consisted of a series of earthworks. "The fort soon completely changed its character under the incessant labour bestowed upon it by Pearson's men, under the vigilant supervision of their chief. It now became a six-angled enclosure, about sixty yards wide having a ditch eighteen feet deep while its breadth was twelve feet. At the bottom it was studded profusely with assagai-heads securely planted, and the parapets, carefully rivitted, were proof not only against any musketry fire, but field artillery also. From its southern angles ran out two well built curtain walls, enclosing a fine kraal for cattle and horses. These curtains were well protected by the fire of the angles from which they sprung, while the kraal itself had its own massive gateway and drawbridge".[39]

From the Tugela river, Col Pearson advanced into Zululand and erected a fort known either as Fort Ekowe or Fort Kwamondi. (Fig. 255,256) Here he utilised an existing church with a corrugated iron roof, and small outhouses, to create a large arrow-shaped enclosure with earth embankments, draw-bridges, caponiers and trou de loups. Fort Melville was an oblong building with flanking towers, built partly in masonry, partly with clay, loopholed throughout and surrounded with a ditch and "obstacle". (Fig. 257) It provided accommodation for 200 men. A circular stone fort, Bengough (Fig. 258) was built near Pomeroy and, though other small circular ones existed, such as that later built at Fort Mistake in 1881, (Fige. 259) most were rectangular or quadrangular like Fort Pine at Dundee. (Fig. 260) Fort Amiel, which overlooked the most northerly colonial town, Newcastle, consisted of rubble walls erected around an existing farmhouse, though an armoury surmounted by a framed look-out tower had an English gabled character. (Fig. 261)

While many forts [40] were erected throughout Zululand and Natal during the Zulu war, most "were of the simplest description" and were all designed "on simple traces suitable to the ground without flanking fire, and with musket proof parapets and usually triangular ditches. The ordinary military obstacles, abatis, entanglements etc., were used, where time and opportunity recommended them". Captain Blood R.E. of the Zululand Field Force, thought that "the most interesting buildings which were carried out were the Kafir huts for the hospital at the Lower Tugela. These are 21 feet by 13 feet, by about 8 feet high and were built by natives ... The huts are built of timber, cut in the neighbouring bush, with wattled sides, covered outside with grass, and with thatched roofs".[41]

After the Zulu war, Forts were also erected at Greytown, (Fort Dartnell), and Eshowe (Fort Nonquai). The latter was built to serve the Mounted Police stationed in Zululand. (Fig. 261–266) It has square castellated towers at three corners, single-storey blocks on three sides and a high wall on the fourth which enclose a yard serving as a parade ground for the Zulu mounted police or Nonquai. Its white walls and very fort-like appearance, whilst appealing, are characteristics of the early Portuguese forts of the East African coast, rather than of the military outposts of colonial Natal.

---

39   Story of the Zulu Campaign. Ashe and Wyaat Edgell. p68

40   Amongst them were Forts;
     Lucas, Agnew, Pine, Melville, Whitehead, Napoleon (Zululand), Napoleon (Natal), Marshall, Newdigate, Cherry, Buckingham, Evylyn, Pearson, Williamson, Tenedos, Crealock, Chelmsford (Zululand), Chelmsford (Natal), Durnford (Zululand),Bengough, Northampton, Emtonjaneni, Warwick, Victoria, Nolele, Yoland, Argyle, Albert, Cambridge, Louis, Curtis, Richards and George.

41   British Parliamentary papers, 1880, The Zulu War, Appendix, C.2505, p157.

Chapter 8

Verandas

"At present, there being no protection from the direct rays of the sun, the substantial walls of the observatory become so hot in the day, that it is difficult to secure proper observations until the building is completed by the erection of a veranda to shield the walls and prevent their becoming so intensely heated. Having become thus raised in temperature during the day, the walls owing to their massiveness, require the greater portion of the night in which to cool, and during this time they give rise to convection currents of heated air, which render it difficult to obtain satisfactory observations with the great telescope, or to accurately determine the time with the transit instrument. Application has been made, therefore, for authority to construct a light inexpensive veranda, which would prevent the walls from becoming so intensely heated, by shielding them from the direct rays of the sun, and being itself constructed of thin materials would readily cool down in a comparatively short time..."[1] (EDMUND NELSON, GOVERNMENT ASTRONOMER.)

Edmund Nelson's scientific analysis of the use of verandas, and of their cooling effect on a building during the day and night, is the first such observation in Natal. The need for "light inexpensive verandas" was greater in such a climate than in those of the highlands of South Africa. The very advantage afforded by a veranda, of giving protection to a house during summer in a region like Northern Natal, became a disadvantage in winter. This was probably the reason why their popularity in England was fairly short-lived. In Pietermaritzburg verandas were often used on entrance elevations only. There they provided excellent fields for the expression of the individuality which the Victorians strove for. (Fig. 267–270)

It would seem that there were three major reasons for the use of verandas in colonial Natal. The first was that they provided shady semi-outdoor spaces relating to the house, the garden and the street. (Fig. 271) These spaces could be used for all kinds of activities, but most commonly as places where one could sit, in conversation perhaps, and enjoy the cool breezes. (Fig. 272) Along the coast this was essential. Human comfort in a climate with a high humidity relies entirely on the direct movement of air across the skin. Verandas also stimulated a movement of cool air throughout those rooms of the building which opened onto them, and they in turn were ventilated through other rooms or a passage way. The second reason was that they gave protection to the walls of the house, thus keeping them cool during the day. The veranda-houses in Natal often had verandas around the entire house (Fig. 273–276) and, while those along the North, West and East walls would protect the rooms along those sides, the veranda on the south side could only be justified in that it provided a very cool place in summer. These south-facing verandas may be derived from one of the earliest uses of verandas in primitive dwellings, in that they provided covered access between rooms.[2] They also gave a complete roof to those houses whose formal geometry demanded it. The third reason was that of fashion. A veranda roof relieved the stark simplicity of a colonial house. (Fig. 277) Even the projection of verandas created opportunities for plastic manipulations of building forms. The dark enclosed space of a veranda would set off the light, decorative patterns of iron or timber supports. (Fig. 278)

While originally of thatch, zinc and wood, veranda roofs were later covered with corrugated iron. A few in Pietermaritzburg had tiled roofs. (Fig. 280,287) The early veranda-houses had continuous roofs covering house and verandas. (Fig. 279) These necessitated steep roof pitches, and when cheap ways of providing flashings became available through the introduction of galvanized iron, the veranda roof could be separated from the roof of the house. (Fig. 281–286) Another solution, that of the "berm" roof, was perpetuated with separate roofs of a flatter pitch. Catslides, popular in Regency buildings, were used in Natal until the beginning of the twentieth century. Occasionally the position of the entrance door was emphasised by a pediment, sometimes of curved sheets of iron. (Fig. 288) This also provided opportunities for an entrance porch, supported and enclosed by a riot of decorative woodwork or cast-iron. (Fig. 289,290)

The veranda roof was often supported on single columns, set either at regular intervals, or alternating to relieve a monotonous rhythm, or varied at the position of the entrance door. Double columns were also popular. The column itself had a simple capital

---

1   History of the Natal Observatory. Report of the eleventh council p3. (Edmund Nelson. Government Astronomer.) 1883.

2   See Chapter 4.

and base, and sometimes a central boss. The earliest timber posts were left quite plain, and were lifted up from the floor (and termite attack) on stone or brick pads. The junction of the column and the roof was often achieved with a flat bracket, or diagonal struts. (Fig. 291–294), (Fig. 295–302) These were simple at first but during the 'seventies and 'eighties developed as decorative items in themselves. Later they became part of the fascia, the junctions having been awkward until the two were fused into one. (Fig. 307–313) The early fascias were reminiscent of those on Regency verandas in their translation of the frilly edges of tent-like canvas roofs. Eventually they became on the one hand geometrical, and on the other, more elaborate in their outline. (Fig. 303–306)

Double columns were strengthened with infills of geometrical patterns and sometimes completely filled with a trellis. Balusters and handrails were optional, though most often used when the veranda floor was raised above that of the garden. The earliest houses only used them on the upper floors and these were simple timber uprights fitted in between horizontal railings. Ultimately, they too were decorated. Types varied from the simple vertical balusters which were used both at regular and irregular intervals, to patterns in timber, and profusely decorated cast-iron panels. (Fig. 314–318)

The great range of possibilities available in every part of veranda design made variety the order of the day. A small variation of only one feature would create a different design or pattern, and hence there are rarely identical verandas anywhere in Natal, although there are many standard types. Generally it can be said, however, that the simple patterns and types favoured by the early colonists gave way to more elaborate and pretentious ones later in the century. The elaboration reached its zenith in Edwardian days. Certain buildings of the 'eighties and 'nineties indicate a simplicity which may have been a reaction against this over-ornamentation, and are in spirit with the Arts and Crafts movement in England and the Colonial Revival in America. (Fig. 319,320,321)

The use of decoration on verandas was closely related to available decorative elements. Early variegations were found in light wrought iron or simple timber pattersn. Most timber decoration consisted of geometrical patterns made up of small scantlings. (Fig. 278,316) Sometimes Indian influences are apparent in the patterns of fascias. (Fig. 323) Earlier verandas also exhibit Gothic forms derived from England, (Fig. 324) while later fretwork designs were based on the traditional timber buildings of Scandanavia, Germany and Switzerland. (Fig. 325,328) Indeed these and others were the countries from which most fretwork patterns were imported.[3]

Trellis verandas (Fig. 11,295) probably originated in the Picturesque landscape garden, "to support the shooting tendrils of the vine and gay luxuriance of the passion flower".[3A] They represent the effort to link the house to the garden.

Previous to 1882 most of the cast-iron verandas were imported from England but thereafter they began to be manufactured locally to English designs.[4] Their application, however, was rather more to commercial than to domestic architecture. (Fig. 329–330)

The various house forms which were used appear to have resulted both from traditional colonial techniques in roofing, and the use of verandas. The plans of these houses, however, were based closely on the plans of typical English houses of the time, and are all variations of a central corridor type with rooms leading off both sides. The corridor itself was widened to create entrance halls and other internal spaces; not until larger and more luxurious houses were erected at the end of the century was it done away with as a circulation system. The veranda can therefore be said to have influenced domestic planning only in that it often provided alternative access. A few houses built later in the century have large interleading rooms, with an air of ease and spaciousness about them, which may well be attributed to the influence of the informality of the veranda house.

Though French doors were often used to connect the interior to the veranda, the universal popularity of the sliding-sash window led eventually to the disappearance of the former. The sliding-sash window was, moreover, a more flexible solution to ventilation. Plate glass was commonly used and sometimes surrounded with narrow bands of a tinted or frosted glass, though these were usually to be found only on the entrance door or in the lights above and to the sides of it.

Encaustic tiles were popular as a flooring surface for verandas and entrance halls. The patterns favoured were those of Minton and Maw, and their use was encouraged by Eastlake (1872) who said that "There can be little doubt that the best mode of treatment for a hall-floor, whether in town or country, is to pave it with encaustic tiles".[4A] The colours used were also those recommended by Eastlake and were mostly of the "Etruscan" or "Roman" variety, in oranges, browns and yellows. (Fig. 334) The use of these on verandas, against orange or salmon brick walls provided a delightfully harmonious colour scheme less dazzling than the contemporary "gingerbread" colours of English Victorian. Baked clay tiles were an alternative used mainly in kitchens. Most houses had timber suspended floors inside.

Belinda's AID TO COLONIAL HOUSEWIVES (c 1890) suggested her preference for simple colonial abodes rather than "the drawing room of the average town villa, with its impossible wall paper, stiff, uncomfortable 'suite', mirrored overmantel, and engravings".[5] She also noted that the craze for draping mantelpieces had departed and that "certain quite unnecessary small tables and jardinieres" could be dispensed with. "So many drawing-rooms look as if they might be labelled "For visitors only", instead of being bright, cheerful rooms wherein members of the household can work, read, or play in quietude and comfort".

The dining room was often the largest room in the house. Sometimes the drawing room was done away with altogether and a large "dining-sitting room" served both functions. Belinda noted that "it used to be the custom of South African builders to make the front passage lead straight into the dining-room, so that it was impossible to go from the bedroom to the kitchen or back part of the house without passing through the dining room". She did not find this serious fault in many of the newer cottages, but thought that progress had been made, since "there was a time, however, when comparatively few houses boasted any passage at all. The front door led straight into the drawing or dining-room". She complained of the narrow entrance halls which allowed little decoration, though she had seen "an excellent effect secured with crimson paper and ivory paint; and another attractive lobby had a few good etchings on the walls, against a pale green background, the paint being dark brown". (Fig. 337)

Bedrooms were much simpler in arrangement and furnishing than the public rooms of the house. The four-poster was found to be too hot for the climate. Charles Eastlake thought that "a room intended for repose ought to contain nothing which can fatigue the eye by complexity". He also expressed concern that "many people nowadays prefer, on sanitary grounds, to sleep, through the winter, as well as the summer, in beds without hangings of any kind".[6] Toilets were, until the introduction of patent cisterns late in the century, inconvenient privies located at the rear of the house. Bathing was performed in a large portable tub in the bedroom, or in the country districts, in the nearest stream. The Buchanan's in Pietermaritzburg, had a bathroom in the 'seventies, "To be ahead of the times was a habit of fathers, and in the restored house we had that of which no other house in South Africa could boast — we had a bathroom... with a ten feet by six feet bath of the old Roman pattern, built of bricks, with a couple of steps leading down into it, and water laid on".[7]

Drawing rooms and the principal bedrooms were provided with fireplaces. Surmounted by heavy mantel-pieces and mirrors, these were nearly always situated at right angles to the view window of the room, though occasionally they were located in a corner. Adamesque grates and firebacks were popular in the 'sixties but were soon superceded by heavier types surrounded with panels of painted tiles, with hearths of a similar material. (Fig. 333)

Doors changed with the fashion from four-panelled to six and eight-panelled designs, and back to four-panelled at the end of the century and were either of stained wood or painted white. Handles and fingerplates were of brass or white porcelain.

Most of the principal rooms had dados or wainscotting (often in a dark colour) surrounding the lower half. The wall between the dado and the frieze was papered. Wallpaper designs of the plainer type were preferred to ornate patterns, (Fig. 335,336) though subsequent papering and painting has covered up any strong evidence of this. In the late 'eighties, Belinda found "a delightful dining-room that is papered with plain terra-cotta paper of a particularly rich shade, and around the top of the walls a handsome landscape frieze on a cream ground affords just the right note of relief". She also recommended "that a large patterned paper should only be used for a large room".

Well-polished floors were thought not to need any covering, but when they were covered, this was done with either richly coloured carpets or linoleum "that simulated Japanese matting". Linoleum was generally green. The richer colours of hangings and furniture, which had been made possible by the production of aniline dyes in 1856, gradually gave way to lighter and more subdued shades, often of brown and green. Even the heavy furniture of mid-Victorian period was replaced by lighter types. In Natal, wickerwork and cane furniture was more suitable to the climate than the heavier upholstered English kinds.[8] Heavy curtains changed to lighter ones. "The woman who is going to make her home upcountry will be well advised to take with her a roll

---

3   Bamboo verandas were used in the Fort at Verulam. On one of the houses at Inanda Seminary, light screens of louvres are set as shading devices between the veranda posts.

3a   See Chapter 4.

4   See Chapter 12.

4a   Hints on household taste. C. Eastlake. p160

5   Belinda's aid to colonial housewives. The Colonial Home. p1,2,3.

6   Ibid, Eastlake. p206

7   Natal memories. B. Buchanan. p14

8   "The bamboo and other canes flourish and, together with the strong grasses, it is impossible to believe that, with a little direction, excellent cheap light furniture, suitable to the climate — after the fashion of Chinese and Japanese ware — might be made in Natal. All furniture comes out from England. It is expensive owing to the heavy freights. The plus and velvet seats are hot and uncomfortable". (1891). On veldt and farm. Macnab. p289

of art serge, a roll of Japanese cotton, and another of Madras or other muslin suitable for curtains".[9]

"Sans Soucci" was designed for Harwin in 1883 by a German architect, Albert Halder. (Fig. 346–350) The entrance portico and pediments are German neo-classical, and compare with the fashionable German buildings which were illustrated in the architectural magazines of the period. (Fig. 348) The front garden with its grassed parterre and tall cypresses is clearly an attempt to recreate the character of the gardens of Renaissance Italy. (Fig. 347) A wide veranda, tiled with terra-cotta and yellow coloured encaustic tiles and supported by luxuriant cast-iron work, surrounds the entire house. Halder appears to have been unresolved about which entrance was to be the major one, for though the portico with its grand double flight of steps on the North elevation is certainly the most obvious entrance, that on the east elevation has also a strong connection to the corridor running the length of the house. Simple veranda-houses were popular throughout Natal, their forms being utilized as well for stores and other buildings. (Fig. 351,352) The Customs House at Port Shepstone (1882) consisted of a plain, square block with a light surrounding veranda and a projecting observation tower with a small pyramidal roof. (Fig. 353) Such symmetrical buildings have a directness which is in some senses atypical of Victorian architecture and which can be attributed partly to the stringent conditions in some areas of the Colonies and partly to other factors. Just as the geometrical tracery and strutwork of Natal verandas is to some extent a fulfilment of the contemporary taste for decoration, so too, the symmetry of these houses and other buildings fulfils the desire to build in a formal and predetermined manner. In this way they are the consequence of a marriage between the classical and functional traditions. True veranda-houses were often symmetrical, though occasionally veranda-rooms and projecting gables articulated the continuous overhanging roof. These rooms and light gazebos on rooftops are interesting signs of the development of an architecture suited to the climate. (Fig. 354-355)

In 1882, Robert Sellars Upton designed a house, "Trevean", for Capt Hitchins on a site at Bellair, some distance from Durban. It is likely that Philip Dudgeon also had something to do with the design of the house, for he is known to have designed a warehouse for Hitchins in 1881, and may have entered into partnership with the ailing Upton.[10] "Trevean" is possibly the best domestic example of late Colonial Victorian in South Africa, and is remarkable for the simplicity of its conception and the restraint of its detail. (Fig. 356–360) The major entrance on the east elevation conflicts with the actual entrance from the south. (Fig. 357) This conflict may well have been resolved by the meeting of the two axes in a lantern-lit central hall, though alterations have disguised the original plan. The rooms, however, have a quality of spaciousness and informality which is derived from colonial planning. The cornice detail, perhaps originally of white vertical bars in green railings, cleverly leads the viewer's eye around the house and underlines its horizontal spread. (Fig. 358,360) "Trevean" is the predecessor of a few well designed veranda-houses (some are situated in the neighbouring suburbs), which were erected at the end of the nineteenth century. The billiard room at Trevean, which is a detached building at the rear of the house, is the work of another architect (possibly Street-Wilson) and its superb ornate interior reflects the changing attitudes to design which separate the early 'eighties from the last years of the century. (Fig. 361)

9   op cit, Belinda's aid. p5
10   See Chapter 9.

═══════════════════════════════
═══════════════════════════════

Chapter 9

Philip Maurice Dudgeon

1877-1887

"Since Mr Dudgeon commenced his probationary career in Durban, a marked improvement in the buildings had taken place. He (Councillor Nicol) ventured to say that from his designs, they had in Durban some of the finest buildings to be had in the whole of South Africa, and they stood as a monument to his ability as an architect. Beautiful villas which would be handed down from one generation to another with the name of Dudgeon as their architect".[1] (Natal Mercury)

Philip Maurice Dudgeon was born in 1852 on Lime Hill farm in the district of St Duloughs outside Dublin. He was the youngest son of Samuel and Mary Anne Dudgeon. Samuel Dudgeon, who practised as a solicitor in the city, died in 1853 and according to the terms of his will the farm had to be sold.[2] No trace can be found of Mary Anne and her five children between this date and 1870, when she is recorded as having kept house at Macaulay Buildings in Bath. This she continued to do until 1877.[3] Her three daughters all married men in the British Army, one of whom had been stationed in the garrison in Dublin, but nothing is known of the whereabouts of Philip Maurice.

He would have been eighteen years old in 1870 and might have remained in Ireland or gone to Scotland when his mother went to England. It would be tempting though, to suppose that Bath and Dublin would be the perfect background for an architect with such a love for and command of the vocabulary of classicism. No evidence, however, can be found for this nor any trace of his architectural training. It is quite possible that he may have entered the British Army.

Dudgeon probably left England in the second half of 1876, for he is entered as a passenger on board the Royal Colonial Mail Steamer, "Stettin" which arrived in Durban in January 1877.[4] It seems likely that he thereupon entered the office of Robert Sellars

Upton. Though no direct evidence exists of this, both architects claimed to have designed the Addington Hospital and several other buildings; this together with other factors indicates a partnership or association.

One of his first commissions in Natal was the supervision of St Joseph's Church. It is strange that Bishop Jolivet did not make use of this young architect for other work in his diocese, but rather wrote to Messrs Goldie, Child and Goldie when he needed designs for "altar and altar rails for Bloemfontein and benches for Pietermaritzburg".[5]

Mystery surrounds the design of Addington Hospital. The Natal Government Clerk of Works, Jenkyn, claimed to have designed the building in addition to supervising its erection. Upton may also have had a hand in the design, but Dudgeon was stated to be the architect when the building was completed.[6]

In 1876, Dr Addison had reported on the case for a new hospital in Durban. "I need not again draw attention to the defective accommodation etc., of the present hospital for the comfort and successful treatment of the sick; because there has been placed upon the Estimates for the Year 1877, a sum to provide for a new hospital, which is to be erected at Addington, upon some sloping ground between the town and the Point; and as the vote is large, and the accommodation about to be provided very ample, I anticipate many favourable results from the same".[7] M.H. Gallwey, the Colonial Secretary, called for tenders on April 14 1877. The time for submission of tenders was extended on April 30th.

"The foundation stone of this fine institution on the back beach, and overlooking the waters of the Indian Ocean, was laid last year without any ceremony whatsoever, and the work of the building which was entrusted to Mr J.S. Nicol (who carried out the whole of the contracts connected with it) was commenced on the 1st October. (Fig. 362,363) It is a noble block of buildings, and a more suitable site could not certainly have been selected in this neighbourhood; the style of the building is Italian, freely

---

1   Appendix to the New Town Hall issue of the Natal Mercury. Tuesday Nov, 3 1885.
2   S. Dudgeon's will was proved on 8 June 1854. Public Record Office, Dublin.
3   City of Bath directory, 1870 to 1877.
4   Natal Mercury. 19 January 1877.
5   Jolivet Diary. Archdiocesan Archives, DBN.
6   Natal Mercury, October 29 1878.
     "Mr Dudgeon a gentleman who has distinguished himself in his profession in Durban, is the architect".
7   Natal blue book 1876.
     Report on Addington Hospital by S.W.H. Addison, District Surgeon.

treated. The front of the premises will be very handsome when finished. It is a one storey building, and there is a spacious portico, supported by eight Doric Columns. Inside there is a vestibule, with corridors leading left and right to the various rooms. On the right and left hand sides are waiting rooms, the one for males, and the other for females. The corridors run right down through the building. On the left hand side is a casualty and operating room, 20 feet by 15 feet, and in connection with them is a dispensary; where the out-door patients, as well as those in the building will be attended to. Adjoining this is a consulting room. There are wings on either side of the building, the one for Natives and the other for Europeans. The left will, we believe, be used for Natives. There is a large ward on either side to accommodate from twelve to fifteen patients, and a nine feet four inch veranda runs around the whole building. Next to the large wards there is a smaller one on each side, to accommodate eight to ten patients. The nurses' rooms are next and there are spacious duty rooms. In the front, there are four detached wards two of which are for lunatics. There are excellent quarters for the Matron and Superintendent; and throughout the arrangements seem to be all that could be desired. We should not avoid to state that there are excellent apartments for patients whose friends are prepared to pay for their sojourn at this establishment. The height of the different apartments is the same throughout, and the ventilation is arranged on the most modern system".[8]

An interesting feature of the planning was the use of verandas as access ways and as a means of detaching rooms for lunatics and patients with infectious fevers. The colonnaded front facing the sea (Fig. 364) would appear to be the work of Upton, but the fine ornamental coffered ceiling with egg and dart mouldings is very similar to that designed by Dudgeon for the Standard Bank in Pietermaritzburg. (Fig. 365) The kitchen, a small cubical building set at the rear of the enclosed courtyard is, without doubt, the work of the latter. (Fig. 366) It is a high square volume, tiled almost to its entire height, and surmounted by continuous arched windows. Though, unfortunately, spoilt by numerous alterations over several years, it must have been the finest interior in the hospital.

An upper storey was erected over the whole of the existing building in 1892. Designed by W. Street-Wilson [9] it is notable for the fine quadrangle which is now surrounded by arcades on four sides. (Fig. 367)

The Alexandra Hotel was designed by Dudgeon in 1879. It took the form of a large house with gables and continuous verandas to both floors. The building is unusual for the herring-bone brick spandrels in the gables which give a suggestion of the Jacobean half-timbered expression popular in England with the architects of the Queen Anne revival. (Fig. 368) However, the clarity and overall restraint of the building are indications of Dudgeon's masterly detailing and his "out of step" conservativism. The interior, with its beautiful timber panelling added to the Jacobean-inn character. In 1881, the 'Times of Natal' described the hotel as the finest in South Africa.[10] Visitors to Natal who landed at the Point found the new hotel a welcome addition: "The shimmering heat was intense and we were glad to take refuge in the cool, airy hall at the Alexandra Hotel. The palms, the Hindoos clad in snowy tunics and turbans, looked delightfully tropical".[11]

In 1879 Dudgeon was commissioned to design a Town Hall and Library in Newcastle. The building was to commemorate the memory of the local volunteers who fell in the Zulu War. It took the form of a small, narrow hall with a pedimented gable at the entrance end. While no records exist of Dudgeon's work in 1880, [12] his office was certainly busy in the early months of 1881. Tenders were called in March, 1881 for new warehouses and offices for Messrs James and Hitchins at the Point. Dudgeon was a keen horseman and joined the Natal Turf Club, where it is likely that he met Charles Hitchins who was a club steward. A surviving photograph reveals the warehouse to have been a three-storeyed structure of brick. (Fig. 370) Vigorous arches in the gable ends together with the circular gable vents, suggest Dudgeon's concern with the problem of unifying the facade of such a tall structure. This kind of building though, can be found along the quayside of any Victorian port in England. In 1881 Dudgeon designed a house for Samuel Crowder; Crowder, a member of the Legislative Assembly who had come to Natal in 1874 from Londonderry, built the house himself. Dudgeon was certainly an architect who dealt mainly with the upper crust of society in Natal, for he also designed a house for Harry Esombe. Unfortunately no records are to be found of these buildings. At about this time he received a few commissions for commercial buildings. One of these was a new store for Messrs Sutton Flack and Co in Pine Terrace.[13] (Fig. 371) The facade is interesting for the size of the windows and their elegant proportions. At this time, he also designed a new store for Barnes and Mcfie, additions to the Standard Bank and a new warehouse in Gardiner Street for Randles Bros and Hudson.[14]

In March 1882, competitive designs were invited for a new Town Hall by the Durban Town Council. As early as 1856 the erection of a Town Hall had been suggested by the Finance Committee but the question was "allowed to stand down". In 1858 the idea was again suggested and Upton was instructed to prepare plans for the building, but again the project was abandoned. Another effort was made in 1875 and six designs were submitted in competition.[15] This time the Towns burgesses objected to the proposal and nothing eventuated.

It would appear that Dudgeon's services were employed in the drawing up of the competition conditions, for on August 30 1881 the Town Clerk wrote to him saying: "I am directed by the committee appointed herein to ask that you will be good enough to prepare the plan of site with streets etc, as suggested by you. With reference to keeping back the building so far, on two sides, not three as you state, the Committee are concerned as to what distance back it should be facing West Street, as to either 20 or 25 feet and whether it would be of any advantage? Upon this question please let me know. No stipulation is to be made as regards height. You will also please prepare a plan showing the general rearrangement".[16] Dudgeon's answer to the question is unknown but it may be assumed from his design that he favoured 25 feet. It is significant that at this early stage he was to be so concerned with the position of the building on the site and its relation to the streets and the other buildings around. (Fig. 372)

On October 3rd, Dudgeon received another letter from the Town Clerk expressing the concern of the Government in that it took "exception to your plans ... on the grounds that the offices as shown therein entirely exclude the light from the Sorting Room". He replied to this immediately, saying: "I note you say the Government...! I would beg to remind you that this plan is not mine but was prepared in the Colonial Engineer's Office, as the Government required and was handed to me by your Committee as such, until which time I never saw it. I simply had the plan lithographed as a guide to competing architects, but a footnote says that it is not necessary to tightly adhere to it as long as the same accommodation and convenience are provided. My own plan will entirely re-arrange it; but I think, as in all probability I shall be one of the competing architects myself, you can scarcely call upon me to say how I propose to light the sorting room, [17] though I can safely guarantee that there will be as much light in it as will be required".[18]

A local newspaper [19] commented on the exhibition of designs prior to the awards being made; "There is a feeling of disappointment at the meagre display of the designs for the new Town Hall. Judging from the number sent in, the premium offered by the Corporation seems to have been too small and the accompanying remuneration insufficiently made public, to induce home competition of the first order to which a building of the cost and magnitude contemplated is entitled. As regards some of the designs now on view, whatever may be their merit as specimens of art, sufficient attention has not been bestowed on the requirements of our climate in respect to shade and coolness and the suitability of the building material obtainable to the style adopted. These, although being points of great consequence, have apparently been overlooked in several of the most imposing and attractive compositions, the elevations of which are too much exposed for our long summers". The newspaper went on to expound the virtues of brick as opposed to stucco and compo.

At a meeting of the Town Council on July 7 1882, the fourteen designs were discussed and a short list of five was chosen. A motion was proposed that as none of the submissions had come within the limits of the estimate, no premium should be awarded. This, however, was a minority opinion and Dudgeon's design was awarded the first premium.

The "Architect" (August 26 1882) described the successful design as "a beautiful and effective design in pure classic style. The drawings are tinted in sepia, a very appropriate manner of finishing them ... Such a building should be carried out in stone, otherwise its appearance and stability would not be such as to render it as complete a work of art as it appears on paper ... The arrangement on plan is again second to none and far superior to most of the other designs". An elaborate description was then given of the design by Samuel Musgrave of Hull, which was placed second. Musgrave himself had described his submission as "Gothic of a very early type" with a boldly arcaded portico and a central tower. He complained of the short time which had been allowed for the preparation of designs and proceeded to make up for his few drawings with a voluminous description of every detail in the building and its construction. The "Architect" thought that it looked "too churchy" for a town hall and wondered whether it "is altogether

8   Natal Mercury. October 29 1878.
9   Natal Mercury Aug. 29 1892. and Natal Mercantile Advertiser. Feb. 1891.
10   Times of Natal. Feb. 1 1881.
11   Not unlike those of the Royal Hotel in the 'eighties.
12   Another severe economic depression was experienced in Natal immediately after the Zulu War.
13   Natal Mercury. May 10 1881.
     P. Flack was a committee member of the Natal Club of which Dudgeon was also a member.
14   Natal Mercury. June 3 1881. and Sept. 20 1881.
15   Durban: fifty years' municipal history. Henderson. p117
16   Town clerk's archives, Durban. Letters dispatched. August, 1881.
17   The Town Clerk's remark on Dudgeon's letter; "Still they did'nt say make it a dark hole".
18   Town Clerk Durban. Letters received. 9997, 1881.
19   Natal Mercantile Advertiser. June 17 1882.

advisable to strictly adhere to Gothic in its entirety in many cases".

Dudgeon's design was to face the market-square and was to be set back twenty-five feet from the streets around it, so that it might be viewed as a whole from any one point as if it were a free-standing sculpture. (Fig. 372,373,374) The main hall was to seat 1,200 persons and was encircled by a wide corridor which also gave access to the other ancillary spaces surrounding the hall. The main entrance was to face West Street and the side and rear entrances were to serve the town clerk's and other municipal offices on the ground floor. The post and telegraph office was to be situated on the western side, where the entrance was to be through a subsidiary, but more pleasing portico. (Fig. 456) The entire building was to be executed in plastered brickwork.

The design was based on a form of town hall of which that in Leeds is the prototype.[20] (Fig. 375) It is interesting to speculate too on whether the Portsmouth Town Hall, designed by William Hill in the early 'eighties, (Fig. 376) was based on the Leeds prototype or perhaps influenced, or was influenced by, Dudgeon's design. Another contemporary influence could well have been the Bolton town hall. [20A] However, the description of the Portsmouth version can easily be used to describe the Durban building; "The style of architecture is "classic", and in regard to its general treatment may be more fully described as "Roman" – a style which, being largely borrowed, contains many points suggestive of the former beauties of once exulting Greece. The tower, on the other hand, belongs in its main design to the style of the Renaissance, rendered famous by Bramante, San Gallo and Michelangelo".[21]

Dudgeon was instructed on July 26 1882, to prepare plans, elevations, sections, estimates and a bill of quantities to enable builders to tender. Certain members of the council had expressed the fear that the tower was too high for the building; Dudgeon prepared a perspective to show "that there would be no disproportion between the tower and the building".[22] It is possible that the model which he made was actually a design model and was completed before he won the competition. (Fig. 377) If this is so, it would indicate his tremendous concern for the external form in an almost sculptural sense. The model differs from the final building in the following ways; 1. The niches at the extreme corners of the front elevation are shown containing bas-reliefs; 2. There is sculpture in the entablature over the main entrance loggia.[23] 3. The tower base in the building is slightly higher than that in the model; 4. The corner columns of the tower are square in the building and round in the model; 5. The proportions and height of the tower were increased in the building from those of the model (15 : 31 to 12 : 28); 6.

Semi-circular windows appear in the hall clerestory in the building. It is significant that most of the changes occur somewhere on the tower, and that this is where his critics found fault; the relationship of a tower with a pediment with columns. prostyle in antis, can never be a happy one. Hence the tower, which in itself is a superb example of Victorian design, is seen at its best from the side or the rear of the building. (Fig. 377)

The beauty of the lower part of the building reveals Dudgeon's mastery of proportion and detail, and his faithfulness to the correct Corinthian. A faithfulness which, in the exuberance of the last decades of the nineteenth century, appears conservative, and which in later years was to be decried for its severity. (Fig. 379)

Dudgeon was capable not only of designing well, but swiftly too. On September 20th of the same year tenders for the erection of the building were accepted. Soon afterwards he expressed astonishment when Drew, one of the successful tenderers, requested to see the drawings again and "make assurance doubly sure". When the foundation stone was laid on February 1 1883, Dudgeon declined to take part in a procession of tradesmen and builders as this was "contrary to the etiquette of the profession". In October, he recommended that Inneswell, who had previously been a masterbuilder in England, be employed as a clerk of works and at a generous salary.

The success which Dudgeon had enjoyed in winning the competition, improved his reputation further and on November 27th, the Town Clerk respectfully requested his presence at a meeting under special committee "for the purpose of framing a complete set of Building Bye Laws"; an extraordinary honour for a man of 29 years. Dudgeon seems to have been a man of considerable private means, for besides offering to provide one of the marble columns for the entrance portico, he requested that his account for professional services be made over to debentures. In 1883 Dudgeon suggested that a museum be included in the building, and that the tower be provided with a clock. Few problems beset the course of the erection, and when the usual cracks appeared, he was able to successfully reassure the Town Clerk and Council. The major queries, though, concerned the costs of the building. Dudgeon's estimate was for £36,225 and the building eventually cost £51,259.

In June 1884 he wrote to the Mayor of Durban, probably with tongue in cheek; "The original objection to my design for the Town Hall enjoined by your council was that the tower was too high for the building. To obviate this I omitted the cupola on top of the dome and substituted a cast iron vane which was procured from England and is now here. As I now learn that the Council do not consider the design too high, I have given instructions to have the cupola as originally designed carried out".[24]

The Council Chamber was furnished and decorated by Dudgeon. In his design for the main hall (Fig. 380,381) he once again reveals his fondness for geometrical forms. The character of the space was very much that of the early nineteenth century pump room. The Town Council was extremely enthusiastic about lighting the building with electricity. Dudgeon, however, was not quite so keen. He eagerly seized the first opportunity "to be relieved from all responsibility in the matter", [25] and declined to take any further part in the lighting arrangements. Much ceremony attended the opening of the building. Dudgeon was described by the Governor in his toast as "my friend", and praise was given to the fact that the building had been designed by a colonist. As a direct result Dudgeon was elected a Fellow of the Royal Institute of British Architects in 1885.[26]

Theal thought that the new building "was the handsomest public building in all South Africa, with the single exception of the Houses of Parliament in Cape Town", [27] and that "the splendid pile of buildings do credit to the architect who is not without several other monuments of skill about Durban".[28]

While the Town Hall was being built Dudgeon was involved in carrying out several other commissions. Amongst them were a new shop for Payne Bros and a new veranda for Harvey Greenacre and Co's shop. (Fig. 382) The latter was an elegant, arched cast-iron veranda which successfuly unified the single and double-storeyed parts of the building. On 30 March 1882 Dudgeon received a letter from the Town Clerk which stated that this veranda was not in conformity with the plan approved. This probably reveals Dudgeon's attitude to the expressions of municipal bureaucracy. On another occasion he was reprimanded for not having submitted for approval, plans for a "Bay Beach building".

In April, 1882 tenders were invited for extensions to the Pietermaritzburg Town Offices.[29] These were housed in a single-storeyed building with narrow window openings. Dudgeon's design left the lower floor intact and added an upper floor. The existing window positions were continued vertically and set back between twin pilasters with semi-circular arches. (Fig. 303)

In the same year he designed a Masonic Temple for the East Griqualand town of Kokstad.[30] This building had an assymetrical entrance gable with pediment. (Fig. 384) The most interesting features though, were the semi-circular headed windows which thrust through the string course mouldings and which gave the whole facade a tense character.

Late in 1881, Dudgeon had received a commission to design the new offices of the Standard Bank in Pietermaritzburg. At the time the manager of the bank was Fergus Hathorn, "by no means the conventional Victorian banker, he was a man of varied interests, and something of an amateur architect and draughtsman".[31] Little else is known of the details of this commission, but it can be assumed that as his client was a man of some architectural sympathy Dudgeon was allowed great freedom of design. The result is a splendid building, probably the best in Natal and Dudgeon's own masterpiece. On the 9 January 1882 tenders were invited for the erection of the building.

The design was in the classical style with perhaps a hint of Palladian influence. This style was thought appropriate for commercial and civic architecture in

20   Designed by Cuthbert Brodrick in 1853.
20a   Completed in 1873.
21   Portsmouth Times, 12 August 1890.
22   Town Clerk Durban. Letters received. 9701, 1882.
23   Dudgeon intended the sculpture in the pediment to represent the industries of the country.
24   Town Clerk Durban. Letters received. 13431. 1884. June 20.
25   Town Clerk Durban. Letters received. 15,458. 1885. Oct.20.
26   His membership lapsed after 1886.
27   History of South Africa. 1870—1885. Theal. p215
      The Houses of Parliament were completed in 1884 to the designs of Grieves, based on the original sketches (1873) by the Cape Colonial Engineer, Capt George Pilkington.
28   The building was used as the Town Hall until 1913. The frequent mass meetings held there during the Boer War emphasised the need for a new hall. On the 26 November 1901 it was sold to the Post and Telegraph Office for £100,000. "It would have been impossible to enlarge the Town Hall itself without spoiling entirely the architectural features of the Building". This however was done in 1924 when a disappointing two-storeyed block was added to the rear of the building and large scale alterations were effected to the interior. Lately the topmost cupola has been removed.
29   Tender advertisement. Times of Natal. April 1882.
30   Tender advertisement. Kokstad Advertiser. June 17 1882.
      The Addington Presbyterian church was built from Dudgeon's design. It seated 300 persons and was opened on 10 December 1882. (Natal Mercury 11 Dec. 1882 and Jan. 3 1887) Dudgeon also designed the Pietermaritzburg Almshouses on erf 101, Burger Street. (now 245—250 Retief Street). (Natal Mercury July 27, 1882 and January 25, 1884).
31   Hathorn is said to have designed the new Victoria Club in Pietermaritzburg. (c.1893).

that it reflected the past grandeur of Rome and the Greek polis, and the Florentine birth of modern commerce. (Fig. 385,386) Once again Dudgeon set the building back from the street, a feature which, besides its form, gave the bank immediate individuality. (Fig. 387) The forecourt was paved with black and white encaustic tiles defined with a Greek key pattern. Beautiful cast-iron panels and gates separated the forecourt from the pavement. (Fig. 388)

An entrance portico protected the front door which led directly into a large banking hall. This was surmounted by a central dome with smaller ones at each corner. As in the interior of the Durban Town Hall, pilasters were continued at regular intervals around the walls and gave a sense of tight order to the space. (Fig. 390) This volume was expressed on the exterior in the form of a pyramid roof over a square base with a continuous range of arched windows. A lower hipped roof surrounded the entire building, and articulated the small flanking offices and portico from the main hall. (Fig. 389, 391) Dudgeon employed another favourite device to terminate the corners of the pyramidal roof and thereby emphasized it's set-back from the front wall. These were chimneys topped by semi-circular discs, (Fig. 392) a feature common in Ireland but only to be found in larger buildings around Belfast and contemporaneously in the new Town Hall for Paisley designed by W.H. Lynn.[32]

The arched windows on the front and side elevations, intersecting the string coursing, as they do, give the building a vigorous quality, while the precise mouldings (Fig. 393) in white mortar neatly define the vertical extremities of the building and lead the observer's eye around the salmon brick wall surfaces. Altogether the relationship of salmon, white and maroon is extremely effective in strong sunlight. Details such as the name-plate above the portico, the fine hardwood windows and door frames, and the portico and hall ceilings, are positive examples of Dudgeon's attention: an attention which served to underline and clarify his original concept.

In 1882 Dudgeon was asked by the Natal Government to prepare a design for a new Legislative Assembly building.[33] Nothing came of this project, however, and though no records exist of his design, it is not unlikely that the design submitted by J. Tibbet in 1887 was based on that of Dudgeon's. [34] (Fig. 473) In 1885 he was elected a steward of the Natal Turf Club and also secretary to the Natal Club, for which he designed a new club house in 1885. This was a one-storeyed structure with an elegant front veranda and classicist window and cornice mouldings. At about this time he designed a Gothic house in Pietermaritzburg (385 Longmarket Street.) This house is recognisably "Dudgeon" in the semi-circular

discs surmounting the chimneys and in the elegance of the cast-iron supports to the veranda. (Fig. 395–396) This is his only known attempt at the design of a veranda-house and may explain the unusual complexity of the planning, (Fig. 394) and too, the "facade" entrance elevation, together with a central porch and gable, while the physical entrance occurs arbitrarily at the one side. Altogether, the house has the character of a much earlier age and this is only belied in the large window openings of the bay windows to the two front rooms. (Fig. 398)

Dudgeon's last commission in Natal was the design of a new Collegiate Institute. Tenders were advertised in January, 1886 and the building was completed in 1888.[35] Dudgeon probably left Natal in 1887, however, and it is unlikely that he supervised the erection of the school. Described as Collegiate Gothic and complete with stone-mullioned windows, it is nevertheless the work of a man well versed in classicism. The entrance is set centrally under an oriel window in a gable, and flanked by protruding gabled "pavilions", while a central ventilator emphasises the symmetry and a continuous band of criss-cross, black bricks underlines the horizontality of the facade. (Fig. 399,400,401) An entrance hall leads to a corridor running the full length of the building, and a fine stone staircase leads to the upper floor. Subsequent and disastrous alterations to the rear of the building 1905 and later) have destroyed any indication of its total character, but the building must be regarded as the best example of Collegiate Gothic in Natal. It is also the best example of the use of local salmon brick and tiles.

Dudgeon returned to England after a brief ten years in the Colony. In 1889 he was married to Ada Gunning at Old Wedcombe church in Bath. He lived in retirement in a quaint Victorian house below Prior Park in Bath and died there on the 2 January 1891 at the age of 39 years. His death certificate [36] states that he died of an intestinal haemorrhage brought about by alcoholic cirrhosis of the liver. After his death his widow returned to her home in Wales where she lived comfortably with the £17,000 her young husband had left to her.

---

32   W.H. Lynn's works were also remarkable for their conservativism. The Irish builder. Jan.15 1874.

33   See Chapter 10.
      It is not unlikely that Tibbet was actually employed by Dudgeon as a draughtsman.

34   C.S.O. Letters received 1574/1883 and 1228/1883.

35   Natal Mercury. Jan. 5 1886.

36   Certified copy of an Entry of death in the district of Bath. 13 Jan. 1891.

Chapter 10

Victorian heydey

1879 – 1893

The even tenor of the fourteen years between the Zulu War of 1879 and the establishment of Responsible Government in Natal in 1893 was twice interrupted: by the first Anglo-Boer War of 1881, [1] and by a severe economic depression during the years 1885–87.[2] Apart from a few veranda-houses and the contribution of P.M. Dudgeon, few buildings of any importance were built in the first five years of this period.

Buildings erected by new settlers in both the Wilgefontein and Marburg settlements continued the traditions of settler architecture pioneered in the middle years of the century.[3] In the case of the Norwegian settlers at Marburg, however, their own national traditions were expressed in the form of a church which had a character not unlike a medieval Scandanavian church. (Fig. 402)

In 1882 fifty Trappist monks arrived in Natal from Bavaria and settled outside Pinetown. They called their new settlement Marianhill. Their leader, Abbot Pfanner, described their first buildings as "temporary and used for sleeping rooms and working rooms. Then we separated them by streets and so formed a village with its square, dormitories, refectory, church, chapterhouse, workshops, kitchens, cellar, and workshops for the marschal, the smith, the saddler, the cobbler, the tailor, the printer and the photographer. We built large schoolrooms for 82 boys who are maintained completely by the convent. The

building was in any case necessary against the rains, but our workshops were put up only as need arose for them. We made a mistake by building too small a convent and we did'nt know about the local stone available".[4] Marianhill is the largest "mission" in South Africa and consists of several related institutions grouped together in a village. (Fig. 403,404) At the heart of the village is the Cathedral facing onto a square (Fig. 489) from where several streets lead off to the monastery, workshops, schools, convents and hospital. All the buildings were erected in brick, made by the monks from clay deposits not far off. This, together with the fact that most of the earliest buildings were designed by one man, the 'black abbot', (an engineer) gives the entire complex an overall unity, not unlike the character of a medieval monastery.

Each group of buildings, however, is selfcontained and distinct. A tall brick tower dominates the monastery group, (Fig. 405) at the centre of which is a plain hall-type monastery church with an arcaded cloister with a central fountain adjoining it. Close by are the various workshops. These are essentially functional and unadorned except for their mid-European chimney-tops. The Abbott's house is a simple square building with a superb, arched entrance door. (Fig. 406) The entrance to the monastery is through an elaborate gateway with a brick vaulted archway and a veranda and witch-hat roof at one side. (Fig. 407,408) The Cathedral has twin open towers topped by small domes, and an entrance portico. (Fig. 409) The nave is relatively unadorned in contrast to the sanctuary and altar which have surrounding friezes on timber and mortar in rich and dazzling colours. (Fig. 410) The Convent is an introverted group of building, the facade of which was designed to repel rather than invite. A narrow onion tower pinpoints the chapel within (Fig. 412) and altogether, with the tall surrounding cypresses and the domed shrine on the hill above, the group is remarkably successful in evoking the character of a central European monastery. This is equally true of the whole village, though here and there some concession is made to the Natal climate in the form of arcades and verandas. The execution of the

1   The first Transvaal war of Independence consisted mainly of an invasion of Northern Natal.
2   "These years (1885–87) were among the darkest in the annals of the colony, and probably the only years during which white children were seen barefooted and begging in the streets".
     Portrait of a Colony. A.F. Hattersley. p193
3   Later annals of Natal. A.F. Hattersley. p76–9, 96–9.
4   Pamphlet Marianhill (1887) Abbot Pfanner.

buildings is perfect. The rich quality of the brickwork and of the brick details underline the unified character. (Fig. 411)

In his doctoral thesis on the history of Marian-hill, Father Dahm claims its legitimate succession in the line of the great monastic missionary institutions of Europe. It is said that at one time the monastery had about a thousand monks and was the largest Trappist monastery in the world. Even before gaining its autonomy the institution had begun to spread its branches throughout Natal, [5] but especially in the Western regions of the Colony where there are "many villages, each with its own church and farmlands, its school and the rest — a sort of colony or grange settled from the monastery".[6] By 1909, there were twenty-eight dependent settlements of the abbey, each with buildings of stone or brick and all reflecting the architecture of the abbey as it had reflected the architecture of the original Bavarian monasteries. That at Ixopo has a particularly fine tower at the side of the church (Fig. 413) and the convent is a good example of a double-storeyed veranda-house. (Fig. 414)

Bishop Jolivet recorded the erection of several new Catholic buildings in his diocese during this period. Among them were a priory at Oakford 1885, (Fig. 417) and a new Academy at Newcastle 1892, (designed by J.P. Mumford), (Fig. 415,416) a Sanatorium at Estcourt, 1890, and one on the Berea in Durban, 1892, (designed by Street-Wilson and Barr). A large temporary church was erected in Pietermaritzburg, which being built of brick with a corrugated iron roof had a simple exterior, "but everybody found our church charming in the interior".[7] The Bishop himself carefully supervised each of these new buildings. In 1886, a small chapel and crypt were erected in Durban to the memory of the pioneer Father Sabon. (Fig. 418)

During this period many new churches were erected throughout Natal, most of which were of brick.[8] Two new Presbyterian churches were built in Durban. The Berea church 1884, (W.E. Roberts) is interesting for its liturgical plan adapted to the form of a cross. (Fig. 419) One arm of the cross was provided for the organ and choir while the congregation in the other three arms were directed towards the pulpit and baptismal font in the corner of the crossing. In the case of the new St. Andrew's church, (Fig. 420,421) also designed by W.E. Robarts, the exterior was built of Durban brick and used the currently popular brick mouldings. The interior was plastered and painted white; the brick arch-surrounds and a timber, vaulted ceiling give it a warm and vigorous quality, in complete contrast to the plain exterior.

The New Republics of Vryheid and Utrecht were not yet included in Natal at this time.[9] Each town had a large stone church (1893) situated within a "Kerk plein" and both appear to be the work of the same architect. [10] (Fig. 422, 426) They were both built of local stone and have towers at the entrance in the German tradition. Both are in the Gothic style. The Vryheid Dutch Reformed Church (Fig. 423,424) is the larger of the two and suffers, because of its size, in the relationship between the height of the tower and the length of the building. The unusual plasticity of the buttresses, the fine lanterns and the small dormer ventilators are Victorian characteristics. Both churches are remarkable for their fine stonework, especially when one considers the remoteness of the localities. (Fig. 425)

In the "age of improvement" the predominant Natal culture was a replica of that of the mother country. In 1883 William Peace said that, "In their social life the colonists have naturally reproduced the habits of the people of England. Thus we find that among them are many flourishing institutions, not only for the support of churches and chapels for all religious denominations, and of admirably conducted schools, both of a public and private character, but also of public libraries and reading rooms, debating societies, musical societies, clubs, yacht clubs, rifle associations, benevolent societies; lodges etc..."[11] In Pietermaritzburg the new Athenium (1893) in Chapel Street (Fig. 427) supplemented the Natal Society and other clubs in the town. Visitors were surprised at the elegance of the entrance door set in an equally elegant Adamesque doorway. (Fig. 429) The cast-iron work of the fence (Fig. 428) and veranda are, like the delicate "pastiche" mouldings along the parapet, indications of a future trend rather than a current fashion.

In Durban the Club had been enlarged and improved by the addition of a veranda in 1881. The members though, found refuge from the intense heat of summer, not only on the veranda but also in the upholstered lounge under large fans. (Fig. 431) Drama, opera and light musicals were catered for by the erection of the Theatre Royal in 1882. (Fig. 432) Up to this time theatricals had been staged in simple music halls. Mr Williamson described his new theatre, "steps at the front will lead to the main entrances, while there will be towers at either side of the front, that on the left hand side containing the double staircase leading from the vestibule up to the dress circle, and that on the right communicating direct and only with the gallery, the "gods" being kept entirely separate from the other portions of the audience. By the centre or main entrances, the stalls, the private boxes, the dress circle and the pit can all be reached. Corridors will run between the other walls and the pit and dress circle, so that in the intervals they will form pleasant places for promenade without going into the open air, while from them the first class refreshment room will be reached. The upholstery will be of crimson and the corinthian columns supporting the galleries will be of white with gilt flutings. The auditorium is of a horse shoe shape with each back seat slightly higher than the one in front of it".[12]

A letter to a local newspaper expressed the need for a thorough inspection of the building to ensure that "the public may sit in the pit, boxes, or gallery with full assurance that the building will not fall and that in case of real or false alarm, causing a panic, they will be able to leave the place quickly and without sustaining injury". A deputation of the Town Council visited the building and supported a report by R.S. Upton in saying that the building was one in which the public could place confidence. Upton found that "the arrangements for ingress and egress are admirable", and that the ventilation was ample and, "perfectly under control for any state of weather, and must greatly add to the comfort of the audience, who will enjoy the cooling influence of the air without draughts, as the corridors will prevent them".[13] The mansard roofs to the towers were probably used less for their own fashionable reason than to suggest the character of a Parisienne theatre.

A new masonic temple for the Port Natal lodge was completed in 1893.[14] The building was set back from the pavement and consisted of a hall on the ground floor with offices and other rooms set parallel to it. (Fig. 435) The facade is interesting for the un-English boldness of effect achieved by the attic-storey and its cornice mouldings butting up against the pilasters. (Fig. 433,434) Large discs containing various masonic symbols filled the space above the lower floor windows. A central ventilator emphasised the position of the entrance which was surmounted by a pediment supported on heavy curved pilasters. A further attic storey repeated the fenestration pattern of those below.

Natal was still essentially a sheep farming area in the 'eighties, though the development of sugar along the coast and coal mining in the Northern districts were indications of future expansion. The discovery of gold in the Transvaal accelerated the progress of rail links between the Colony and the Transvaal Republic. The state of the Durban harbour was already a limiting factor in the growth of the colony. In 1882, the Harbour Department stated that its aim was "a harbour accessible to ships of any draught, at all states of the tide, in any weather, by night as well as by day".[15] Although this aim was only achieved after the turn of the century, the gradual effect of the improvements effected was the development of Durban as the economic hub of Natal.

This prosperity was expressed in the numerous commercial buildings erected in Durban. Shops, offices and warehouses had changed from those of earlier years. No longer were they simple functional solutions to the problems of providing spaces close to the street where trade could be carried on. Pretensions in the form of more and cruder ornament spread over facades. Two features were nevertheless still inherent in town buildings. One was the fondness for arched openings and the other for plastered surfaces. These, however, with their profusion of ornament, exhibited little of the flat unbroken surfaces of previous generations. Indeed mouldings around window and door openings and heavy incised rustication combined to give an overall texture to walls. Signs, perhaps, that such surface patterns were thought more interesting by their designers than the logical explanation of wall and roof elements. Maybe this is why P.M. Dudgeon's designs, by contrast, appear to be so rational.

Gables made their first appearance towards the end of the 'eighties, affording wonderful opportunities for more elaborate facade design; they rarely had any logical relationship to roofs.[16] Fig. 437,439) Eastlake stated the emerging problem of shop design very clearly, "Some attempts at architectural display are occasionally made in the way of shop fronts. But here a certain practical difficulty attends the designer. However elegant the superstructure may be, it has one drawback; it must be resting on nothing, or, at least, apparently on nothing; the aim of every modern retail dealer being to expose his goods for sale behind a single sheet of plate glass".[17] This applied not

5   Reichenau Monastery was founded as early as 1886.
6   Reichenau, Lourdes, Centakow, Marianthal and Maria Ratchitz were but a few of the outposts.
7   Jolivet Diary.
8   Baptist churches; Pinetown 1883, Pietermaritzburg 1884. Methodist churches; Newcastle 1881, Howick 1879, Ladysmith (1) 1881, Ladysmith(2) 1891, Dundee 1886. Anglican churches; Newcastle 1880, Pietermaritzburg (St Luke's) 1882. Estcourt (2) 1882, Stanger 1888, and Ixopo 1883.
9   Vryheid, Utrecht and part of Wakkerstroom were included in Natal in 1903.
     A history of Natal. E.H. Brookes and C. de B. Webb. p158
10 Possibly an architect in the Transvaal Republic. A Dutch Reformed Church was erected in Dundee in 1884.
11 Our Colony of Natal. W. Peace. p32
12 Landmarks of old Durban. S.A.B.C. p52
13 op cit, Landmarks of old Durban. p53
14 Probably designed by W. Street-Wilson.
     The building was destroyed by fire a few years after it was built.
15 They were South Africans. J. Bond. p98
16 Decorated gables had become popular in Britain during the "Queen Anne revival".
17 Hints on household taste. C. Eastlake.

only to the ground floor, but also, to the upper floors; there larger window openings crowded the mouldings closer together on the remaining solid wall surfaces and really necessitated a quite different approach to facade design. (Fig. 436)

The eventual solution was already at hand in the light frameworks of verandas. While this period is, like the preceeding ones, notable for the relative absence of verandas to shop fronts and commercial buildings, [18] those which had such adjuncts were at an even greater disadvantage. For a two or three-storeyed masonry block supported visibly only by light cast-iron veranda posts requires to be designed in an equally light way. (Fig. 439)

There appear to have been two trends in facade design which may or may not have been stimulated by these problems. The first was to provide a vigorous large scale sub-structure at the ground floor (Fig. 440) while corner turrets and gables relieved the heaviness of a flat wall surface in addition to providing the desired "picturesque" quality. The other is evident in the kind of building which has its roots in the functional tradition. The African Boating Co built a four-storeyed barracks for stevedores in Point Road which displays a refreshing rationale. (Fig. 441) Flat-arched openings spaced close together leave a narrow underlying framework of wall surface. Parapet columns accentuate the vertical frames and the separate floor structures are expressed as horizontal bands of projecting stanchion ends between window openings.

By the early 1890's rail links between the coast and the hinterland of South Africa led to the development of Durban and the adjacent coast as a holiday region. Hotels were erected which were often two-storeyed buildings with light encircling timber verandas. As early as 1863, a scheme had been suggested for providing public baths in the Bay. These were not altogether successful. In 1891, Councillor Cowey proposed to erect a public swimming bath on the market square. W.H. Powell F.R.I.B.A., newly arrived from London, prepared the plans for the building. It was to contain a swimming bath to be supplied with sea water from the Bay, and elaborately equipped Turkish baths. (Fig. 444) "The institution consists of swimming baths, 80 feet long and 30 feet wide surrounded by 52 dressing rooms; slipper or private baths, numbering 21, and possessing all the most modern accessories; and the Turkish baths section containing three heating rooms which register temperatures of 110 degrees in the first, 190 degrees in the second, and 250 in the third. The accessories of a Turkish bath are all provided, viz, massage room, three heating rooms, a plunge bath, hot, cold, needle spray shower baths, and a retiring or cooling room containing 14 private boxes and six outside couches. The interior of the whole building is inlaid with ornamental tile and lighted by electricity".[19]

Public parks had been laid out in Durban in the mid-eighteen sixties. In response to a request from the Athletic Clubs of the town, the Council laid out an oval in Albert Park and erected a Pavilion early in 1889. (Fig. 445)

In Pietermaritzburg a Produce Hall and Grandstand were built (1893) for the Royal Agricultural Society where they have served the annual shows for over seventy years. A new Market Hall had been put out to competition in 1884. Included in the design was a new borough police station and lock-up. J.S. Brunskill was the successful architect. He chose to separate the two functions entirely and designed a two-storeyed police station with a portico facing onto Commercial Road and a bell-tower projecting from the Longmarket Street elevation. Both the gable over the entrance and the tower sit extremely uncomfortably over the building. Brunskill may have learnt something from Dudgeon about tower design but seems to have completely ignored the latter's corner treatment on the Durban Town Hall. The Market Hall was set back from Commercial Road on the Market Square and is altogether a finer building. (Fig. 446) The symmetrical roof form with its clerestoreys creates a spacious and well-lit hall. The exterior suffers from a similar mixture of brick and "imitation stone" as the police station, though it would appear that the peculiar arched niches crossing the brick and mortar surfaces were some kind of attempt to link the two materials

The new Ladysmith Town Hall (1894) was designed by R. Walker and is a miniature version of Dudgeon's Durban Town Hall.[20] (Fig. 447,448) Once again, however, it was the form rather than the detail which was borrowed. Some twenty years later interesting internal alterations were carried out. The hall was rebuilt at the rear and a pleasant entrance atrium took its place.[21] (Fig. 449,450) The Newcastle Town Hall (1898) was designed on similar lines by William Lucas. (Fig. 451) The tower and dome have a strange papery quality while visually they have almost entirely flattened the pediment over the entrance portico. (Fig. 452)

Pietermaritzburg had hankered for a Town Hall for many years. In 1855, John Moreland had prepared the elevation and ground floor plan of a proposed design for the Town Council.[22] In 1860 Prince Alfred laid the foundation stone of the new building next to the site of the old Voortrekker Raadzaal. Nothing came of this scheme, however. [23] On the 5 February 1891, Sir Charles Mitchell relaid the foundation stone for a building which was to have a hall to accommodate 2,000 people. The council had invited interested persons to compete and the successful competitors were Street-Wilson and Barr. Nothing is known of Percy Barr but Street-

Wilson had come to Natal in 1886 after practising first with Robert Hesketh and later on his own in London. The practise which he had set up with Barr in Durban was described by the Colonial Secretary as being the best in the colony.

The building was said to be in "a quaint blend of Tudor, Flemish and Florentine styles", [24] which suitably sums up the mixed style of late Victorian days. (Fig. 458) A tall clock tower with a obelisk roof pin-pointed the crossing of the two major streets in the town and a two-storeyed block of offices with balconies encircled the hall. (Fig. 459) Entrances to the building were from Church Street and Commercial Road. Street-Wilson's perspective reveals his intentions to have been changed in the course of the erection. (Fig. 453) In particular, the square block containing the clock and chimes, which in a sense is vaguely reminiscent of Barry's Westminister Palace, (but not nearly as successful) is completely spoilt by the niggardly gables above it. Street-Wilson had no doubt acquired his fondness for decorated gables from Hesketh, an architect who had climbed enthusiastically onto the Queen Anne Revival bandwagon. The building can only be judged from the present phoenix-like reincarnation, but original photographs of the interior reveal the influence of Dudgeon's Durban Town Hall. (Fig. 455) A similar arrangement of galleries and stage were built, though the lower stage drum was an improvement on that in Durban. The four manual organ with its 84 stops, which was the largest in South Africa at the time, appears decidedly unhappy against the flat panelled ceiling. The latter was no improvement over that in the Durban one. The Council Chamber was described as a fine room which had French casements along one side leading out onto the shady balcony. The main entrance hall in Church Street which had a large antecedent vestibule, contained "a grand staircase".

On the evening of 12 July 1898 the building was almost totally destroyed by fire. Street-Wilson was also commissioned to design the new building which was to be three-storeys high and was to cost £100,000.[25] Though this design was based closely on the original building, he had learnt by his mistakes. (Fig. 459) The corner tower has a more pleasant outline and is more effectively balanced in the three-storeyed building with the extended portecochères over the main entrances. (Fig. 456A) The circular clock face was moved lower down the height of the tower and the softly rounded corners were continued the full height up to an open timber fleche. Gables, domes and turrets break the outline of the roof and pinpoint the corners and entrances. The alternating horizontal salmon brick and mortar strips play delightfully against the vertical fenestration patterns.

Altogether, the exterior has a richer and softer feeling than the 1893 building. The interior is Street-Wilson's master-piece. (Fig. 457) Not many architects are given two opportunities to show their skills with the same building but in this case it paid off handsomely. The large and grand organ, majestic in outline, was made the focus of the whole space and splendidly counterbalances the sweeping curves of the ceiling. The stage too, was designed to link the organ to the floor level. Even the Viennese chairs appear to have been carefully chosen to harmonize with the space. The building has served not only as a visual enhancement to the centre of Pietermaritzburg but also in an auditory way. The quarter-hourly chimes and Sunday morning carillon may be heard from as far away as the distant suburbs of the town.

Albert Henry Hime, who had become the Colonial Engineer in 1875 and who had previously had experience in Bermuda on the construction of bridges, delegated his authority to several members of his staff. In Durban C.H. Jenkyn was the clerk of works. This post involved not only the supervision of buildings in the area but their design as well. In Pietermaritzburg Alfred Singleton and later Charles Snell occupied the equivalent posts. The first architect in the Colonial Engineer's office was C. Bompas who entered the Department in 1888.

In Durban, Jenkyn's two largest designs were the new Customs House and a Water Police Station.[26]

18   Perhaps this can be accounted for by the problems of dark display windows under projecting verandas.

19   Durban. Fifty years municipal history. Henderson. p144

20   In November 1891, plans were called for a New Town Hall. Six designs were submitted. Moses Holmes design was placed first but as the cost far exceeded the intended amount (£1,000) it was abandoned.
     Once again plans were called in August 1892. The dimensions of the new hall were to be 65 ft. by 35 ft. and the building was to be of stone. A history of Ladysmith. K.C.M.

21   The tower of the town hall was severley damaged during the Boer War siege of Ladysmith. W. Lucas was commissioned in 1902 to carry out the renovations.

22   Natal Witness. April 13 1855.

23   A competition for a town hall was also advertised in 1880.

24   Ingram also said that "The style is free Renaissance, and as this has had as it were a new birth in Britain, grown up from modern needs, it can only be described as Victorian, with piazza and balconies, designed to especially suit the scorching suns of Natal".
     The story of an African city. Ingram.

25   Completed in 1901 and opened by the Duke of Cornwall and York.

26   Jenkyn also designed Central Gaol in Dbn.

Jenkyn had served his apprenticeship under Alexander Gordon and after this had "supervised the construction and shipment of works of a varied description to the Colonies" and "a lighthouse in a difficult position on the east coast of Newfoundland". The new Customs House (1884) had an entrance portico with four Tuscan columns supporting a plain pediment. (Fig. 460,461) This gave access to a large customs hall, which is the best part of the building, and several other spaces at the sides of the hall. The roofs, (Fig. 462) which were originally of slate, build up in a pyramidal development from those above the outer spaces to that over the main hall. Altogether, the building has a character of the kind to be found in Scottish buildings at the beginning of the Victorian era.[26A] The Water Police Station, (Fig. 463) not far away, was built of brick and presented a heavy dome-topped tower and semi-circular pediments at the corners.

Alfred Singleton designed the new Boy's Preparatory School (Fig. 464) and Girls Model School in Pietermaritzburg. Both buildings were in the colonial idiom. Narrow classroom wings which surrounded "quads" were terminated with simple projecting gables and the roofs were punctuated by low "dormer" ventilators. He also used tall gables in the Courthouse in Estcourt (1887) and that at Dundee (1888).[27] The former (Fig. 465) had a projecting veranda with an entrance porch while the latter (Fig. 466) had a semi-circular pediment over the arched entrance doorway. Singleton was evidently very conversant with the colonial style, for his design for the Colenso toll house, (1879) (Fig. 467) could be easily mistaken for a house of the early 'fifties. The Ladysmith correspondent of a Natal newspaper said that, "on the Colenso side (of the Tugela bridge) a fashionable looking Tollhouse has been built whose eyes look in every direction".

The Asylum on Town Hill in Pietermaritzburg was also the work of Singleton. However, Hime might have found time between the sittings of the Legislative Assembly to look in on the progress of the work. Singleton himself had designed the original building in 1876.[28] At the time it was decided to concentrate on the completion of one portion of the plan and this was finished early in 1880. Extensive additions were built in 1889 and probably consisted of a variation on the original design. (Fig. 468) The central double-storeyed block had a projecting portico and a roof-turret capped with a fine cast-iron crown. This block contained the administrative offices; from the entrance hall corridors ran off to the side wings and the veranda quadrangles. The long front facade was terminated at each end with double-storeyed blocks having simpler timber roof lanterns. (Fig. 469) Singleton once again used his "dormer" ventilators and supported the projecting

eaves with turned brackets, corbelled out from the walls. The buildings are particularly notable for the panoramic views they enjoy over the town, something which Singleton must have thought important, for the entire building is raised up on a terrace to overlook the surrounding trees. (Fig. 470)

Hime himself designed the Mounted Police Barracks in Alexandra Road, Pietermaritzburg.[29] (Fig. 477,472) These had been begun in 1878 but numerous disruptions caused them to be completed only in 1890. The entrance gable and lantern with a tunnel guarded by heavy timber doors, and the verandas were introduced in the course of the work but the original plans were carried out without material deviations.

New plans were prepared and fresh tenders were invited for the Legislative Assembly building in 1886. The winning design was that of James Tibbet. His drawings were revised by Charles Snell [30] for, "when the quantities were taken out, it was found impracticable to follow that gentleman's plans in their entirety".[31] The building is one of the finest in Pietermaritzburg. (Fig. 473,475) J.S. Little, a visiting Englishman, thought that "it would put to shame, as far as internal arrangements are concerned, our palace of Westminister".[32] A contemporary prototype of the lifted-up prostyle can be found in the Clark Hall (Fig. 475) at Paisley (by W.H. Lynn) and the similarity goes further than that. In both buildings the base is heavily rusticated and the fenestration of the upper floor is divided into small square openings above large French casements leading out onto the balconies.

In the Legislative Council Building corridors ran down both sides of the main assembly hall and led to the various offices of the legislative councillors. The hall was panelled in dark timber, and the hangings and upholstery were of crimson velvet. Semi-circular clerestory lights were arranged along the two long sides of the space. A ladies gallery was added in 1890. The building was completed with elegant cast-iron fences and gates surrounding the whole site (Fig. 476) and a marble statue of Queen Victoria, executed by Sir J.E. Boehm was set on a pedestal in front.[33]

26a   Perhaps this can be explained by Jenkyn's earlier associations with Alexander Gordon.
27   Courthouses were erected at Richmond in 1880 and at Ladysmith in 1888.
28   C.E. Report Natal Bluebook 1876.
29   C.E. Report Natal Bluebook 1878 to 1890.
30   C.E. Report Natal Bluebook 1886.
31   Supplement to Natal Mercury June 22 1887.
32   South Africa. J.S. Little p249
33   In 1901 extensive additions were erected to the one side of the Legislative Assembly Building, but the additions with the copper dome on a high base do not have the same quality as the original.

In the precincts of this new seat of Government, law 4 of 1893 "to provide for the establishment of Responsible Government in Natal", was assented to by the Governor on July 3 1893. Analysis of the expenditure on Public works and buildings after this period indicates a tremendous increase from 1892 (£23,060) to £150,887 in 1898 and £405,855 in 1902. The deepening of the harbour mouth in Durban and the subsequent development of the port, together with the new rail link to the Transvaal brought about a boom period which was to transform the entire Colony.

PART TWO

Chapter 11

Town and village

"Another moment, and we are running up the narrow channel that lies between the lofty bluff and woody point. Only a few seconds and our sluggish craft, tugged by a row-boat, chanting a lively air — has fairly entered the unrivalled "Harbour Bay" — a sheet of water of at least ten thousand acres, completely land-locked by the Bluff and Berea Ranges, except at the narrow inlet, which too, by a sudden bend is lost to view once you enter.

Fancy yourself thus floating on a vast lake of deep, transparent water, eight or ten miles in length, walled in right and left by masses of unbroken forest (evergreen), stretching up mountain sides almost to the bright blue sky; then carry your powers of imagination still further, and picture this vast lake growing wider and wider as it stretches inland, till it terminates in a succession of slopes, extending from the waters edge to a distant chain of mountains, connecting the bluff with the Berea hills. Fancy, moreover, these slopes dotted over with thriving homesteads, with cultivated fields, with thousands of acres of wild, waving deep green grass, with droves of depasturing cattle and herds of noble deer. Add to the picture also a thriving seaport town, reposing at the foot of this slope, under the shade of the dense bush...(1850)[1] (Fig. D)

G.H. Mason's enthusiastic description of Port Natal indicates two features which were common to most of Natal's towns and villages. The first was the complete dominance of the natural environment over the man-made settlement. The second was the close relationship of the town to the surrounding agricultural region. (Fig. 487) Besides the very earliest settlement at Port Natal, where the settlers were traders, hunters and missionaries, many towns and villages originated as agricultural centres.

Just as their predecessors in the Cape had established towns as "fountainheads of regional community life", [2] so both the early Dutch and English settlers who were scattered throughout the Colony founded towns which became established centres of religion, jurisdiction and trade.[3] The Voortrekkers were each allowed one erf in Weenen and Pietermaritzburg in addition to the large farms given to them on their arrival. Another motive for the birth of a town was defence. Pietermaritzburg remained as a palisaded laager for two years before a permanent settlement was begun. Later, frontier posts such as Estcourt (Bushman's River) and Harding in 'No-man's land' developed as small villages around a small fort.

Some immigration schemes were conceived as settlements where the immigrants would farm smallholdings and live close to each other in villages. At the centre of such a village there would be a school and church. These schemes were only successful where the nature of the land allowed such intensive usage. The German settlement at New Germany thrived and by 1876 it was said "to consist of a considerable number of small comfortable-looking homesteads grouped around a large chapel".[4]

But perhaps even more successful was Verulam. Theophilus Irons had drawn up regulations for the erection of houses on town lands.[5] He and the Committee were advised by W.J. Irons to reserve certain of the most suitable parts of the town for the erection of public buildings, a school, a church, and a site for a cemetry. Irons gave further instructions concerning the village; "I will forward a design for a school house and church by the next vessel. You know my idea has always been to have the streets planted with rows of trees on each side, giving a uniform and picturesque appearance".[6] Verulam became the stronghold of Wesleyanism in Natal and developed as a busy centre for the sugar, cotton and coffee plantations in the district.

Other immigration settlements had proved disastrous and the great proportion of immigrants returned to the only towns in existence, Durban and Pietermaritzburg.[7] A few, however, remained behind (as in Richmond) and their little settlements gradually developed into villages.

A few other villages originated as missions where the nucleus already existed in the form of a few houses surrounding a church and school and perhaps a trading post.[8] Later, towns developed in the northern districts as a direct consequence of coal mining.[9]

The Dutch who had remained in Northern Natal during the 1840's set up the Klip Rivier Republic which disintegrated in 1847. Several of the more resolute Republicans decided to settle in an area where they could be rid of British Administration. In 1854 the Zulus gave them permission to graze their cattle in an area to the Northwest of Zululand. Here they settled and formed a Republic known as Utrecht. Constant suspicion of the Zulus, however, gave the Republic a perpetual sense of insecurity. In the 'fifties "they settled down to quarrel with one another in good old Trekker style". By 1862 their capital, Utrecht, was a "dreary little town of about twenty houses, a church built in 1854, one hotel and a court house". (Fig. 488) The later New Republic of Vryheid, (1884) was almost a part of the Transvaal to the extent that the two towns Vryheid (1884) and Paulpietersberg (1896) were both laid out by the "Landmeter Generaal" of the "Republiek van Zuid Africa", Johann Rissik. Both were Dutch gridiron plans [10] (Fig. 489) with the usual vast Kerk and Market squares formed at the centre of the layout with the major streets crossing at the corner of the "Kerk Plein". Another recorded township which the Boers laid out in Natal was one at St Lucia Bay in 1884, "which caused the British Government to send a gunboat and plant the Union Jack there".[11]

The task of laying out the new villages and towns in the Colony was entrusted to the Surveyor General, W. Stanger, though apparently he was often fully occupied elsewhere and the work was given out to Surveyors such as John Moreland and Thomas Oakes. The usual plan adopted was a rectilinear one. Broad streets were laid out with large blocks with little or no consideration for the topography. (Fig. 490–492) The other common feature these villages have is their proximity to a river or stream.

Those towns which still retained an essentially Dutch population such as Greytown and Ladysmith were arranged around a large block, originally intended as a Market square, though they have had numerous uses since. (Fig. 491,492) The Surveyors themselves named the streets, not forgetting to give at least one street their own name or perhaps that of their wife.

During the course of colonial development, settlers, who had for some reason or another established some communal facilities in an area, would petition the Government to lay out a township there. In such cases (Mt Moreland, Port Shepstone) existing buildings and property would be the starting point and probably account for certain rather complex town plans.

In 1847 a Government Commission was appointed to divide the country into magistracies. As a result of this several towns came into existence. Greytown was planned as the centre of the Umvoti district in a place where an old wagon drift crossed the river. In 1850 Thomas Oakes surveyed the town on the farm of L.J. Nel. (Fig. 491) John Bird was appointed to lay out a capital in the Klip River district. After due examination the site was chosen on the farm of one van Tonder. (Fig. 492) It was proclaimed as a town on 20 June 1850 and huts were erected to house the magistrate and his staff and a force of twenty-four Zulu policemen. Lieutenant-Governor Benjamin Pine named it Ladysmith in honour of Sir Harry Smith's wife "in order that it may be a suitable partner for the Dutch settlement at Harrismith on the further side of the Drakensberg".

Newcastle was chosen by the Colonial Government as a capital for the most Northern district in 1864. Much argument surrounded the selection of the site, which had several disadvantages. The water supply was unpredictable and there was no building stone or timber for use as fuel. However, a sale of erven which took place on 16 March 1864 was well attended, though the courthouse was the only building to be erected for some years thereafter.

Pietermaritzburg had been laid out in 1839 as the principal town of the Republic of Natalia.[12] (Fig. E) The site on the Bushmansrand was almost flat and a gridiron plan was laid out with the longest streets running from North-East to South-West. A large Market Square was set out at the centre of the town where the main street, Church street crossed the road to the Port, Nel street. (Fig. 493)

The erven were "each one hundred and fifty by four hundred and fifty feet in size, thus large enough for a garden and an orchard".[13] The town also had a commonage, a hundred and twenty square miles in extent. Trekker planning, indeed, may be seen to be the precursor of the consistent Victorian attitude of independence. Perhaps the desire to be a free-hold owner was a continuation of that tradition in England or maybe a reaction against eighteenth-century neighbourliness. Whatever the reason, immigrants preferred

1	Life with the Zulus of Natal. G.H. Mason. p44
2	Early nineteenth century architecture in South Africa R.B. Lewcock. p390
3	Such towns as Greytown, (1850) Pinetown, (1849) York, (1850) Weenen, (1839) Camperdown (1885) and Bulwer, (1889).
4	Natal, A history and description of the Colony. Henry Brooks.p76
5	See Chapter 4.
6	History of early Verulam. M. Park (M.A. Thesis) p272
7	Other immigration settlements were at Howick (1847), York, (1850) Richmond, (1850) and Byrnetown, (1850).
8	Hermannsburg, Empangeni and Eshowe.
9	Dundee, Glencoe and Hattinghspruit.
10	These town plans appear to have been derived from the plan of Worcester in the Cape Colony. Utrecht and Vryheid were officially incorporated into Natal in 1903.
11	History of the Vryheid District. F. Wilter.
12	See Chapter 2. Pietermaritzburg has ever since been the capital of Natal.
13	Progress of South Africa. Theal. p246

the policy of one man, one site. This gave considerable impetus to the development of the free-standing veranda house with its essentially independent character.

Every proprietor of an erf in Pietermaritzburg was bound to pay a proportionate tax to defray the expense of leading water to the town from the "Kleine Bosjeman's" river. (Fig. 493A) The water was conveyed along furrows down the Zwartkop valley to the western extremity of the settlement, where it was divided so as to run through the main streets.

The first public buildings (Raadzaal and Church of the Vow) were built on and adjacent to the Market Square. (Fig. 494) The erection of the gaol on the town square was a continuation of the Medieval European tradition which had been commonly used in the Cape earlier in the century.[14] The most substantial houses were originally erected around the Market Square. This remained the centre of the town until the Wesleyan Church buildings and the Government school were built around Chapel street, between the Market Square and Fort Napier.[15]

The large erven with their free-standing houses surrounded by gardens gave the streets a somewhat different character from that of those towns in the Eastern Cape where the streets were defined by walls of houses.[16] The earliest Dutch houses, however, were built close to the street in continuation of eighteenth century traditions.

The selection of the site for the Capital town was not effected without criticism. The Rev J. Archbell thought that "its denuded appearance not merely detracts from its beauty, but actually stamps deformity upon its appearance, whilst its entire lack of fuel, which is not to be found within fifteen or twenty miles of its site, must for ever prevent it attaining superiority as a place of residence or becoming a commercial importance ... It does not require much penetration to perceive that, with so many and decidly superior inland sites, it never can become the metropolis of the colony or the emporium of trade". By contrast he proposed that "Port Natal possesses advantages which cannot be described in too striking colours: its contiguity to the bay; its superabundance of fuel, as well as large timber; its inexhaustible supple of water from four rivers ... all point out the great importance of the locality. In short, the whole, whether viewed in reference to quality or position, presents as it were, material of the most suitable quality, waiting only to be transformed, as art or fancy may deem best, into one of the most populous and delightfully situated towns on the coast of Africa".[17]

Capt Allen Gardiner had laid out a plan for Durban in 1835.[18] (Fig. 495) The town was to be situated next to the Bay. A system of long streets crossed by shorter ones with alternating rectangular and square blocks was to be the starting point for the town. The four squares, one of which was to contain a church at its centre, and the houses built adjacent to the streets are characteristics of eighteenth-century planning. Perhaps the most interesting aspect of Gardiner's plan is its similarity to that actually laid out by Wahlberg and G.C. Cato early in 1840.[19] (Fig. 496) The latter, however, only had one square. Gardiner had allowed for street-widths of 80 feet but those laid out by G.C. Cato were 100 feet in width. According to Russell this distance was governed by the length of a wagon and a span of oxen and the space required to turn in.[20]

The Market Square was for long regarded as the centre of the town. The Wesleyan Church and later St Paul's were built adjacent to it. However by its very size it created problems. It seems that the earliest buildings were erected on the eastern side of the town and later developments spread further westward up Smith and West streets. The large sandy square became an effective barrier between the East-enders and West-enders and was to lead to much jealousy and controversy.[21]

At first houses, shops, schools and churches stood close together in the towns. The few industries were generally located outside of the towns close to good supplies of freshwater or, as in the case of building materials, where natural stone or clay was found in great abundance.[22]

In Pietermaritzburg an exclusive residential area soon developed at the Western end of the town. This was centred around Government House and Fort Napier where the social and cultural life of the town was most evident.

The rapid suburbanization of Durban was a very British feature. Even before pressures of land shortage and high prices forced home builders away from the centre of the town it was thought to be fashionable to live on the Berea hills overlooking the town (1852.) In 1855 the Durban Town Council decided to lease 150 acres on the Berea. The period of lease was to be fifty years and lessees were required to erect a building to the value of £25 on each 2½ acre site. The first sale of freehold sites was held in January, 1856, when fifty acres were sold.

The general plan of the Borough made by Thomas Oakes in 1846 had comprised an area of over seven thousand acres and by 1854 the Government had made several grants amounting in all to 853 acres. The Councillors, however, were not satisfied as they required considerably more than 1,000 acres for grazing the oxen used for wagon transport alone. In 1862, the land reserved for the Harbour Commission at Addington was acquired and lots were put up for sale. It is interesting to note that the earliest houses in the township faced away from the sea. The development of Addington, however, was stultified owing to the fact that no municipal funds were available to provide the necessary lighting, sanitation and water facilities.

Poor transport and non-existent roads between the town and suburbs, however, encouraged the development of an exclusive residential area close to the town and the bay, in the region of St Andrew's street. In 1879, Mr H.R. Collins of the Durban Tramways Company Limited, applied for the permission of the Town Council to lay a tramline along the streets of the Borough and to work a passenger tramway from the Point Road to the Berea Toll gate. The resultant Law 19 of 1880 authorised the company "to work the same with cars and animal power for the conveyance of passengers and parcels". This service supplemented an earlier omnibus service between Grey street and the Point. By 1885 a network of Tramways [23] had developed between the town and the Berea and created sufficient impetus for the rapid suburbanization of the town.

While the first railway in Durban, which ran from near the Market Square to the Point, had not served as a commuter service, the new rail link between the Port and Pietermaritzburg (1880) created the opportunity for town workers to live further and further away. As a result the hills along the Umbilo River, which had always been admired for the pleasant breezes which blew up the river from the sea, were rapidly developed.[24]

The effects of these expansions allowed large open areas to develop around the periphery of the central business area. In Pietermaritzburg most of this was taken up by parks and gardens which have been largely the reason for its "garden city" character. In Durban these fringe areas became useful places for warehouse and light industrial developments, and cheap housing. In 1897 it was said that "Durban, whose fortunes have been driven by her merchants, is the best town in South Africa. There is no poverty, there is no dirt, and, though the situation is low the death rate is small. The first object of the merchants has been to secure a large forwarding trade to Johannesburg. The second, to settle a large white population — British if possible — in Natal as consumers of European goods. To this end great encouragement is given to artisans and mechanics, and what with the scheme by which these men easily become owners of their own houses and gardens, good and cheap education for children, a free reading room, and excellent baths, the working class in Durban is better off than anywhere else in Africa".[25]

Another result of the suburban spread was the decentralisation of amenities such as security. By 1880, there were twelve Police stations in the Borough of Durban. The great number of roads had necessitated the application of tolls to those who

used them and toll houses were situated at all the entrances to the town. In Pietermaritzburg the extensive area of the original town plan and its slower development discouraged the creation of suburbs until the 'nineties. In the residential parts of the original town centre, however, one senses a semi-suburban atmosphere and an essentially English one, with the intermittent public-house set amongst the houses.

The growth of the Natal town and village was extremely haphazard. The original rectilinear layouts were simple solutions effected by persons with little qualification for the task. It would seem that the major advantage of a simple rectangular system of streets and erven was in the actual surveying of the town. A complex pattern of land usage developed over this grid and eventually outgrew the initial dimensions of the town and extended into the surrounding countryside. In Durban, Addington was laid out in the form of a grid running parallel to the beach and at an acute angle to the streets of the Town. This kind of patchwork planning resulted in a sewing together of such systems at their junctions which, though interesting within the framework of the town, created severe problems at a later stage when the motor vehicle was introduced. Tramways

14   Early nineteenth century architecture in South Africa. R.B. Lewcock. p399
15   Natal settlers. A.F. Hattersley. p32
16   Port Elizabeth and Grahamstown.
17   Annals of Natal. VOL 11. C. Bird. p657
18   See Chapter 1
     Before going to the Portsmouth Naval College in 1807, Gardiner had exercised his ingenuity in drawing plans for cutting the French fleet out of Rochelle harbour.
19   The sale of land on the Point in 1837, reveals a complete disregard for Gardiner's proposals.
20   The history of old Durban. G. Russell. p66
21   See Chapter 7.
     "Mr G.C.Cato either owned or was agent for owners of the major portion of the Erven at what was then designated the "East End of the township". It was his opinion that the proximity of the Point both by water and road would ensure its establishment and prosperity, consequently the prices of those Erven were raised accordingly". Ibid, Russell.
22   Cradle days of Natal. Mackeurtan. p253
23   The Durban tramways were electrified in 1898. The suburb of Scottsville in Pietermaritzburg had been settled in the 'nineties, "though its leap forward in development came only ten years later with the inauguration of an electric tram service". Pietermaritzburg Panorama A.F. Hattersley.
24   Rossburgh, Sea View, Bellair, Hillary, Escombe, Malvern and Northdene.
25   On Veldt and Farm. Macnab. p97

and railway lines by virtue of their need for continuous routes have cut across the original ox-wagon layouts of the towns and villages.

The hallmark of the nineteenth century was variety. In the Colony of Natal the large erven and the development of the freestanding veranda-houses mitigated against architectural unity. In the residential streets of the towns this unity was partially restored by shady avenues, hedges and garden walls. (Fig. 502) The latter were architectural extensions of the houses beyond. Plastered walls with intermittent columns surmounted by urns and elaborate entrance gateways, usually of cast-iron, reflect and sometimes are used as a counterpoint to the architecture of the house. (Fig. 503,504)

At the centre of the town where the smaller, subdivided sites and the closer relationship of the buildings to each other provided possibilities for unifying the street, the very opposite was actually carried out. (Fig. 501) With few exceptions each building retains a separate identity and shouts its purposeful difference in an overall civic cachophony.

The choice of different styles for different functions, such as Gothic for churches and Classical for commercial buildings gives an essential richness to the townscape but underlines the variety and disunity of the town.

Urban unity, however, can be found not in the framework of the towns but in the fabric of the buildings. Perhaps Pietermaritzburg developed into the finest Victorian town in South Africa and one of the finest in the colonies as a direct result of the continuity of salmon brick wall surfaces. With such a unifying medium set within a rectangular system of streets the diversity of style and variety of building form attained their full richness without destroying the coherence of the whole.

Both Durban and Pietermaritzburg were laid out "on a scale commensurate with future expectations, rather than with present requirements".[26] They therefore remained as large collections of scattered buildings interspersed with wild bush and cultivated gardens for many years. (Fig. 505)

A visitor to Pietermaritzburg in 1849 described the town, "as consisting of white houses, scattered at intervals over a ridge occupying the centre of a valley ... the first object that attracted our attention was the burial ground, which bore a clearer testimony to the salubrity of the climate than to the cemetry building taste of the inhabitants".[27] Most visitors and newly arrived immigrants found the town to be picturesque with the neat hedges of pomegranate and quintz enclosing the cultivated gardens. Pietermaritzburg retained the character of a large garden up until the twentieth century, though even from the centre of the town today the long vistas of the main streets are terminated by the surrounding agricultural land.

(Fig. 506) In 1852 Charles Barter commented; "Were the experiment of planting trees tried on a large scale, and should it prove successful, I know of no greater boon that could be conferred on the town or its inhabitants. A want of shade is at present one of its chief natural deficiencies, no slight one beneath the rage of an almost tropical sun. This want supplied, the now open and bare looking market place surrounded with a cool and shady promenade, the entrances to the town and some of the streets planted in avenues, and each erf contributing its quota of varied foliage, Maritzburg would be one of the prettiest and most delightful, as well as one of the best situated and planned of colonial cities".[28] By the end of the 'fifties this deficiency had been remedied to some extent by the planting of oaks, willows and seringa. The latter were planted around the entire Market Square (Fig. 494) and along the southern side of Church and Longmarket Streets. (Fig. 507,508) Their shade in the main streets was eventually supplemented by the erection of verandas to the shop fronts.[29] Most of the residential streets were planted with avenues of Australian gum and seringa, though the latter have been replaced by jacarandas. The Australian gums were considered to answer the two-fold purpose of shade and lighting conductors! Together with the bordering sluits of running water, these wide avenues were a continuation of the Dutch character of many Cape towns and villages.

In Durban the whole town was covered a foot deep with white sand and the only foliage evident was the virgin bush. Its irregularity was also found to be picturesque by the first English immigrants, though their enthusiasm for the town must be attributed largely to the beauty of the Bay and the surrounding hills. The irregularity was the result of the fact that "no attention had been paid to enclosing the property on either side of the streets; so that the town appeared like a confused mass of dwellings, pitched almost indiscriminately".[30]

The early efforts of the pioneers were directed at keeping the natural bush under control, and when this was achieved vegetable gardens were commenced. By 1860 the gardens "of oranges and lemons, pineapples, bananas, coffee, cotton and indeed every known production from the English water-cress to the rare exotic" [31] had given way to flower gardens. The settlers brought with them the traditions of Regency and early Victorian gardening. These gardens consisted largely of brightly hued and multi-coloured shrubs set between flower beds of "hardy annuals", while through them gravel paths led apparently aimlessly. Later in the century the more exotic sub-tropical plants became popular and many gardens can still be found in Natal with their flowing lawns and tall palms. (Fig. 360) In 1853 West street (Durban) "was pretty well filled up on either side by detached tenements of divers heights and sizes, but all the other parts of the town were just thinly sprinkled over with stores and cottages. The street did not even give us an apology for its lack of footpaths".[32] Various experiments with sod pavements had been tried unsuccessfully. Eventually brick was resorted to and that in turn gave way to artificial stone (concrete).

It was thought at the time that there were few towns which could boast longer or straighter streets than Durban and Pietermaritzburg. The Natal Mercury thought that "If these streets were hardened, paved, and lined continuously with shady trees, we would back them, arched as they would be by the sunniest of skies, and thronged by many hued men of all continents and races against those even of imperial Paris".[32A] (Fig. 509) A certain Mr Jameson was responsible for the planting of "Brachylaena Discolor" in the Durban streets after 1868. These replaced the earlier seringas which had not grown well. (Fig. 509A)

In May 1862, it was decided to improve the barren Market Square in Durban. Competitive designs were invited for an ornamental garden. The plan of G. Seymour was carried out in 1863 and when completed it was described as a "beautiful oasis of shady paths and green lawns in the centre of the business portion of the town". (Fig. 511) The square was provided with a bandstand in the same year, where the "Durban Rifle Guard Band offered healthful and social recreation every Saturday".[33] The Alexandra Park in Pietermaritzburg was designed and laid out by Napoleon Wheeler during the 'seventies. With its two cast-iron bridges and ornamental bandstand and pavilion, its delightful oval and various gardens it is a 'worthy' Victorian extension of the town. (Fig. 512,513,544)

In the smaller towns and villages of Natal the wide shady streets and the large gardens situated even in the business centres, indicate the acceptance and utilization of the natural environment. (Fig. 514,515) In 1905 though, Cathcart Methven issued a challenge to town-planners in Natal when he said; "Some of the municipalities, especially in the younger towns fortunate enough to have been endowed by nature with exceptional natural beauties and a topography which lends itself to artistic treatment, have a great opportunity in front of them, if they can only be brought to see it. If such inestimable natural beauties are made the most of, then the municipalities have a wide field before them, which will demand greater effort, and an even broader and more liberal conception as regards public improvements, than in the past".[34]

Perhaps the most important aspect of the development of the towns and villages in Natal was the popular attitude to convenience and comfort. Verandas were extended over pavements to shelter shops and shoppers alike from the elements whilst at the same time they provided a bazaar-like extension of shop wares in the street itself. (Fig. 516) Visually they gave unifying horizontal elements to the sides of streets. Indeed the background buildings, by their very independence and vertical assertion, reveal a partial fulfilment of Pugin's dream of the medieval town. (Fig. 517)

Lanes and arcades criss-crossed the centres of the towns, providing cool and quiet retreats from the bustle of the main streets and additional shop and office space within the large urban blocks. In Pietermaritzburg, law suits, converted drains and private rights of way have resulted in a labyrinth of circulations between Church and Longmarket streets. (Fig. 518) The arcades which were built at a later date in the Indian quarter of Durban must surely be amongst the finest civic spaces in South Africa. (Fig. 519)

One feature of Natal towns and perhaps the most delightful of all was the jin-ricksha. (Fig. 520) By 1904, Durban had 1,700 such vehicles and 2,000 Zulu pullers.[35] Between their appearance in 1893 and their eventual supercession by the motor car after World War 1, they contributed greatly to the commuter services of the expanding towns while at the same time providing a colourful and eminently sensible way of communication in a sub-tropical climate.

26   More annals of Natal. A.F. Hattersley. p116
      "and yet we could not fail to perceive that the selection of the spot and the original design had been the work of no mean masters of their craft, and that it was something more than a mere inland village which they contemplated". Dorp and Veld. Charles Barter.
27   op cit, A.F. Hattersley. p116
28   op cit, C. Barter.
29   These verandas have become to be such an essential civic device that parts of the town where there are none have suffered economically.
30   More annals of Natal. A.F. Hattersley. p82
31   op cit, Hattersley. p82
32   Natal Mercury. 1863 October 2.
32a   op cit, Natal Mercury.
33   Durban, 50 years of municipal history. Henderson.
34   Report S.African advancement of science. 1905. Presidential address. p41
35   Schooners and skyscrapers. E. Rosenthal. p128

Chapter 12

Building materials and techniques

One of the major influences on Victorian architecture was innovation made possible by the new technologies, either in the form of new materials or in new applications of old materials. The architectural history of the period is almost as marked by the complete indifference to innovation observable in many architect-designed buildings.

Colonial architecture was shaped and influenced by available building materials, materials dug by the settlers from the soil of their new country, or procured in limited quantities from the mother country. The building techniques were most often based on age-old European traditions, and were at first influenced by the existing customs of the natives or immigrants from other parts of the country. Later, local traditions, based on the experience of colonial craftsmen and builders, left their stamp on the buildings of Natal.

At first, builders used the natural materials which were most easily obtained. Mangrove poles, impervious to white ants, or light yellow-wood poles, were used as a framework in the wattle-and-daub huts. Brush provided the wattling and the walls were plastered with several coats of mud and dung. The tree runner was used to tie the poles together. This was called "mtwazi" [1] by the Zulus and "was cut in long pieces, beaten or bruised with a stone, laid in water to separate the strong strands of fibre, and used at once while still damp. It made an excellent and durable twine".[2] Internal walls in these houses were built of laths of reeds and plastered over with "daagah".[3] A similar technique was used for constructing ceilings, though the earliest houses had ceilings of "bafta" [4] tacked to battens.

The few attempts to build sod houses utilised a composition similar to "daagah". This was composed of "clay or ant-heap, tempered with sand and cow-dung, trampled into mud by Natives, and served in balls or buckets to the operator, according to the consistency required", [5] Cob consisted of a mixture of "daagah" and straw which was trampled in layers about a foot high. When the walls were dry the loose ends of straw were cut off and a protective coating of lime-plaster applied to the surface. It seems that the first unburnt or green bricks were made in a similar way, though they were more liable to cracking, and deteriorated rapidly under the hot sun and heavy rains; they were used mainly for internal walls.

When more permanent buildings were erected, burnt brick and stone were used as walling materials. Stone was used for foundations. The early fear of building on the Durban sand was such that when the Block House was erected on the Point in 1847, a foundation "of concrete, lime and ironstone gravel, 4 ft. in thickness" [6] was provided under the building. Capt C. Gibb R.E. found stone on top of the Bluff. In Pietermaritzburg he noted that the material was also close at hand.[7] Harding thought that the stone used for building by the inhabitants of the town was a "slate of a friable kind, which falls to pieces on exposure to the weather".[8] Newly-arrived masons, however, found soft sandstone deposits near the town, and several buildings were successfully erected of this material. Gabriel Eaglestone was the best stone-cutter and mason in Natal for many years;[9] the fine stonework and carvings of St Peter's church bear testimony to the care of his craft.[10] In 1852 the Presbyterian congregation was provided with stone by the municipality for the rubble walls and free-stone plinth of their new church.[11]

Harding also found during his preliminary excursions into the country that "sandstone and shale are the prevailing rocks in the northern part of the district. The sandstone is an excellent building stone, which works well under the chisel and can be obtained in large masses".[12] In Ladysmith and Newcastle this stone has been used extensively in buildings ever since. But perhaps the most successful application of this material in Northern Natal can be found in the Dutch Reformed churches in Utrecht and Vryheid.[13] The masons who executed these buildings were the Crankshaw Bros of Newcastle.[14] Deposits of a good building stone were also found near Estcourt and in the District of Alfred. In the latter most of the early buildings were built of a hard sandstone which has a rich brown and red face when carefully dressed.[15] Mortar joints became more deeply recessed as fashion demanded, though more interesting poly-chromatic effects were obtained by the variegation of brown, blue and grey slates in the wall surface.[16] The stone walls of St Mary's church in Richmond were said to have been built without any mortar at all.[17]

It is significant that the available stone in Natal was generally used in Gothic buildings; except for those areas where it was easily obtained in great quantities this stylistic use eventually gave way to brick.[18]

It is possible that the Pistorius family in Pietermaritzburg had made burnt bricks in addition to tiles, but shale was easily obtained for use as a walling material, and their efforts may have been solely directed at filling the demand for a roofing material. The earliest recorded use of burnt brick in Natal was that in the Block House on the Point in 1847.[19] These bricks would have been brought to Natal from Cape Town or Port Elizabeth. Up till the 'sixties many materials were allowed duty free into the Colony; brick and fire-brick were included.[20] The influx of British immigrants between 1849 and 1851 created a demand for bricks, and several brickyards were established.[21] The first bricks made in Durban were expensive and poor in quality.[22] Those made in Pietermaritzburg "were not of the popular brindled colour and, without the addition of lime, proved to be lacking in durable qualities".[23] Buildings not built in brick or stone were listed as dangerous by the Natal Fire Assurance and Trust Company: those wishing to insure them found the premium three times the amount for that of a stone or brick structure.[24] This gave renewed impetus to the brick industry, The Government and the Municipalities found it necessary to establish their own brickyards, and for the purpose imported brick-making machines.[25]

Facebricks, though unpopular, first appeared in Pietermaritzburg in the 'fifties. These were red in colour, but newly found deposits of a yellow clay soon produced a salmon orange brick. The Government brickyards purchased a "brick pressing machine" [26] in 1869, and thereafter it became possible to make every wire-cut brick almost identical in colour and texture and precisely true. The general opinion was one of great delight, and the uniformity and regularity began to be carefully sought after as deliberate effects. As a result flush mortar courses became absolutely regular and slightly smaller, and the overall character of brickwork was that of an even

1 History of old Durban. G. Russell. p90
 See Chapter 4.
2 Reminiscences and memories of early Durban and its pioneers. C. Anderson. p10
3 A clay mortar. The word is probably from the Xhosa "daka" meaning dirt or mud. Early nineteenth century architecture in South Africa. R.B.Lewcock. p378
4 Unbleached calico. op cit, Russell. p92
5 op cit, Russell. p91
6 British parliamentary papers. 15, 1847, p167
7 British parliamentary papers. 15, 1847, p12 no.6.
8 S.G.O. April 3 1846.
9 W. Watson, David Garbutt and Jesse Smith were masons amongst the newly arrived immigrants.
10 The British settlers of Natal. A.F. Hattersley. p320
11 See Chapter 5.
12 S.G.O. April 3 1846.
13 See Chapter 10
14 Their work extended throughout Northern Natal, the Orange Free State and the Transvaal.
15 A history of the Alfred district. B.E. Camp.
16 Such as St Peter's Church in Pietermaritzburg.
17 A history of Richmond from 1839 to 1937. S.W.B. Shepstone. p25
18 A deposit of marble was found on the north bank of the Umzimkulu River in the early 'sixties. In April, 1866, Dr Sutherland and Jesse Smith inspected the deposit in an effort to secure large blocks of marble to send overseas. Bazley was the first to exploit the stone commercially (1880) and small coasters were sent up the river to remove slabs to Durban. It is possible that some of the marble (most is Carrara) in the Emmanuel Cathedral in Durban comes from this area.
19 British parliamentary papers. 15. 1847. p167
20 Natal Blue Book. 1863. Schedule of goods allowed duty free into the Colony. Bricks and firebricks; Cement (Portland and Roman); Lime; Machinery used exclusively in the preparation of timber and in the making of bricks and tiles; Pig iron; slates for roofing; tiles (flooring).
21 In Durban on the Umgeni, at Greyville and Curries Fountain and at the back of the Berea. In Pietermaritzburg at the foot of Town Hill and at the present site of the Coronation brickfield. Amongst those involved in the manufacture of bricks were, Hogg, Bristow, Peacock, Maxwell, Chatterton and Ratcliff.
22 History of old Durban. G. Russell. p92
23 The British settlement of Natal. A.F. Hattersley. p215
24 Advertisements. Davis' Almanac. 1864.
25 50 Years municipal history of Durban. Henderson. p8 and 11. Mechanization had replaced the manual process of manufacture in England in the early 1860's soon after the introduction of the Hoffman Kiln (1858).
26 C.E. 1889/1869. A straw chaffing machine was acquired for the Brickyard in 1883. C.E. 4210/1883.

machine-made texture.[27] Only later were the subtle varieties of Georgian and Early Victorian brickwork sought after and rougher facebricks began to be produced. The salmon bricks are partially responsible for the human, intimate quality of many Pietermaritzburg buildings; a quality which is essentially anti-monumental.

By 1866 there were 27 brickmaking establishments in the Colony.[28] In the outlying districts, where there was no good building stone, small kilns were erected to burn the limited quantity of bricks required in the locality. As early as 1854 a magazine erected at Weenen was built of burnt brick arches, 1 ft. 6 in. thick, in lime and sand mortar.[29]

During the first half of the nineteenth century there was a predilection for hiding brickwork behind plaster or stucco. The broad sweeping effects of Regency architecture encouraged the use of stucco, and by the end of the period several patents for external rendering were in existence.[30] Loudon stated that "the object of covering the outside of the walls of cottages with cement is generally to imitate stone".[31] To suggest mortar courses the walls were decorated with a pattern of incised lines.

In 1843, Capt Gibb wrote to his commanding officer saying; "Limestone I have not yet been able to find on the Bluff; but there are shells at its base, which when burnt and mixed with the lime we have been using on this side (the Point), would make excellent lime; and for rough work, there is a red clay on the spot similar to that used in buildings on the Eastern Frontier (of the Cape), which might be useful".[32] The brick walls of the Point Blockhouse were to be set in lime mortar and rendered with "rough cast dashing" and whitewashed. Lime kilns had been operating at Congella since the days of the Republic of Natalia, [33] and later these were supplemented by kilns at Cato's Creek.[34] Neither could supply the quantity needed and supplies were imported from the Cape and Mauritius. Shell-lime had been extensively used in the Cape Colony, [35] and was used in Durban as a rendering to prevent the attack of the saline atmosphere on bricks and mortar.

In a few cases early settlers plastered and whitewashed their houses with a lime which was dug out of the ground and produced "a good cream colour".[36] Large quantities of cement, however, were imported from England and the Cape mainly for use in Durban. The Natal Society building and several others in Pietermaritzburg, however, also had stucco and ornamental renderings.[37] C.J. Cato tested the quality of two kinds of cement offered for sale in Durban in 1851 and reported that "both the Medena and Roman cement are of very inferior quality. Of the two the Roman is the preferable".[38]

The early houses of the Dutch and English settlers had plastered walls, which in their hand-applied unevenness reflected the character of eighteenth and early nineteenth-century Cape architecture and the small cottages of rural England. Mouldings above doors and windows and those on gables must too have had a similar quality. These eventually gave way to the more precise finishes and mouldings executed with wood floats and steel trowels.

Walls were traditionally whitewashed in the Cape and in England. Many references are to be found to Pietermaritzburg in the 'forties as a town of whitewashed gables.[39] Limewashing was an annual task, for being impermanent, heavy rain soon washed it off. The addition of Russian tallow made it less soluble. Later, pigments introduced in the course of the slaking, allowed stone colours to be applied to complete the effect of imitation stone renderings. Limewashing, however, persisted as a finish to the interior of simpler houses.

The British settlers had brought wall papers with them and these were said to have been conservative in comparison to contemporary English fashions. It is not known, however, whether Charles Eastlake's recommendations on their use were followed. "There should be one dominant hue in the room, to which all others are subordinate. This will admit of many variations of shade, passing from green to blue, or venetian red to brown, without requiring absolute uniformity of tint throughout".[40]

In 1864 Davis' Almanac recommended a wash for outside walls which would render the house impervious to white ants and other insects. It consisted "of 1½ bushels of grey lime, 1½ bushels of Roman cement, 6lb. of copperas, 6lbs. of soft soap, 6lbs. of sulphur, and as much yellow ochre as will bring the whole to any desirable colour".[41]

Floors were originally of earth pounded hard and smeared over with cow-dung sometimes mixed with ox-blood. Burnt brick and square clay tiles eventually superceded mother earth.[42] Flag stones were imported in large quantities during the 'sixties, though these must have been intended mainly for paving. "House for sale" advertisements of the early 'fifties indicate that by this time many houses had boarded floors. These were suspended about three feet above ground level and consisted of imported 6in. or 4in. pine or local yellow-wood board.

A local specification for a hard floor for kitchens and outbuildings of 1864 suggested that housebuilders should "mix well washed gravel, lime and hot gas tar together and in such proportions as will render a black mortar. If laid on three or four inches thick, it will last for years and be always dry, and free from white ants. A layer of very small stones or coarse gravel underneath, if the ground around is low, would be all the better".[43] Perhaps the nicest floor material used in Natal during the nineteenth century were encaustic tiles.[44] These were reserved for veranda floors, though sometimes used internally in halls and corridors. Their hardwearing quality and low thermal receptivity made them ideal for the former.[45] Generally they were imported from England, and in particular from Herbert Minton and St John, of Stoke-upon-Trent.[46]

In the 1880's French parquetry floors came into fashion in England but only reached Natal in the late 'nineties. Eastlake recommended the use of parquetry floors borders for "with such a border projecting two or three feet from the wall all round, the carpet need not be carried into the recesses and corners of a room, but may be left square at the sides".[47]

Timber was not plentiful in Natal, and in the few places where there were forests, supplies were rapidly exhausted. From the very earliest times sawying was therefore a lucrative industry. The timber trees were found in two localities; "the thick bush of the coast, from which many of the harder woods of small size are derived, and the forests of the mountain tops, where the trees are densely packed into the kloofs and ravines of the hill sides at a high elevation and where some of them attain to considerable size... One of the best known, and upon the whole most generally useful, of the Natal woods ..., is the yellow-wood of the colony, (Podocarpus falcatus) or geelhout.[48] The wood is of a light yellow colour, of a very close and compact appearance, and works easily and well while it is still moist; but when dry it cuts jaggedly and unevenly across the grain ... It shrinks more than any other wood employed for constructive purposes: beams of it shorten as much as half-an-inch in twenty feet. It is very generally used for building purposes, where it can be efficiently protected from wet, and all the commoner kinds of house-hold furniture, such as tables, and the internal fittings of houses are made of it. It is in this sense the 'deal-wood' of Natal".[49]

Or the local woods which had been used in the Cape, yellow-wood (Podocarpus thunbergia) was one

35 Early nineteenth century architecture in South Africa. R.B. Lewcock. p378
Finishes such as terra-cotta were only introduced into Natal after 1900.
36 Arbuthnot memories. (Private collection Arbuthnot family). p14
37 A plan and elevation of the new Natal Society building was submitted to the Surveyor General's office by Hughbert Baker in 1851. S.G.O. 111/1/6, 150. 1851.
38 S.G.O. 111/1/5, 78. 1851.
39 See Chapters 2 and 3.
40 Hints on household taste. C. Eastlake. p119
41 Davis' Almanac 1864.
Ant guards of galvanized iron were introduced in the 'nineties. Damp proof coursing was often of slate though later replaced by asphalt and bitumastic felt.
42 Natal Bluebooks. 1860–1870. Import lists.
43 Davis' Almanac. 1864.
44 See Chapter 8.
45 "The modern application of encaustic tiles is by no means confined to the ecclesiastical purposes for which they were mainly used in medieval times ... Some of the most eminent architects of recent years have exercised their skill in the production of designs more suitable for domestic purposes; and pavements of these tiles, combined with other kindred manufactures, have become an almost universal part of the permanent decoration of the better class of public and private buildings, for which they are also largely exported to the colonies and foreign countries, superceding the perishable forms of flooring, and at the same time rendering unnecessary any decorative coverings". Encylopaedia Brittanica (1896 edition) Encaustic tiles. This reference also includes a complete description of the manufacturing processes.
46 Concrete was also used as a flooring material as early as 1847 (The Block house on the Point) though mainly for verandas thereafter. The drawing for the Block house at Estcourt (Fort Durnford) in 1874, specified a suspended ground floor consisting of sneezewood joists supporting a boarded timber floor and boarding below the joists with a concrete infill between. This was not actually built.
47 Hints on household taste. C. Eastlake. p109
48 Also "Podocarpus Elongata".
49 Natal. A history and description. Brooks and Mann.
(Chapter. Timbers of Natal.)
"there were the remains of saw pits, dug at the instance of one James Kingshurst, formerly a ship's carpenter of the brig Sarah Bell, who in the dawn of civilization, cut down most of the fine straight yellow-wood trees to be found there, to convert into planks for building purposes".
A history of old Durban. G. Russell. p141

27 In 1890 the Pietermaritzburg Town Council offered to swop the Government with office accommodation in the new Town Hall for bricks from the Government brickyard. They ordered 250,000 external and 1,000,000 internal pressed bricks. C.E. 1824/1890.
28 Davis' Almanac. 1866.
29 S.G.O. 111/11/30. 1854. (98)
30 Amongst them were Baker's Roman cement (1796), Portland cement (1825) and Hamelin's mastic (1817).
31 Encylopaedia of cottage, farm and villa architecture. Loudon. 528, p260
32 British Parliamentary papers, 1843, 15. 6. p12
33 British Parliamentary papers, 1847, 15. p167
34 Lime was still being manufactured at Congella in the 'nineties.

of the most important, and hence the Voortrekkers readily used it for their first buildings in Pietermaritzburg. It was used for doors, window-frames, floors, ceilings and rafters. Most of this wood was cut in the Karkloof and Dargle valleys. A load of forty one-inch boards, twenty feet in length cost 150 S' in 1851.[50] Capt Gibb had found timber for flooring and for all common purposes on the Bluff in abundance, but did not think that any "could be procured of sufficient length for tie-beams etc.".[51] He also noted the absence of wood around Pietermaritzburg, which fact he thought would be "a serious drawback to the town".[52]

For structural purposes sneezewood (Ptoerozylon Utile) and stinkwood (Laurus bullata), both of which attained to a considerable size, were employed. The latter was thought to be "almost as good as oak for church fittings", [53] and extremely suitable for external use. While other Natal hard woods such as Tambooti and Umzimbiti were used mainly by waggonmakers, lancewood, whitepear, milk-wood, essenhout (South African Ash), wild olive and Umsini were all applied in some way in building.

The greatest problem in the use of timber in Natal has been the prevention of termite attack. While the termite antheaps had provided useful material for plaster and mortar, the insects themselves attacked any form of timber in buildings, "so that floors, posts, and even roofs had to be renewed".[54] The wattle-and-daub huts of the early settlers were particularly prone to the ravages of the termite, and to keep them out of walls, a low plinth of Stockholm tar was painted around the exterior. This was not effective and only more permanent structures of brick delayed their destructive progress towards the structural timber in the buildings. In 1866, creosote was advertised as a measure against white ants, though its intense smell mitigated against its use for anything other than concealed work. The gumresin of sneezewood was said to make it comparatively safe from insect attack.[55]

By 1866 there were thirteen saw mills in the Colony. One of these, at Memel, advertised boards, planed, tongued and grooved by machinery. Good softwood and hardwood had been imported in enormous quantities between 1858 and 1875. Most of this came from England and Prussia (Danzig deal) but substantial quantities are recorded [56] as arriving from Bombay, the Cape, South Australia, Sweden and the United States of America. Indeed, not only bulk timber but entire building elements such as doors, windows and perhaps veranda "lace" were imported from the latter. Later, imports were also received from Norway, Russia, Canada, Belgium and Burma, and large timber merchants were established in Durban. By 1880 these companies were producing mouldings, doors, windows, stair balusters,

decorative bargeboards and veranda posts and fascias. [57] All of these had been, until this time, imported from other countries. Fretwork and moulding machinery gave impetus to the use of timber for verandas for which cast-iron had began to be almost as economical and readily available.

Cheap doors and sliding sash windows, [58] principally of American manufacture, had done away with the locally handmade yellow-wood types favoured by the Voortrekkers and early British settlers. Both sash and casement windows were used by the Voortrekkers. A few of these windows have heavy surrounding frames set flush with the surface of the external wall, which reveal their eighteenth century roots. French casements and panelled internal doors varied in the number of panels according to fashion. Most imported American doors were four-panelled. Complete with machine-made bolection mouldings and architraves, they became accepted as standard items of building and began to vary only in the colour of the stain and the design of doorknob.

For external woodwork, dark green paint [59] or a dark timber stain were considered most desirable. Towards the end of the century, however, white window and door frames and white balustrading and verandas were found to be most effective in the strong sunlight when viewed against the salmon brick walls. Occasionally light grey colours were used on timber and cast-iron verandas, though the most popular colours for the latter were also browns, greens and black.[60]

The most interesting development in the use of windows in Natal is the size of window panes. The Voortrekkers had brought glass with them to Natal from the Cape, and as late as the 'sixties small Dutch glass sizes were still referred to in Natal.[61] To the first English settlers glass was a luxury replaced temporarily by calico. In England oiled cloth and linen canvas had been traditional substitutes in rural areas. The invention of plateglass [62] had led the early Victorians to regard uncluttered view windows as a great advance over the Georgian and Regency windows which were sub-divided into small panels by glazing bars. The latter, however, were used for a long time in Natal, for the expense of plate glass made its use feasible only in shop-fronts. As early as 1853 sheet glass 32in. by 42 in. was advertised in Durban, [63] but the sizes 9in. by 7in. and 8in. by 10in. continued to be popular until superseded by the 10in. by 12in. and 16in. by 24ins. sizes. Ultimately, through the development of less expensive processes which served to increase the determination to be rid of the obstructive bars, large sheets of rolled glass were produced. In Natal these were imported up until the twentieth century. Their first application was in the centre or viewing portion of the window, and they were surrounded by narrow bands of glass, sometimes stained or frosted. This tradition was continued and translated into scored lines and shot-blasted and etched patterns.

Stained glass had been used in the early Gothic Revival buildings in Natal, but consisted mainly of panels taken from ruined medieval buildings in England and Europe. The development of cheap tinting and texturing processes allowed even the poorest householder to have a small surrounding panel of coloured glass in the doorway. Some interesting designs and patterns are to be found in a few Indian-owned houses in Natal where there are Islamic motifs in greens and golds on the glass. These were said to have been imported from India.[64]

Thatch, made from the "beautiful Tambooti grass", [65] was used extensively as a roofing material in Natal by the early settlers. Besides its fashionable use as a rustic material and its traditional use in the domestic architecture of rural England, thatch was readily available and made an extremely suitable roof for the warm climate of Natal. Thatching was a trade carried out mostly by Zulus, though, amongst the 1850 immigrants there were two English 'thackers', W. Granger and Petty, who became renowed for their craft at Port Natal.[66] The thatch was secured by lengths of wild rattan sewn on to the wattle battens of the roof, by rope yarns, though in the first instance konotie fibre, or strips of wet bullock hide, had been in vogue. The ridge was protected by a plastered cap of daagah, tarred and whitewashed. Most thatched roofs were hipped.[67]

Where there were no ceilings under a thatched roof, the inner face of the thatch was sometimes finished with matting fastened by laths.[68] Early ceilings were of matchboarding or plastered laths made of reeds. The constant fear of fire and the high insurance rates for thatched buildings, in addition to the fact that they were ideal places where snakes and insects could hide and white ants ravage, led to their eventual disappearance.[69]

The Dutch in Natal, in their efforts to create an urban environment (and quite possibly having had bitter experiences of thatched roofs in the Cape), set about the manufacture of roofing-tiles. For this purpose the Volksraad made a grant to Pistorius of a piece of land at the foot of Town Hill for use as as tile-yard.[70] On his arrival in Pietermaritzburg, Capt Gibb found that "roofing materials are to be procured in the village".[71] This must have been a reference to Pistorius' tiles for they were supplied to the camp in large quantities for the buildings at Fort Napier.[72] These tiles were probably those known

50   The Hull Advertiser, 2 May 1851.
51   British Parliamentary papers. 1847 p12 no. 6
52   British Parliamentary papers. 1847–48. (980) p13,14.
53   op cit, Brooks and Mann.
54   op cit, Brooks and Mann.
55   op cit, Brooks and Mann.
56   Natal Bluebooks. 1858–1875 inclusive.
      In 1858, £1,363 worth of yellow-wood was exported from Natal but by 1860 this had dropped to £209 and thereafter stopped entirely.
57   Davis' Almanac. 1858–1860.
      Fretwork machines were invented in America in the early 'fifties.
      Twentieth century impressions of Natal. 1906. Hunt Leuchars and Hepburn, Harbrow and Co, Johannedals, J.J. Egeland, W.F. Johnstone, Mitcheson and Killbrunner, and the Victoria Saw Mills.
58   Sliding sash windows, which were probably invented in Holland, were first used in any quantity in England at Chatsworth in 1676.
      Cast-iron sliding sashes were specified for Fort Durnford in 1874. See Chapter 7.
59   "probably the association of green with the idea of coolness is sufficient to explain its persistent popularity in hot climates".
      Early nineteenth century architecture in South Africa. R.B. Lewcock. p418
60   Papier-mache and cast-iron ventilators, some of which are of fine Art Nouveau patterns, can be found in houses built in Natal after 1895.
61   Natal Mercury, Advertisements, 1853.
62   Plate glass was a French invention made in England under French supervision in 1773.
      The cost of this fine polished glass was so high that half a century elapsed before its commercial production became feasible in 1838.
      The pattern of English building. A. Clifton-Taylor. p328
63   Natal Mercury, Advertisements, 1853.
64   Greytown. Personal.
65   Reminiscences and memories of early Durban and its pioneers. C. Anderson. p10
66   A history of old Durban. G. Russell. p92
67   op cit, Russell p92
      A treatise on thatching in Davis' Almanac of 1864 gave particular emphasis to hipped roofs.
68   Estimates for repairs to Government House, Pietermaritzburg. S.G.O. 161, 1854. 111/1/9.
69   Fleming diary. Sat. 27 1851. "In the course of the week a great many lightning conductors have been put up throughout the town".
      Thatched buildings were listed as "dangerous" by the Natal Fire Assurance and Trust Company. Davis' Almanac. 1860–1864.
70   Carl Pistorius records that together with his father and brother "I made a lot of tiles there with my own hands, without machinery of any kind".
      See Chapter 2.
      More annals of Natal. A.F. Hattersley. p114 and Natal memories. B. Buchanan. p68
71   British Parliamentary papers. Sept. 5 1843, 15. p12 no. 6.
72   op cit, Hattersley. p114

in England as "plain" tiles.[73] Such tiles would have to be laid so that there would be at least two thicknesses of tile over every part of the roof. Each lap would also be required to be pointed with mortar. Good hand-made tiles in England would have a slight camber in both directions. This would have the advantages of allowing the tiles to conform more readily to the slight irregularities of the roof timbering, and give an overall irregular effect. Perhaps some of these requirements were not fulfilled, which might explain why several roofs in Pietermaritzburg were re-covered with pantiles in the early 1850's. Two Lincolnshire men, James Smartfit and Henry Chatterton began the manufacture of pantiles and Broseley tiles in 1851.[74] The pantiles were 13½in. by 9½in; a dimension decreed by an Act of Parliament in the time of George I.

A pantile covered roof was considerably lighter than a plain tile roof, since the pantiles needed only a single overlap. The flatter pitch meant a saving in roofing timber, an important consideration in early colonial buildings. Later nineteenth century combinations of flat and rounded tiles developed into the patent Roman tiles. These are to be found on buildings in Natal which date from the 'sixties and 'seventies, and were sometimes used in intricate patterns.[75]

Tiles made from the same clay which gave the salmon colour to Natal bricks were used mainly on buildings in Pietermaritzburg. The Government brickworks acquired a tile press in 1877 (Wade and Cherry's tile Press), and the first building to use the precisely cut tiles was the Town Hill lunatic asylum. [76]

Another early roof covering was slate. Between 1849 and 1865 enormous quantities [77] were imported into the Colony from the Cape and England. The mechanical cutting of Welsh slate was an industry set up as a result of the peace-time conversion of war factories after the Napoleonic Wars; [78] by the 1830's slates were being exported to the colonies. Countesses (1ft. 8ins. by 10ins.) and Duchesses (2ft. by 1ft.) were the sizes favoured in Natal.[79] Later, slabs of slate were obtained from the Impanmbinyoni quarry, and in one instance the Court House at Umzinto [80] was built entirely, walls and roof, of this material. Though used up until the 'seventies, slates were thereafter gradually replaced by the less expensive corrugated iron.

One of the other roof materials used in Natal was shingles. A load of teakwood shingles was expected from Moulmein on the "Ina" in 1850, but no reference has been made to such an early application of the material. At the end of the century though, they appeared on buildings of the Queen Anne Revival and the late Colonial style. Zinc roofs were used on buildings erected by the English settlers. A Pietermaritzburg builder, Fleming, recorded that in 1851 he went to Durban "and went through several of the merchants, enquiring the prices of slate, zinc and iron for roofing. I find zinc will come in fully as cheap as anything. Eventually decided on pan-tiles". [81] A certain Mr Currie of Durban was said to have perfected a "mode of zinc roofing with overlapping waterproof joints. These roofs were fixed by him on buildings at several sugar mills and served their turn until replaced by imported corrugated galvanized iron".[82]

In England, corrugated iron was first applied to building in the form of cast sheets. These were described at the time (1838) as "one of the lightest, most elegant and from the particulars furnished, the most economical, description of roof..."[83] The corrugations were in the form of a zigzag profile, 3ins. in depth, and users were advised to fill the joints with cement or putty and coat the final roof with tar or paint. Loudon refers to the use of the material in Russia in the 1830's and records that these sheets were 2 feet 4ins. wide by 4 feet 8ins. long. He claims that the engineer Walker was the inventor of corrugated iron.[83A] Great stress was placed on its structural properties; "a single sheet of iron, so thin that it will not continue in a perpendicular position, will, after undergoing the process of corrugation, bear upwards of 700 lbs. weight without bending in the least degree".[84] To increase the strength of sheets they were curved, a feature which appeared in the first uses of corrugated iron in Natal.[85]

Iron had been used in the Cape as early as 1847, [86] and on the arrival of the first Byrne immigrants to Natal in 1850 it was already in evidence on a few Durban roofs. Its durability and economy were largely responsible for its eventual widespread use, though the voracity of termites may have caused its original introduction. The earliest sheets were small and thick and fluted at both edges. These were known as Morewood's tiles and advertised for the fact that they "require no fitting, they are very easily fixed, and 20 tiles cover 100 super feet".[87]

Rolling processes were perfected in the late 'fifties and larger sheets began to be manufactured. The English Builder's and Contractor's Price book for 1864 mentions that "No's 16 to 22 (Birmingham Wire Gauge) are the thicknesses generally adopted for roof covering in England, but large quantities of 24 and 26 gauge are exported to the Colonies".[88] Such names as Gospel Oak and Tupper and Co's soon appeared in Natal. The latter was advertised as "specially adapted to the climate of India as it will not expand or contract like zinc or lead".[89]

The availability and relative cheapness of corrugated iron made it an ideal roofing material for Natal, and on verandas and houses it allowed the continuation of the development of the colonial style. The most common colours used for painting such roofs were red and green. Green was recommended by Loudon in the 'forties.[90] Later in the century metallic grey and silver paints were developed and became popular because of their heat reflecting properties.

Loudon had also observed that the material could be used for door and wall panels, and indeed as a covering for framed houses.[91,92] Such wood and iron houses were later derided as belonging to "a tradition of domestic architecture based on the corrugated-Ironic style".[93] During the 'seventies and 'eighties they began to be erected all over the colony; "one day we see a wagon ... on the ground a number of pieces of timber (scantlings and boards), also door and window frames, and pieces of a small building on which the pieces of corrugated iron will form the roof. After a few days time the building is so far complete that it provides shelter in case of rain. A few days more and we see a lean-to on one side, a few days after that another lean-to on the other side; the whole building being divided into compartments, and having a veranda on each side, forming a comfortable house for a family to live in".[94]

Large iron structures such as bridges and lighthouses were imported throughout the Colonial period. Towards the close of the century, bandstands, staircases and civic furniture, all of cast-iron (and more often than not from Macfarlane's of Glasgow) were chosen from the British catalogues for parks and public spaces.[95] Most cast-iron work used for verandas had been selected in a similar way. Only in the 'eighties were iron foundaries established locally. Iron in the form of girders spanning between solid masonry walls was used in buildings of more than two storeys in height, [96] but no iron-framed structures besides those mentioned were erected until after 1900.[97]

By 1893 buildings in the Colony of Natal were strongly influenced by machine-made materials, the

73 The pattern of English building. A. Clifton-Taylor. p254
74 The British settlement of Natal. A.F. Hattersley. p216
75 As in Government House, Pietermaritzburg. (Fig. 231) and Collegiate Institution, PMB (Fig. 193)
76 See Chapter 10.
   C.E.O. 1786/1877.
   Singleton himself had recommended the purchase of a tile press.
77 1858, £228; 1860, £644; 1862, £927; 1863, £853; 1864, £628; 1865, £517; 2875, £300.
78 Early nineteenth century architecture in South Africa. R.B. Lewcock. p319
79 Davis' Almanac. 1855–1865.
80 Arbuthnot autobiography. p16

(Private collection. Arbuthnot Family.)
81 Fleming diary. 1851. (Killie Campbell Museum.)
82 A history of old Durban. G. Russell p257
   Zinc was also used for roof ridging though it was expensive. Lead and Copper roofs were later applied to the domes of buildings such as the Legislative Assembly buildings in Pietermaritzburg. (Chapter 10.)
   The major use of such metals, however, was in plumbing.
83 The architect's magazine and journal. Vol.V Feb. 1838. p66
   This is a specific reference to "corrugated cast-iron" by Hutchinson, an engineer.
83a Encylopaedia of cottage, farm and villa architecture. Loudon. 429. p205
84 op cit, Loudon. p205
85 Lamport and Holt. Chapter 5.
86 The growth and government of Cape Town. Laidler. p310
87 Advertisement. Natal. Robinson. (1863)
88 Builders and contractors price book. 1864.
   Mention is also made of circular, corrugated, galvanized, tinned iron roofs of 14–24 gauge. The sizes of the sheets were 6ft. x 2ft. and 8ft. x 3ft. Painted corrugated sheets were also available at the time.
89 Advertisement. Natal. Robinson. (1863).
90 Encylopaedia of cottage, farm and villa architecture. Loudon. 429. p205
91 See Chapter 5.
92 Early Victorian architecture in Britain. H.R. Hitchcock. p122
   Various prefabricated iron buildings are said to have been dispatched to Natal for the use of the English immigrants. See Chapter 4.
93 The progress of architecture. W. Paton.
   Natal Mercury Pictorial.
94 Our Colony of Natal. W. Peace. p38
   In 1886 John Nicol a contractor of Durban advertised "wood and iron buildings for construction up country". By 1900, firms such as William Harbrow of London contracted "to erect residences, bungalows, cottages, farmhouses and buildings, churches, chapels, mission halls, stables, pavilions, club rooms, drill halls, and sheds (iron framed or timber framed)" of corrugated iron.
   Natal illustrated. 1900.
95 The Band Stands in the Market Square, Durban, and Alexandra Park, Pietermaritzburg; The Vasco da Gama memorial clock, Point Road, Durban; and the spiral staircase, Legislative Assembly building, Pietermaritzburg are among the best examples of such imported cast-iron-work in Natal.
96 See Chapter 10.
   Wrought Iron brackets were sometimes used as veranda supports.
97 In 1887, a concrete building was erected as a new house at a Convent on the Bluff. Bishop

precise and evenly textured character of which sets them apart from the earlier hand-made artefacts of human settlement. The entire building process had been revolutionised through the advances of technology. No longer were doors, windows and other building elements made by hand on the site, but manufactured anonomously elsewhere on production lines and assembled as rapidly as possible. The wide variety of choice of such elements, however, mitigated against dull uniformity. Even those trades which were of essence 'in situ' became streamlined. The precise and hard character of such architectural detail bears the stamp rather of the new tools of technology than of the subtleties of the traditional craftsman.

Jolivet visited the mission and recorded that "the house of concrete promises to be a success. The roof of concrete is already over two rooms", Jolivet diary 17 August 1887. (Archdiocesan Arcnives, Durban.)
Earlier (1859) concrete blocks were made for the facing of the railway wharf at the Point in Durban.
The story of old Durban. G. Russell. p400.

Chapter 13

Architects, surveyors and engineers

"The demand for architecture attracts the architect, and slowly, perhaps, but surely, the low-roofed, flat-looking, unattractive Colonial town begins to don a new garb. The wattle and daub period has passed away, and the period of stone and brick buildings has commenced. The rule of thumb architect, or, more correctly, constructor, returns to his legitimate business, and his place is taken by the trained architect, who aims at combining scientific skill with artistic capabilities. In this renaissance or transition period, good and bad architects, capable and incapable architects, are generally to be found, and the result is often to be seen in the strange admixture of finely-proportioned and well-designed buildings side by side with other structures in which incapacity and the absence of all sense of artistic perception are written in plain letters from the roof to the basement".[1]

During the nineteenth century several changes occurred which completely transformed the process of design and the execution of building contracts in the English-speaking world. The concept of the architect as a professional man arose. A nicer clarification of his duties to both client and contractor emerged, and the design process became framed within codes of conduct. Particular scales of renumeration were alloted to various aspects of the architect's duties. The long-standing traditions of pupilage developed into a system of apprenticeship, and eventually at the end of the nineteenth century formal academic training was established. The enlightened patron's of the eighteenth century had been displaced by the architecturally uninformed client-entrepreneurs, or, in many cases with disastrous results, by building committees composed of well-meaning, though ignorant, laymen. On the building site the general contractor co-ordinated, through his foreman, artisans and tradesman, who no longer always took the care and interest displayed by their predecessors, the individual master craftsmen.

Amongst the Voortrekkers who settled in Natal

were a few who had been engaged in building in the Cape Colony. The Pistorius family seem to have been involved in all aspects of building; design, manufacture and erection. The kind of architecture which resulted from such a system was a distinctly human one. Local traditions developed when the mind which had conceived the whole determined the dimension of a moulding, or chose the colour of a door on the real building and not merely on paper.

Among the soldiers of the British Regiments stationed in Natal were Royal Engineers and many who could show skill in building and plastering. Thomas Greene was amongst those soldiers who were found useful for the buildings required in Pietermaritzburg; "I was recommended for the task of building houses for the officials of the town".[2] Until the arrival of the British settlers in 1849, the men of the 45th regiment, the Sherwood Foresters, were responsible for the erection of not merely the necessary military buildings but also most of the buildings in Pietermaritzburg. The Royal Engineers like Capt Gibb continued the utilitarian traditions of British military architecture. These were taken up by subsequent Colonial Engineers, who had also received the rigorous and straightforward training of the Royal Engineers.

Besides the few English tradesmen who had come to Natal from the Cape during the 'forties, there were many who called themselves carpenters and masons among the British immigrants. Those who were genuine artisans would have found work easily in the towns. However, several people who had no previous experience at building were induced by the great demand for immigrant housing to turn their attentions to the production of building materials and building construction.

Fleming, a builder who had worked for the London Missionary Society at Somerset East in the Cape, came to Natal in 1845 and brought with him nails and glass. His journal is a fascinating record of early buildings in Natal. Besides designing the buildings he erected, he developed a system of contracting, whereby, as he stated; "I find all labour, bricks, stone and sand, the employer to find all timber, thatch, glass, paint and nails etc.,"[3]

Among the British immigrants of 1849 and 1850 were several engineers and surveyors. The termination of work on the railway constructions in England probably accounts for their emigration.[4] Hughbert Baker, James West and John Basely were all Railway Engineers and Surveyors. Of the architect-surveyors, the only one who practised as an architect to any extent in Natal was Robert Sellars Upton

1   The Natal Mercury, February 9 1905.
2   More annals of Natal. A.F. Hattersley. p72
3   Fleming diary. 1845–1853 (Killie Campbell Museum).

(1809–1883.) Indeed the early characteristics of Durban architecture [5] were to a large degree influenced by the work of this "abrupt classicist" who, "thoroughly versed in the theory and practise of architecture, prided himself upon correctness of style and solidity of construction as his leading principles".[6]

Christopher Joseph Cato, a pioneer of Durban, was a man of diverse interests but perhaps the most interesting of the early architects of Natal.[9] He had, unfortunately, no qualifications as a surveyor or architect, though the following extract from a letter written by him to the Surveyor-General reveals his ambition, "If I am not intruding on your time, I will explain my meaning about the appointment of Government Architect. I wished you to be kind enough to get me appointed by the Governor and gazetted as such. Then any work the Government does I should be paid for by percentage or a salary, while the works are being carried on. In that manner I should be able to take the superintendence of other works. I think you will understand my meaning". [10]

From 1845 to 1850 the Surveyor-General and his staff were concerned mainly with land settlements and disputes. The first, Dr William Stanger, had worked as a geologist member of the Niger expedition in 1841 and later joined the Roads Department of the Cape Colonial Government. His main interests were said to have been botanical, and though trained as a surveyor his architectural ability was limited. Indeed the work of his successors John Bird and Dr P.C. Sutherland bears similar characteristics in its simplicity and conservativism. In a sense such limitations of qualification were a distinct advantage in the "age of reform" and much of the architecture carried out by these surveyor-architects laid a sound basis for the development of a colonial style, which itself was characterised by restraint and a down-to-earth functionalism. From its very inception, the Surveyor General's department introduced the system of competitive tendering; many tenders submitted in the early 1850's reveal the hazards of building outside of the recognised towns.[11]

George Loveday, who arrived on the "Hebrides" in May 1850, [12] called himself an architect, though he named his eldest son "Richard Kelsey" after his surveyor friend whose chief claim to fame was the monument he designed to King William. It may have been Loveday who was the architect responsible for the clever fretwork details of the first Catholic church and the additions to Government House in Pietermaritzburg.[13] A descendant, however, has claimed that besides these two he also designed St Peter's Cathedral, the Presbyterian Church and the Masonic Hall.[14]

Anyone who was in the slightest way connected with the erection of buildings called himself an architect. James Harding, who advertised as an architect and builder in Pietermaritzburg in the 'sixties and 'seventies, and thereby provided a "packaged deal", found himself in the local law courts in 1881 when his tenuous occupation proved the impossibility of acting in both capacities.[15] A certain Bowers Janion, who seems to have been an estate agent, considered himself an architect as well; "J.B.J. having recently inspected some of the most modern buildings in England is prepared to introduce improvements here without any material increase in the ordinary cost".[16]

Architects had to resort to the courts when clients failed to pay the necessary professional fees. During a courtcase in 1882, when an architect, F.J. Alexander, was attempting to claim his fees, the judge observed that anyone in the Colony could call himself an architect, a fact which made judgements on such matters extremely difficult.[17] However, P.M. Dudgeon's practise was referred to as having set a precedent in the Colony in the matter of professional fees, [18] and the case was decided on this basis. To clarify the law relating to architects in Natal, Law 38 of 1884 was passed. This laid down that "an architect shall mean any person who has duly fulfilled the articles of his indenture to a qualified architect, or who prepares designs and specifications for buildings, or who executes or supervises the erection of the same. Any person who is employed to perform work usually done by an architect as herein defined, shall be required to take out an architect's license".[19]

Building legislation had been introduced in Pietermaritzburg in 1855 and in Durban in 1861, [20] and the initial by-laws were directed towards the control of the construction of buildings rather than the relationship of buildings to each other. Only fifteen years previously in England, two bills had been introduced in Parliament to prevent houses being built back to back without an intervening space between, or being constructed below ground level. The Times had thought this, "a reckless and wanton invasion of property and liberty".[21] By 1878 the laws surrounding the erection of buildings in Durban had reached the stage that builders were compelled to submit plans for approval. Dudgeon found this a considerable inconvenience, for on one occasion the Town Surveyor's office retained his plans for four days! [22]

The wide increases in the volume of building in the Colony resulted in a shortage of skilled labour. In 1858 the Umzinto Sugar Co was inaugurated by men from the Cape who brought with them "several high salaried Chinamen to build houses for them".[23] In 1875 two Chinese carpenters were under the employ of the Colonial Engineer and were stationed in Estcourt. After the 'eighties, however, a considerable number of artisans were brought to Natal by the Government from England and Scotland.[24] By this time mission stations had commenced the training of Africans as tradesmen. The Edendale Wesleyan Mission trained young boys as carpenters, joiners and wagon-makers, and the mission at Inanda trained carpenters, masons, plasterers and bricklayers.[25]

While a system of pupilage had probably existed in the offices of such architects as Upton since the arrival of the first British settlers, the architect's law of 1884 encouraged prospective architects to fulfil their articles of indenture in the office of a recognised architect. William Robarts, who ran an extensive practise in Durban during the 'eighties and 'nineties, was one who trained several such young architects.[26] During the 'nineties, however, William Street-Wilson (who may have taken over P.M. Dudgeon's practise) was the best known architect in the Colony and probably in great demand amongst colonial pupils.[27]

The entire design and contractual process of building was based closely on that in England. Information given on drawings was reduced to a bare minimum and supplemented by thorough specifications, while details were worked out on the site by the architect.

The Colonial Engineer's Office, which had taken

---

4   Some of the surveyor-architects who arrived with the British Immigrants were:

   Tatham. Edmund.
   Tatham. Robert. (sons of Charles Heathcote Tatham).
   Moreland. John.
   Anderson. Robert.
   St John Greene. Lawrence.
   Ridgeway. Rowland.
   Waddington. Henry.
   A few found no scope for their vocations and turned to other interests. St John Greene is said to have "Invented, patented and manufactured 'Nutrine'."
   The dawn of Durban. A. M'Crystal.

5   See Chapters 5, 6 and 7.

6   The Daily News. May 7 1883 (obituary).

7   Durban Town Clerk's archives. H. 1573. April 5 1860. and, History of old Durban. G. Russell. p328 The post was taken over by H. Waddington.

8   50 Years municipal history of Durban. Henderson. p8. W.E. Robarts was appointed Borough Surveyor in 1877.

9   C.J. Cato came to Natal in 1839 and is said to have designed the crest and seal of Natal.

10   S.G.O. 111/1/5. May 4 1851. This appointment was not carried out.
     An interesting footnote to the letter proffers the advice of his colonial experience on tendering, to John Bird, the Surveyor General, "If

there should not be any tenders given in it would be as well to estimate the work tender for the materials separately and hire men to do the work — as in Cape Town and the frontiers, it would be quite as economic". (Alterations to H.M. Custom's House).

11   Surveyor General's office. Vol. A. Index to Tenders. 4, 21, 22, 49, 80, 81, 82, 189, 192, 231, 235, 237, 239 and 241.

12   Diary G. Loveday. (Killie Campbell Museum).

13   Chapter 5. and Chapter 7.

14   Papers relating to Loveday diary (Killie Campbell Museum).

15   The Times of Natal. Feb. 4 1884.
     "The Chief Justice in delivering his judgement expressed the opinion that it was a most unwise and dangerous thing to have an architect and a builder in one and the same person".

16   Newspaper advertisements, 1880.

17   Times of Natal. July 13 1882.

18   1½% for sketch plans and full 5% for drawings and supervision. Letter Dudgeon to Town Clerk, Durban. July 26 1882. (Durban Town Clerk's archives).

19   Ordinances, Laws and Proclamations of Natal, 1843—1889, comp. and ed. by C.F. Cadiz, R. Lyon and W. Broome. p1557. In 1889 a dispute arose as to whether or not architects from the Cape and Transvaal wishing to submit an entry in the Pietermaritzburg City Hall competition were required to pay the usual licences. C.E.O. 1494/89.
     An architect's registration bill came into effect in Natal in 1905.

20   Ordinances of the Colony of Natal. Vol. 11. Jan. 1 1856. Dunbar Moodie.

21   The Victorian home. R. Dutton. p30

22   Letter from Dudgeon to Town Clerk, Durban. 19 Dec. 1881. (Town Clerk's archives, Durban).

23   Arbuthnot autobiography. p19 (Arbuthnot Family collection).

24   C.E.O. 4357. Oct. 25 1875.

25   These Africans were generally employed in buildings erected for Africans. Later the Springvale, Church of England Mission and Marianhill monastery set up industrial and building schools. Private institutions who required artisans in Natal often brought them out from England or Europe especially for the purpose. Fr. Henry Lenoir, who had built the Church of Holy Cross in Liverpool (designed by A.W. Pugin) was brought to South Africa in 1876 by Bishop Jolivet to build churches for him throughout his diocese. St Mary's Church in Kimberley was one result of his labours.

26   W. Robarts became the first president of the Natal Institute of Architects in 1901.

27   The first attempts to introduce some kind of formal architectural training were made by the Natal Institute in 1903 and 1904 when classes in architecture were given at the Natal Technical College.

over the design of Governmental buildings from the Surveyor General's Office in 1864, used standard specifications and building contracts for their numerous works throughout the Colony.[28] Though many of these buildings indicate the standard building solutions worked out by men who were both loathe to depart from conventionality and in some cases intellectually unable to do so, type plans were only used by the Colonial Engineer after 1903. This was done upon the recommendation of the Civil Service Commission, who stated that: "One of the most important matters in connection with the Public Works Department is the absence of any proper type of Government buildings. There should be a standard plan for a school, post office, gaol, court-house, etc. When this plan has been agreed to... it should serve as a model for all buildings of the same class for some time to come".[29] In 1905 the Assistant Engineer reported that "the Ben Johnson type of Elementary school, approved by the London school board and modified to suit climatic conditions in this colony was selected as a type school".[30]

This was the age of the catalogue and pattern book. One could choose entire buildings from such catalogues as Macfarlane's of Glasgow. Every machine-made building element or ornament could be selected in this way; just as building styles and house-plans were from Regency times selected by the building public from pattern books and encyclopaediae. In a certain sense such a system of choice left little originality to the architect, though in other ways this could only be of advantage to architecture. The economic limitations of colonial building programmes necessitated that cheap, which generally meant simpler, examples were chosen.

Architectural design in the Colony of Natal was based on the traditions of English civil and military architecture and though influenced at first by the established traditions of the Cape, it became to be flavoured by the popular fashions of British and European architecture. While movements such as the Picturesque may be seen to be the forerunner of Cubism, and of the nineteenth century tendency to query and violate recognised stylistic precepts, and hence may be said to have laid the necessary groundwork for the development of the modern movement, the unrecognised Colonial style, with its essential functional basis and restraint, may be regarded as one of the important bridges between the architecture of the nineteenth and twentieth centuries.

28   C.S.O. 237/1954, 1864.
29   Report on the civil service of Natal. 1903. p65 86.
30   Annual report of the P.W.D. of the Colony of Natal. 1905. p32

REPORT OF THE GOVERNMENT ASTRO-
NOMER OF NATAL. 11th Council, 1883.
L.H.M.
DURBAN TOWN CLERK'S ARCHIVES; Let-
ters received and dispatched: 1854–1893.

Bibliography

B: MANUSCRIPTS AND JOURNALS.

SHEPSTONE JOURNAL. N. ARC.
DIARY OF CONGELLA. Carl Behrens. K.C.M.
REMINISCENCES OF EARLY NATAL.
Thomas Greene K.C.M.
THE FANNIN PAPERS. K.C.M.
EARLY DAYS IN NATAL. W. Lister (Bird
Papers N.ARC)
ACUTT CHRONICLE. K.C.M.
HISTORY OF EARLY VERULAM.
1850–1860.
(M.A. THESIS) M. PARK. N.U. PMB.
FIRST IMPRESSIONS OF NATAL BY A
PERTHSHIRE PLOUGHMAN. 1853. K.C.M.
LETTERS, SOPHIE GRAY TO DEAN GREEN
(1864) Anglican Church Archives. N.U. PMB.
DIARY OF BISHOP ALLARD. O.M.I. Arch-
diocesan Archives. DBN.
CORRESPONDENCE BETWEEN J.E. METH-
LEY AND J. METHLEY. 1854. K.C.M.
FLEMING DIARY, K.C.M.
DIARY OF BISHOP JOLIVET O.M.I. Arch-
diocesan Archives, DBN.
R.I.B.A. MEMBERSHIP LISTS. 1875–1895.
R.I.B.A. Library. London.
ARBUTHNOT MEMORIES. Arbuthnot family
collection.
DIARY G. LOVEDAY. K.C.M.

A: OFFICIAL DOCUMENTS.

BRITISH PARLIAMENTARY PAPERS RE-
LATING TO THE SETTLEMENT OF NATAL
XV. 1843.
BRITISH PARLIAMENTARY PAPERS RE-
LATING TO THE ZULU WAR. XLII
1879–1880.
SURVEYOR GENERAL'S OFFICE ; Letters re-
ceived and dispatched. 1846–1860.
SURVEYOR GENERAL'S OFFICE ; Tenders
for the erection of buildings. 1846–1860.
S.G.O. 111/11/30
COLONIAL ENGINEER'S OFFICE ; Letters re-
ceived and dispatched. 1860–1889.
COLONIAL SECRETARY'S OFFICE ; Subject
index to letters received. 1846–1893.
PUBLIC WORKS DEPARTMENT ; Subject in-
dex to correspondence. 1890–1905.
REPORT ON THE CIVIL SERVICE OF NA-
TAL. 1903.
NATAL BLUE BOOKS. 1858–1905.
          Including the Surveyor Gen-
          eral's Reports, 1858–1862;
          Civil and Colonial Engineer's
          Reports, 1863–1894;
          Public Works Department Re-
          ports, 1894–1905.

C: NEWSPAPERS AND MAGAZINES.

GRAHAMSTOWN JOURNAL 1837.
DE NATALLER 1844–1845.
AFRICANA NOTES AND NEWS. 1955–1965.
CAPE MONTHLY MAGAZINE. 1872 Vol. IV,
V.
THE KOKSTAD ADVERTISER. 1882.
THE PORTSMOUTH TIMES 1890.
THE NATAL COURIER 1863–1864.
THE NATAL WITNESS 1849–1850, 1855.
THE NATAL MERCURY 1853–1855.
1875–1889. 1891–1892. 1903–1905.
THE TIMES OF NATAL. 1880–1882.
THE DAILY NEWS. (NATAL MERCANTILE
ADVERTISER). 1853 and 1865–1870. 1882,
1891, 1893.

THE NATAL INDEPENDENT 1854.
THE ARCHITECTURAL MAGAZINE AND
JOURNAL. 1838. vol. V.
AMERICAN ARCHITECT AND BUILDING
NEWS. vol. XI, 1888.
THE IRISH BUILDER. 1870—1880.
FRAZER'S MAGAZINE. 1875.
CITY OF BATH DIRECTORY. 1870—1891.
THE BUILDER. 1875—1885.
THE ARCHITECT. 1875—1885.
DAVIS' NATAL ALMANAC. 1863—1909.

D: WORKS.

1   General, Natal and South Africa.

REMINISCENCES. C.J. Anderson. 1946.
STORY OF THE ZULU CAMPAIGN. W. Ashe
and W. Edgell. 1880.
SOUTH EAST AFRICA, 1488—1530. E. Axel-
son. 1940.
THE DORP AND VELD OR SIX MONTHS IN
NATAL. C. Barter. 1852.
BELINDA'S AID TO COLONIAL HOUSE-
WIVES.
ANNALS OF NATAL. Vol. 1 and 11. J. Bird.
1888.
NATAL 1846—1851 by an old inhabitant. (J.
Bird) 1891.
THEY WERE SOUTH AFRICANS. J. Bond.
1956.
TREKKING FOR SOULS. J.E. Brady.
NATAL, A HISTORY AND DESCRIPTION OF
THE COLONY. H. Brookes and Mann. 1876.
A HISTORY OF NATAL. E.H. Brookes and C.
de B. Webb. 1965.
PIONEER DAYS IN NATAL. B. Buchanan.
1934.
NATAL MEMORIES. B. Buchanan. 1941.
TO THE SHORES OF NATAL. T.V. Bulpin.
1953.
ANGLICANS IN NATAL. Burnett. B.B. 1953.
HISTORY OF THE ALFRED DISTRICT. B.E.
Camp.
THE PATTERN OF ENGLISH BUILDING. A.
Clifton-Taylor.
TEN WEEKS IN NATAL. J.W. Colenso. 1855.
J. SHEDDON DOBIE. S.A. JOURNAL.
1862—66 ed. by A.F. Hatterlsey.
MY AFRICAN HOME. 1852—1857. E.W. Feil-
den. 1882.
THE DIARY OF HENRY FRANCIS FYNN.
(1803—1861) Comp. and ed. by J. Stuart and
D. McK. Malcolm. 1950.

NARRATIVE OF A JOURNEY TO THE
ZOOLU COUNTRY ... Undertaken in 1835.
A.F. Gardiner. 1836.
MORE ANNALS OF NATAL. A.F. Hattersley,
1936.
LATER ANNALS OF NATAL. A.F. Hattersley.
1938.
PIETERMARITZBURG PANORAMA. A.F.
Hattersley. 1938.
THE NATALIANS. A.F. Hattersley. 1940.
PORTRAIT OF A COLONY. A.F. Hattersley.
1940.
THE NATAL SETTLERS. A.F. Hattersley.
1949.
THE BRITISH SETTLEMENT OF NATAL.
A.F. Hattersley. 1950.
A HOSPITAL CENTURY. A.F. Hattersley.
1955.
OLIVER THE SPY. A.F. Hattersley. 1959.
DURBAN: FIFTY YEARS' MUNICIPAL HIS-
TORY. W.P.M. Henderson. 1904.
A BRIEF HISTORY OF METHODISM AND
OF METHODIST MISSIONS IN SOUTH AF-
RICA. W.C. Holden. 1877.
TRAVELS AND ADVENTURES IN EASTERN
AFRICA. N. Isaacs. ed. by L. Herrman. Van
Riebeeck Society, Nos. 16 and 17. 1936—37.
SIR ANDREW SMITH. Kirby 1965.
THE GROWTH AND GOVERNMENT OF
CAPE TOWN. Laidler.
LANDMARKS OF OLD DURBAN. S.A.B.C.
1948.
SOUTH AFRICA, A SKETCH BOOK OF MEN,
MANNERS AND FACTS. J.S. Little. 1884.
HISTORIC NATAL AND ZULULAND. H.C.
Lugg. 1948.
THE CRADLE DAYS OF NATAL. G. Mackeur-
tan. 1931.
ON VELDT AND FARM. F. Macnab. 1897.
DRIE HONDERD JAAR NASIE-BOU IN
SUID-AFRIKA. Malherbe.
LIFE WITH THE ZULUS OF NATAL. G.H.
Mason. 1855.
ZULULAND. G.H. Mason. 1862.
THE DAWN OF DURBAN. A' M'Crystal.
THE NEW COLONY OF PORT NATAL. J.E.
Methley. 1849.
ORDINANCES, PROCLAMATIONS RE-
LATING TO THE COLONY OF NATAL. VOL
1 and 11. D. Moodie. 1855.
NATAL ILLUSTRATED. 1900.
THE VOORTREKKERS OF SOUTH AFRICA.
M. Nathan. 1937.
OUR COLONY OF NATAL. W. Peace. An
emigrant's guide.
THE PRESBYTERIAN CHURCH OF PIETER-
MARITZBURG. 1850—1950. Prof. A. Petrie.

MARIANHILL. Abbot Pfanner. 1887.

VOORTREKKERMENSE (ed. by G. Preller).

NATAL. Sir J. Robinson. 1863.

NOTES ON NATAL. Sir J. Robinson. 1872.

A LIFE TIME IN SOUTH AFRICA. Sir J. Robinson. 1900.

SCHOONERS AND SKYSCRAPERS. E. Rosenthal. 1963.

NATAL: THE LAND AND ITS STORY. G. Russell. 1891.

THE HISTORY OF OLD DURBAN. G. Russell. 1899.

A HISTORY OF RICHMOND FROM 1839 TO 1937. S.W.B. Shepstone.

BACKGROUND TO ESTCOURT. C.F. Shuter.

ENGLISHMAN'S INN. C.F. Shuter. 1963.

THE PROGRESS OF SOUTH AFRICA IN THE 19TH CENTURY. G. McC. Theal. 1900.

A HISTORY OF SOUTH AFRICA (1834–1854) G. McC. Theal. 1922.

SOUTH AFRICA. A. Trollope. 1878.

TWENTIETH CENTURY IMPRESSIONS OF NATAL. 1906.

KULTUURSKATTE UIT DIE VOORTREKKER TYDPERK. G.H. van Rooyen.

TONGAATI. R.G.T. Watson. 1960.

HISTORY OF THE WESLEYAN CHURCH OF SOUTH AFRICA. J. Whiteside. 1906.

HISTORY OF THE VRYHEID DISTRICT. F. Wilter.

CHANGING IDEALS IN MODERN ARCHITECTURE. P. Collins. 1965.

CHURCH BUILDERS OF THE NINETEENTH CENTURY. B. Clarke. 1938.

THE GOTHIC REVIVAL. B. Clarke. 1928.

RURAL RESIDENCES. J.B. Papworth. 1840.

A HISTORY OF CAST IRON IN ARCHITECTURE. W. Gloag and D. Bridgewater. 1948.

ROMANTICISM AND AMERICAN ARCHITECTURE. J. Early. 1959.

SAMUEL BLACKETT. M. Herman. 1963.

DECORATIVE CAST IRONWORK IN GREAT BRITAIN. R. Lister. 1960.

ARCHITECTURE, AMBITION AND AMERICANS. W. Andrews. 1955.

AN ENCYCLOPAEDIA OF COTTAGE, FARM AND VILLA ARCHITECTURE. Loudon. 1833.

THE DEVELOPMENT OF ENGLISH BUILDING CONSTRUCTION. C.E. Innocent. 1916.

THE PATTERN OF ENGLISH BUILDING. Clifton-Taylor. 1962.

VICTORIAN CITIES. A. Briggs. 1961.

HINTS ON HOUSEHOLD TASTE. C. Eastlake. 1872.

HIGH VICTORIAN DESIGN. N. Pevsner. 1951.

THE VICTORIAN HOME. R. Dutton. 1954.

VICTORIAN TASTE. J. Gloag. 1962.

ART AND ITS PRODUCERS. W. Morris. 1892.

THE SEVEN LAMPS OF ARCHITECTURE. J. Ruskin. 1849.

THE DARKENING GLASS. J. Rosenberg. 1961.

2   Architecture, Town planning and the visual arts.

EARLY NINETEENTH CENTURY ARCHITECTURE IN SOUTH AFRICA. R.B. Lewcock. 1963.

AN INTRODUCTION TO VICTORIAN ARCHITECTURE. H. Casson. 1948.

THE REGENCY STYLE. D. Pilcher. 1947.

A HISTORY OF ENGLISH ARCHITECTURE. Kidson, Murray and Thompson. 1962.

VICTORIAN ARCHITECTURE. Ed. by P. Ferriday. 1963.

EARLY NINETEENTH CENTURY ARCHITECTURE IN BRITAIN. H.R. Hitchcock. 1954.

ARCHITECTURE, NINETEENTH AND TWENTIETH CENTURY. H.R. Hitchock. 1958.

H.R. RICHARDSON. H.R. Hitchcock. 1936.

ARCHITECTURE SINCE THE REGENCY. Goodhart-Rendel. 1953.

VICTORIAN ARCHITECTURE. R.F. Jordan. 1966.

3   General

THE AGE OF IMPROVEMENT. A. Briggs. 1954.

VICTORIAN PEOPLE. A. Briggs. 1959.

EARLY VICTORIAN ENGLAND. G.M. Young. 1934.

THE VICTORIANS. Sir C. Petrie. 1938.

THE AGE OF REFORM. R. Hofstadter. 1956.

SOUTH AFRICAN REPUBLIC

TONGALAND

• Volkrust

Charlestown

• Paulpietersburg

UTRECHT

• Utrecht

• NEWCASTLE

ORANGE FREE STATE

• Vryheid

NEW REPUBLIC

• Dundee

• Glencoe
(Biggarsburg)

• Harrismith

• Melmoth

ZULULAND

LADYSMITH •

• Empangeni

• Bergville   • Colenso

• Weenen

• Eshowe

• Estcourt (Bushman's River)

• Kranskop

NATAL   Greytown •

BASUTOLAND

• Umvoti

• Weston (Mooirivier)

York • • New Hanover

New
Guelderland

Fort Nottingham •   • Karkloof

• Stanger

Dargle •   • Howick

• Wartburg

• Umhlali

PIETERMARITZBURG

• Tongaat

Edendale •   Verulam •

Drakensberg

• Boston Thornybush •

• Inanda

Himeville •

Camperdown •

• Mount Edgecombe

• Underburg

• Byrne   • Cato Ridge

• Bulwer

Pinetown

• Richmond

• DURBAN

• Donnybrook

• Creighton

• Isipingo

• Ixopo

Umzimkulu

• Umkomaas

• Umzinto   • Scottburgh

• Harding

Marburg •   • PORT SHEPSTONE

Drawn by
Ruth Bowie

MAP OF NATAL
(late nineteenth century)

DRAWINGS AND PHOTOGRAPHIC ILLUSTRATIONS

a (above)
Pelham Crescent, South Kensington,
London. 1820 - 1830. G. Basevi.

b (left)
'A Cottage Orné', 1818, from 'Rural
Residences' by J.B. Papworth.

c (below)
'An English Town of 1440', from
A.N.W. Pugin's CONTRASTS. 1841.

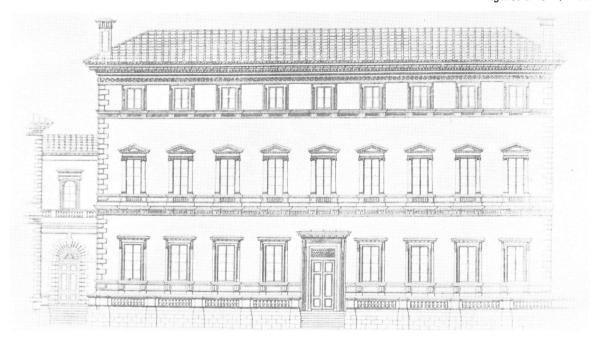

d (top)
Elevation, The Reform Club House,
Pall Mall, London. Sir Charles Barry.
1838 - 1840.

e (centre)
The Foreign Office, London. (1860 -
1875) Sir Gilbert Scott.

f (left)
House, 170 Queen's Gate, Kensington, London. 1888. R.N. Shaw.

1 (above)
Farewell's Camp at Port Natal. c 1825. (L.H.M.)

2 (below)
The Settlement at Port Natal. 1835. (L.H.M.)

3 (above)
Umlazi Mission Station. 1836. (K.C.M.)

4 (below)
Drawing of Congella. c 1840. (L.H.M.)

5 (left top)
House Burger's. (Later the Colonial
Offices) Church St., PMB.

6 (right top)
The Church of the Vow. PMB. Photograph c 1870. (N. Mus.)

7 (left centre)
Pulpit, Church of the Vow.

8 (below)
Raadzaal, PMB. 1841. (K.C.M.)

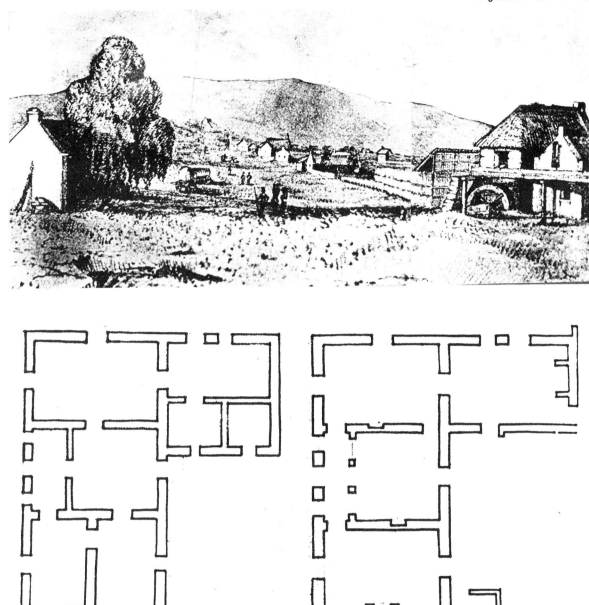

9 (above) : Drawing of Pietermaritzburg in 1841. Upper Church Street showing Visagie's
Mill at the right. (N. Mus.)

10 (below) : A comparison between the original drawing of the Dutch Reformed Pastorie
of 1842, at the left, and the Salvation Army Men's home of 1950 by C.F. Shuter.
(Natal Witness, May 14, 1950)

11 (top) : The Dutch Reformed Pastorie. PMB. 1842. (Ogilvie Collection)

12 (left above) and 13 (right above) : House at the corner of Boom Street
and Clayton Ave., PMB. (Ogilvie
Collection)

14 (above)
House Cloete. c 1842. PMB. Watercolour by P.L.G. Cloete. (O.H.M.)

15 (centre)
House Moodie, PMB. c 1865. See
Fig. 14. (N.Mus.)

16 (below)
'Little Saxony'. P. Otto. Otto's Bluff.
c 1842. Watercolour by P.L.G. Cloete.
(O.H.M.)

17
18
19
20   21

17   'Upper Saxony' c. 1853, from a water-colour by Capt. R.F. Garden. A house built some ten years later not far from the original dwelling. See Fig. 16. (K.C.M.)

18   Captain Smith's camp at DBN. 1842. (L.H.M.)

19   Fort, DBN. 1843. (L.H.M.)

20   Magazine, Fort, DBN. 1845. (Don. Lib.)

21   Barracks, Fort, DBN. 1845. The veranda roof was originally supported on wooden poles. (Don. Lib.)

22 (right) 23 (below) 24 (left above)
Fort Napier, PMB. The water-tower was built later in the century.
The picture below is from a watercolour by Capt. R.F. Garden (K.C.M.), c. 1846.

25 (above)
House Boshoff. Longmarket St., PMB. (Facing Market Square) 1844. (Ogilvie Collection)

26 (below)
House Martin West. PMB. 1845. (Ogilvie Collection)

27 (left top) : Fanlight, House Martin West. Church St., PMB. (Ogilvie Collection)

28 (right) : House Kritzinger, Cnr. Pine and Loop Streets, PMB. (N. Mus.)

30 (left, lower) : Detail of Kapsteilhuise on an eighteenth century Cape Farm. ('Pictorial atlas of the history of South Africa' by J. Ploeger and A. Smith).

29 : Dutch houses, central Church St., PMB. (Photograph c 1865) (Ogilvie Collection) Refer also Fig. 505, Left.

31 (left top) : Greytown. (Photograph 1860's) (K.C.M.)

32 (right top) : Stoepkamerhuis. Umkomaas. (K.C.M.)

33 (above) : Dutch Reformed Church, Ladysmith, 1849. (K.C.M.)

34 (below) : Government House, PMB. from a watercolour by Hughbert Baker. (Public
record office, London.)

35 (above) : Wesleyan Mission House. Cnr. Chapel and Church Streets, PMB. Refer Fig. 36.
    (N. Mus.)

36 (below) : Chapel Street, PMB. (AQUATINT O.H.M.)

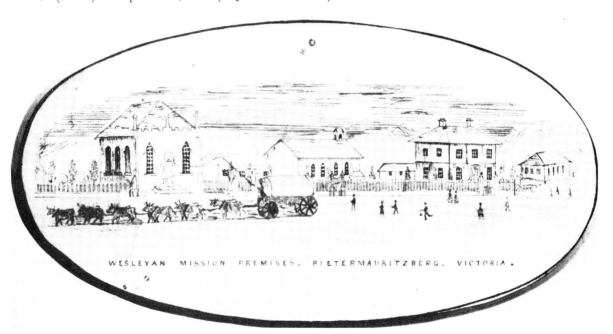

WESLEYAN MISSION PREMISES, PIETERMAURITZBERG, VICTORIA.

37 (left)
The Wesleyan Chapel, PMB.

38 (below)
Crown Hotel, Commercial
Rd, PMB. 1849. (Ogilvie
Collection)

Figure 39 / 99

39   Plan and Elevation, Government Schoolroom. Longmarket St., PMB.
      1849. (N. Arc.)

40 : Government Schoolroom, PMB. (Olgilvie Collection). 42 : 'Mr. Best's House at Port Natal', 1848. Pencil Sketch by Capt. R.F. Garden. 41 : Block House, Hospital Hill, Point, Durban, 1846. (O.H.M.) 43 : Chiappini's warehouse, (Customs House) Point, DBN. (L.H.M.) 44 : House Saunders. Tongaat. 1849. (Tongaati, Watson).

40   41

43   44

42

45 (left top)
A Settler house. (R.B. Lewcock)

46 (above)
Typical Zulu hut construction.

47, 47a, 48 (below)
Houses, DBN. c 1850.

49 (above) : Manor House. G.C. Cato. DBN. (L.H.M.)

50 (below) : House Hillary, DBN. 1851. (WATERCOLOUR L.H.M.)

51(Above) House Feilden, DBN. 1850. From 'My African Home' by E. Feilden.
51a (below): House Lindley, Inanda, 1849. Pencil sketch by Capt. R.F. Garden, K.C.M.

52   53
54   55
56   57
58

52 : Anglican Church, Byrne. 1850. (L.H.M.).   53, 54, 55 : Houses PMB. Early Fifties.
(N. Mus. and Ogilvie Collection)   56, 57 : Houses DBN. Early Fifties. (L.H.M.)
58 : House Binns. DBN. (L.H.M.)

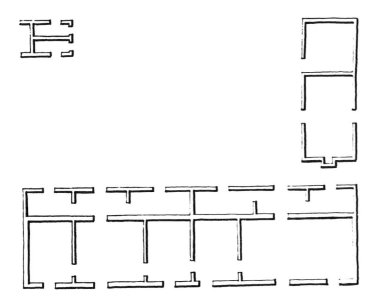

59

60

61   62

59 : House plan, DBN. 1853. (Drawing N. Arc.) Reconstructed by the author.

60 : Plan, houses Dacomb. DBN. 1852. (Drawing N. Arc.) Reconstructed by the author.

61 : Ground and first floor plan, house Savory DBN. 1851. (Drawing N. Arc.) Reconstructed by the author.   62 : House Savory, DBN. (L.H.M.)

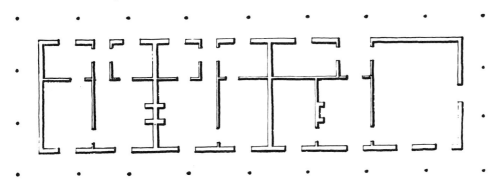

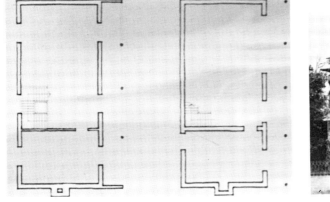

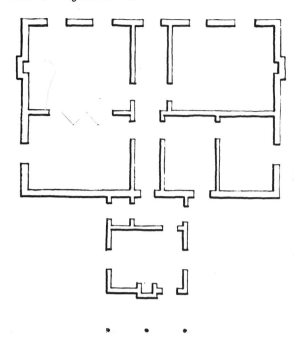

63   64

65

66   67

68   69

63 : Plan, house Goodricke. Smith St., DBN. 1854. (Drawing N. Arc.) Reconstructed by the author.   64 : House Goodricke, DBN. (L.H.M.)   65 : Houses Umkomaas, Photograph c 1860. (K.C.M.)   66 : Botha's Hotel, Botha's Hill. 1850. (N. Mus.)   67 : The Phoenix Hotel, West St., DBN. 1850. (L.H.M.)   68 : Stores, West St., DBN. 1851. (L.H.M.)   69 : The Magistracy, Ladysmith. 1854. (N. Mus.)

70 (above) : Corrugated iron warehouse, Lamport and Holt. 1850. Reconstruction by the
author. (L.H.M.)

71 (below) : Middleton and Wirsing. Cnr. Gardiner and Smith Streets DBN. (L.H.M.)

72 (above) : Royal Hotel, central Smith St., DBN. (L.H.M.)

73 (below) : Congregational Church and manse, Smith St., DBN. R.S. Upton. 1854.
(WATERCOLOUR L.H.M.)

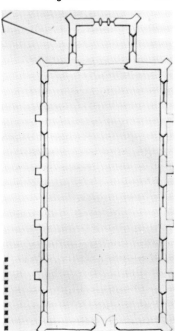

74 (above left) : Intended Elevation of St. Paul's Church, from a Chart
of Port Natal. ('Old Durban' by G. Russell.)

75 (above right) : Reconstructed plan. St. Paul's Church, DBN. R.S. Upton.

76 (below) : St. Paul's Church, DBN. R.S. Upton. 1853. (L.H.M.)

76a (top) : St. Paul's Church, DBN. 1880. (L.H.M.)

77 (below) : St. Peters Church, PMB. 1851 - 1857.

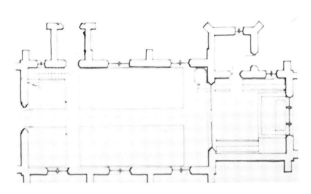

78
Plan, St. Peter's Church, PMB. 1851 - 1857.

79
Gargoyle, St. Peter's Church, PMB.

80
Carved heads, Chancel, St. Peter's Church, PMB.

81
Interior, St. Peter's Church, PMB.

82
East Window, St. Peter's Church, PMB.

78	79
80	
	81
82	

83 (above left) : St. Peter's Church, PMB.

84 (below) : Colenso's Chapel at Bishopstowe. (N. Arc.)

86 (above left) : St. Mary's Church, Longmarket St., PMB. 1860. (Ogilvie Collection)

87 (above right) : St. Mary's Church, PMB. After 1889.

88 (below) : Presbyterian Church, PMB. 1851. (Left) The buildings in the centre and at
the right were the gaol and Raadzaal respectively. (WATERCOLOUR K.C.M.)

89 (above)
Presbyterian Church, PMB. Before
1873. (N. Mus.)

90 (left)
Presbyterian Church, PMB. After
1873.

91 (above left)
Catholic Church, Loop St., PMB. (R.B. Lewcock.)

92 (above right)
Fretwork, elevation, Catholic Church, PMB. (R.B. Lewcock.)

93 (left)
St. Mary's Anglican Church, Richmond, 1853. (N. Mus.)

94 (below)
House Colenso, Bishopstowe. (Ogilvie collection)

95 - 98   95   96
Houses PMB. 1850's (N. Mus. and   97
Ogilvie Collection)
                               98

99   99
Plan of proposed Government House,
PMB. (N. Arc.)

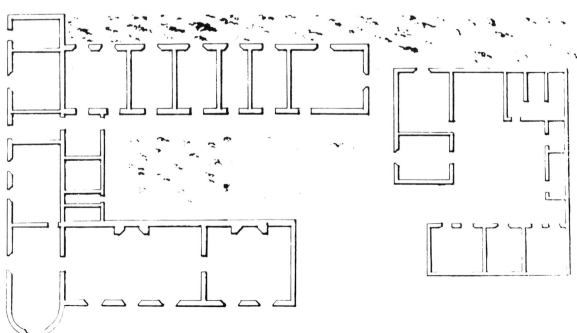

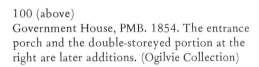

100 (above)
Government House, PMB. 1854. The entrance
porch and the double-storeyed portion at the
right are later additions. (Ogilvie Collection)

101 (left), 102 (bottom left), 103 (bottom right)
Houses, PMB. 1850's (N. Mus. and Ogilvie
Collection)

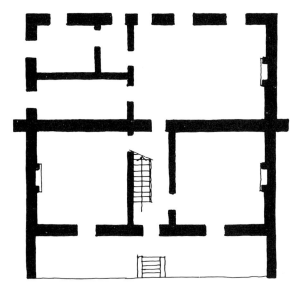

104 (top)
House, Mooi River. c 1855. Drawing by Sarah
Churchill. (N. Mus.) refer also Fig. 17

105 (above)
House Archbell, Longmarket St., PMB. c 1855.
(Ogilvie Collection)

106 (left), 107 (below)
Plan and Elevation of house, 121 Loop Street,
PMB. (Meas. Dwg. Author.)

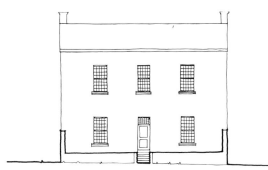

108	109
110	111
	113
	112

108
House, 380 Prince Alfred St., PMB.
c 1855. (Ogilvie Collection)

109
Shop, Cnr. Commercial Rd., and
Longmarket St., PMB. (N. Mus.)

110, 111, 112
Commercial buildings, PMB. 1855.
(K.C.M. and Ogilvie Collection)

113
Stables at House 'Mkondeni. (Ogilvie
Collection)

114
Farmhouse, Baynes Drift, near PMB.

115
Mason's Mill, Plessislaer.

116
Windmill, Ridge Rd., DBN. 1855.
(K.C.M.)

117
Eastern Mill, PMB. (N. Mus.)

114   115

116

117

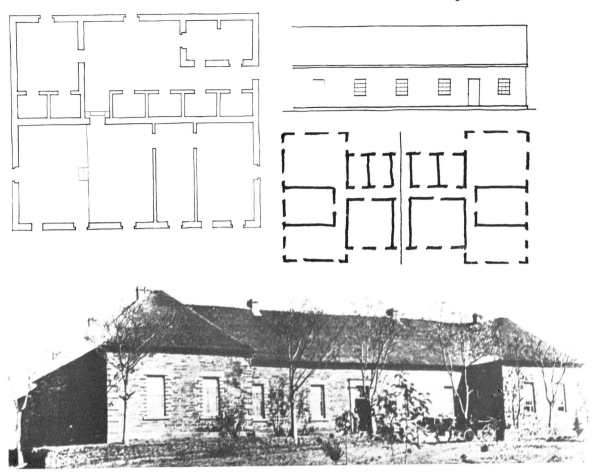

118, 119   Plan and elevation of district courthouse, Umvoti. (Dwg. N.
           Arc.) Reconstruction by the author.

121   Rough plan of Grey's Hospital, PMB. (N. Arc.)   123   Sugar Mill, Tongaat. c 1865. (Tongaati, Watson.)

122   Grey's Hospital, PMB. (N. Arc.)   124   The Queen's bridge, Umgeni River. 1864. (L.H.M.)

118	119
	121
122	
123	124

125 (right)
Gaol and Police Station, DBN. H. Waddington.
1861. (L.H.M.)

126, 127 (below)
Hospital DBN. R.S. Upton (L.H.M.)

128	129
130	131
132	

128 Fort Cross, 1861. (O.H.M.)

129 Parker Wood and Co., DBN. 1860 (L.H.M.)

130 (Left) Acutt and Leslie, Gardiner Street., DBN. (L.H.M.)

131 Durban Club. 1861. R.S. Upton. (L.H.M.)

132 R. Acutt, West St., DBN. 1860. (L.H.M.)

133 (above)
Crozier and Louch, West St., DBN.
(L.H.M.)

134 (left)
Dickenson and Co, and S. Crowder
(Left), West St., DBN. (L.H.M.)

135	136
137	138
139	140

135   West Street, DBN. (The building on the right dates from the late seventies. (L.H.M.)

136   Shop, central west Street, DBN. 1859. (L.H.M.)

137   Challinor's West St., DBN. (L.H.M.)

138   Leeds House, West St., DBN. (L.H.M.)

139   Masonic Hall, Gardiner, St. DBN. 1859. E. Tatham. (L.H.M.)

140   The Natal Bank, West St., DBN. 1860. C.J. Cato. (Dwg. L.H.M.)

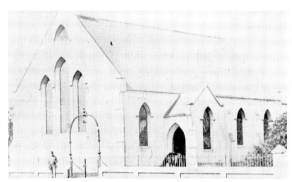

141   Caney's buildings, DBN. (L.H.M.)

142   The Natal Bank, Church St., PMB 1858. C.J. Cato. (Ogilvie Collection)

143, 144   Metropolitan Methodist Church, Chapel St., PMB. (N. Mus.)

145   Methodist Church, West St., Durban. 1858. (L.H.M.)

146   Methodist Chapel, Berea, DBN. 1866. (L.H.M.)

141	142
	143
	145
144	146

147 (opposite above)
Methodist Church, Richmond. 1860

148 (opposite below)
Methodist Chapel, Shafton Grange, Karkloof.
(Now St. Mark's Anglican Church) 1858. (dwg. L.H.M.)

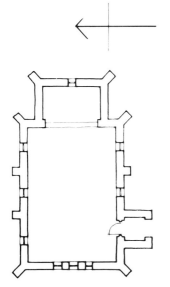

149
Plan, Methodist Chapel, Shafton Grange.

150
Methodist Chapel, Shafton Grange.

151
Entrance door, Mehodist Chapel, Shafton
Grange.

152
Anglican Church, Mt. Moreland. Adams. 1857.
(N.U.P.)

153
St. Thomas' Church, DBN. 1864. (L.H.M.)

149	150	151	154
152		153	Prefabricated Gothic; St. Augustine's Church,
154			DBN. (L.H.M.)

155   Dutch Reformed Church, Market Square, PMB. E. Tatham. 1857. (N. Mus.)

156	157
158	
160	159
161	

156
Dutch Reformed Church, PMB.

157
Dutch Reformed Church, Greytown. 1861.
(K.C.M.)

158
Gabled House, Greytown. c 1885.

159
Church, Kwa Mondi. (K.C.M.)

160
House Colenbrander, New Guelderland. 1860.
(N. Mus.)

161
Overport House, Berea, DBN. 1860. (N. Arc.)

162, 163   Overport House, DBN. (L.H.M.)

164   The Gothic Hall, Overport House, DBN. (L.H.M.)

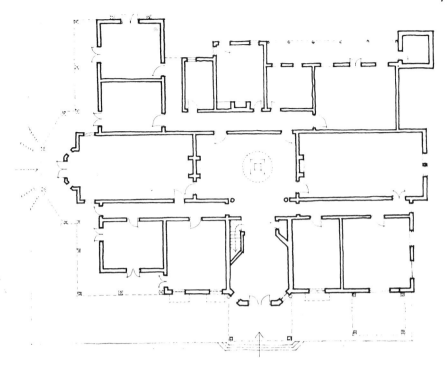

165 (above) : Reconstructed plan, Overport House. DBN.

166 (below) : Plan, House North, Northdene, 1861.

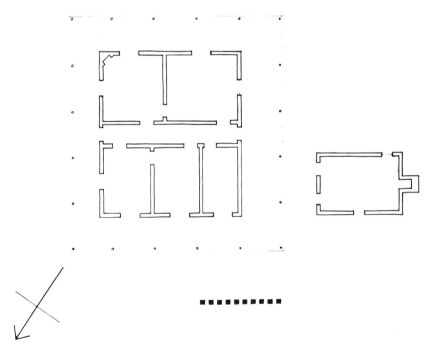

167 (above), 168 (left), 169 (below) : House North. (R.B. Lewcock).

170 : The Magistracy, Umzinto. 1865.   171 : House, Boom St., PMB. 1862.   172 : Warrington House, Church St., PMB. 1859.   173 : House, Pietermaritz St., PMB.   174 : Cottage, Carbineer St., PMB.

	170
171	172
173	174

175 : House, PMB.   176 : House Berg St., PMB.   177 : House
Sutherlands. 1861. (Ogilvie Collection).   178 : House, Chapel St.,
PMB. (R.B. Lewcock.)

175   176

177

178

179 : Farmhouse, Dargle. (L.H.M.)   180 : Leaded-light window, House, Loop St., PMB.   181 : Houses and shops, Longmarket St., PMB. 182, 183 : Plan and elevation of a proposed cottage. C.J. Cato. c. 1865. (Drawings L.H.M.)

179

180   181

183   182

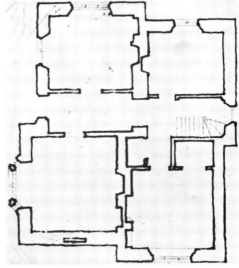

184 (right)
Elevation of a proposed villa. C.J.Cato.
c.1865. (Drawing L.H.M.)

185 (centre)
Courthouse and Post Office, PMB. P.Paterson.
C.E. 1864.

186 (bottom)
Courthouse and Post Office, PMB. (N.MUS.)

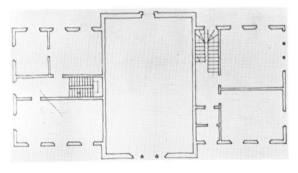

187

188   189

190

187
Courthouse, DBN. P.Paterson. C.E. 1865-1866. (L.H.M.)

188
Front elevation of Courthouse, DBN. (Drawing L.H.M.)

189
Plan of Courthouse, DBN. (from Drawing L.H.M.)

190
Lighthouse, Bluff, DBN. 1864. P.Paterson. C.E. (L.H.M.)

193 (above) and 194 (opposite): Collegiate Institution (Boy's Model School) PMB, 1862. P. Paterson. C.E. (N.MUS.)

192 (above): Public Library and Reading Room, Market Square, DBN.
R.S. Upton. 1879. (L.H.M.)

194
191   195
196   197

Fig. 191: Library, York. 1871.
195 : St. Mary's School, Richmond. c. 1869. (Ogilvie Collection). 196 : St. Mary's Church and Presbytery, Loop St., PMB. 1875. (N. MUS.) 197: St. Mary's Presbytery, Loop St., PMB. (Now Convent of the Holy Family) 1875. (R.B. Lewcock.)

198	199
200	
201	
202	203

198 Convent of the Holy Family, Loop St., PMB. 1876.

199 St. Charles College, Loop St., PMB. 1875-1876. (N. Arc.)

200 Durban Collegiate Institute, M. Holmes. 1878. (L.H.M.)

201 Girls Collegiate School, Quadrangle, Burger St., PMB. F.J. Alexander. 1878. (N. MUS.)

202 Girls Collegiate School and Hall, Burger St. elevation. PMB. (R.B. Lewcock)

203 Interior of St. Saviour's Cathedral, PMB. 1868. (N. MUS.)

204 (top) : St. Saviour's Cathedral, PMB.   205 (above left) : Pulpit.
St. Saviour's Cathedral, PMB.   206 (above right) : Baptismal Font, St.
Saviour's Cathedral, PMB.

208 (top left) : Macrorie House, Loop St., PMB. 1852, 1867.   209 (top right) : Gable, Macrorie House, PMB.   210 (centre left) : St. Patrick's Church, Umzinto.   211 (centre right) : Interior, St. Patrick's Church, Umzinto.   212 (left) : St. Luke's Church, Howick. 1868.

213 (top) : St. Matthias Church, Estcourt. 1872. (N. MUS.)

214, 215 (lower left and right) : Ebenezer Chapel, Ebenezer St., PMB.
1865. (N. MUS.)

216   217
218   219
220

216 : St. John's Church, Longmarket St.,
PMB. 1878. (N. MUS.)   217 : Baptist
Church, West St., DBN. 1874.   218 :
Methodist Church, West St., DBN. R. Ridge-
way. 1877. (L.H.M.)   219 : St. Cyprian's
Church, DBN. 1877. (L.H.M.)   220 : Bel-
fry, St. Cyprian's Church, DBN. (L.H.M.)

221	222
223	224
	225

221   Wesleyan Churches, Greytown.

222   Wesleyan Chruch, Dundee.

223.   Lutheran Church, New Germany.

224   Lutheran Church, Clairmont.

225   Lutheran Church, Dundee.

226, 227 : St. Joseph's Catholic Church, Dbn. (L.H.M.)

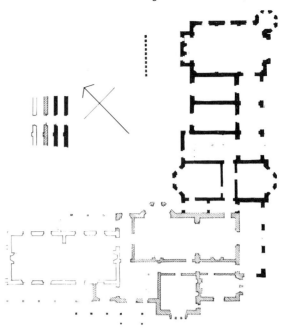

228 (above left)
Sanctuary, Holy Cross Church,
Liverpool. 1859. A.W. Pugin. 'History
Of Holy Cross Parish'.

229 (left)
Emmanuel Cathedral, DBN.
W. Street-Wilson. 1901.

230 (above right)
Plan, Government House, Longmarket St., PMB. 1852-1892.

231 (above)
Government House, PMB. 1867. (Ogilvie Collection)

232 (left)
Porte-cochère and mounting block. Government House, PMB. 1867. (Ogilvie Collection)

233 (below)
Government House, PMB. 1878. (Ogilvie Collection)

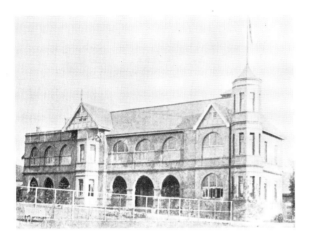

234   236

235

237

234   Additions to Government House, PMB. 1888 and 1890. (Ogilvie Collection).

235   Portsdown House, DBN. c 1856. R.S. Upton. (L.H.M.)

236   Caister House, DBN. 1867.

237   Manor House, Ridge Rd., DBN. (L.H.M.)

238 (top) : South elevation, Coedmore.
1875. (Dwg. R. Keating).   239 (above left)
Coedmore, DBN.   240 (above right) :
Tower Buildings, West St., DBN. (L.H.M.)
241 : (left) : Hotel Harding. (L.H.M.)

242	243
244	245
246	

242 Dykes Mill, Verulam. 1869. (Don. Lib.)

243 Shop, Timber St., PMB. (R.B. Lewcock.)

244 McDonald Bros., Longmarket St., PMB.

245 Burnham's Store, West St., DBN. (L.H.M.)

246 Randall's Bros., West St., DBN. (L.H.M.)

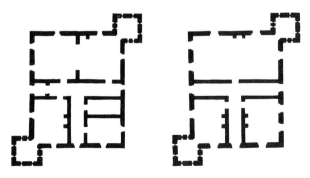

247, 248 (above) Blockhouse (Fort Durnford), Estcourt, 1874.
(N. MUS.)

249 (left) Plans, Fort Durnford,
Estcourt. (From Dwgs.
Estcourt Town Engineer)

Figures 250 - 251 / 155

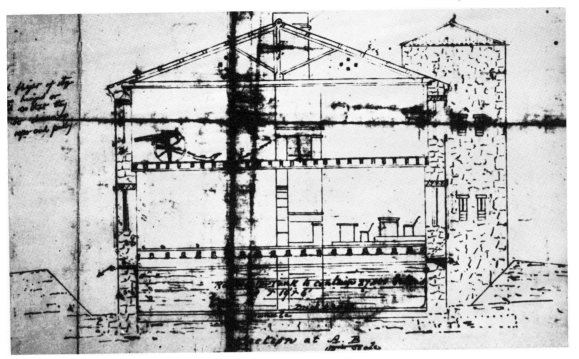

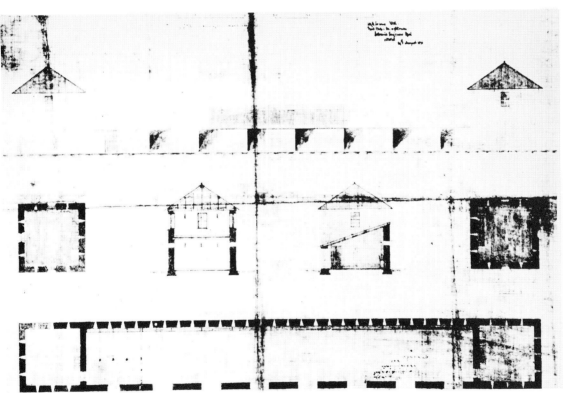

250 (top) : Section, Fort Durnford, Estcourt. (Estcourt Town Engineer)
251 : Design for Stables and Picquet Rooms, Fort Durnford. 1874.
('Estcourt Town Engineer').

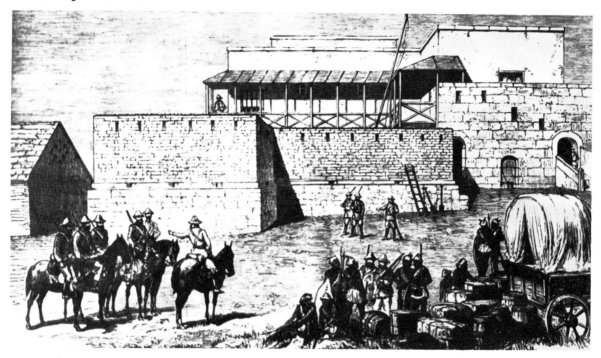

252 (top) : Verulam, Laager, 1879. (London Illustrated News, 'The Zulu War'.)   253 (above), 254 (overleaf) : Laager, Greytown. 1879. ('The Zulu War', London Illustrated News, 1879).

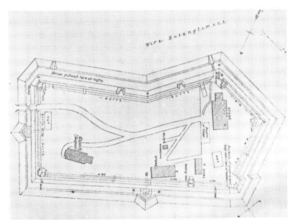

254

255   256

257   258

255, 256 : Eshowe, Fort Kwamondi, 1879.
(B.P.P. 1880, c 2505.)   257 : Fort Melville,
1879. (London Illustrated News, 'The Zulu
War', 1879.)   258 : Fort Napoleon, Zululand. (Dwg. G.I. Thompson. K.C.M.)

259   260

261

262

263

259 : Fort Mistake, Biggarsberg, 1881.
(K.C.M.)   260 : Fort Pine, Dundee. 1879.
(K.C.M.)   261 : Fort Amiel, Newcastle.
1879. (N. MUS.)   262, 263 : Fort Nonquai, Eshowe. c 1882. (K.C.M.)

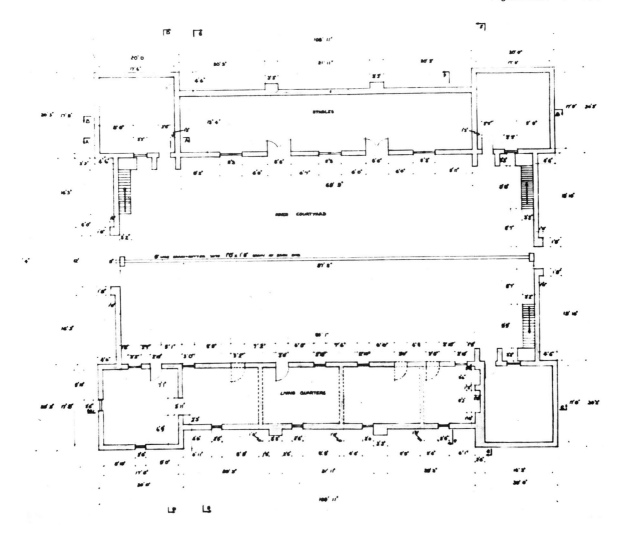

264 : Measured drawings, Fort Nonquai. (C. Coetzee.)

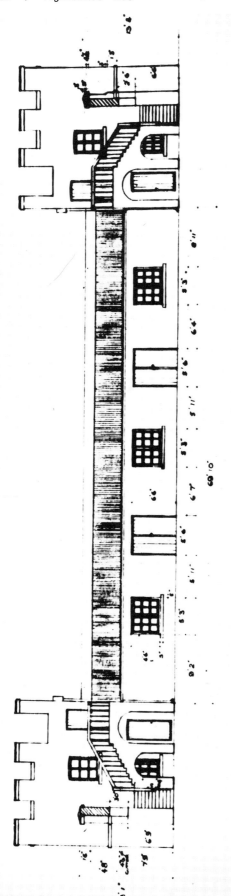

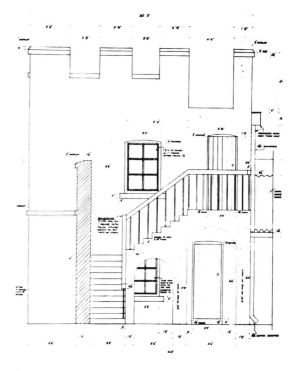

265, 266 : Measured drawings, Fort Nonquai (C. Coetzee)

267	268
269	270
271	
	272

267-270 : Houses with front verandas, PMB.
1860-1900. (R.B. Lewcock.)   271 : House
Howick.   272 : A late nineteenth century
veranda. (L.H.M.)

273 : Veranda-House, Estcourt.   274 : Veranda-house, Newcastle.
275 : Veranda-house, Willowfountain, 1882. (Ogilvie Collection).
276 : Veranda-house, Greytown.   277 : Veranda-house, Wakesleigh
Drive, Bellair, Durban.

273	274
275	276
277	

278 (top)   : Veranda-house, Harding. 'Twentieth Century Impressions
                Of Natal'.

279 (above) : Veranda-house, Willowfountain. c 1860 (Ogilvie Collec-
              tion.)

280 (top)
House M'kondeni, PMB. 1862. (Ogilvie Collection)

281 (left)
Domestic building forms in Natal, 1824-1893.

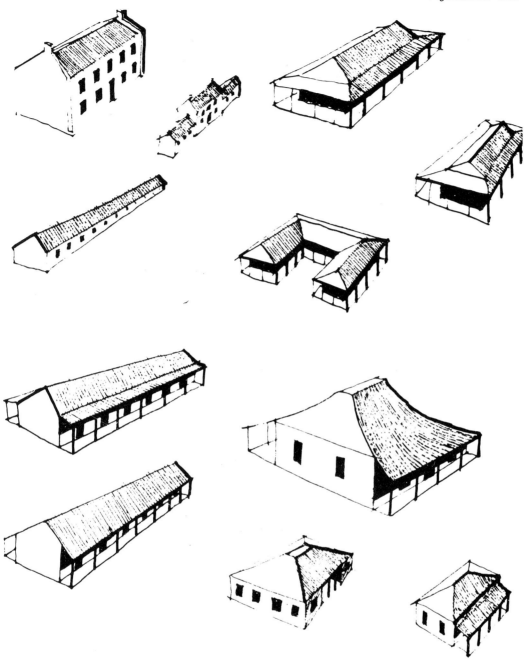

282, 283
Domestic building forms in Natal, 1824-1893

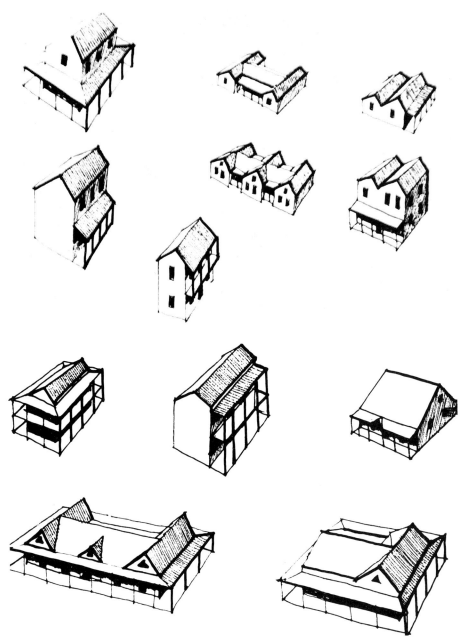

284, 285
Domestic building forms in Natal, 1824-1893

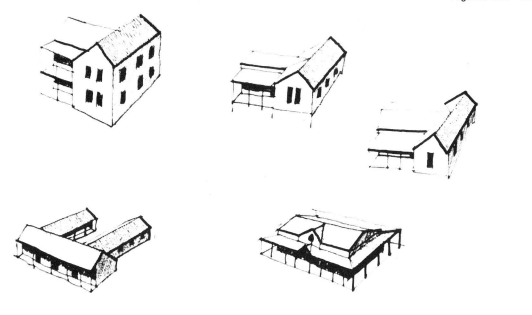

286 (top)
Domestic building forms in Natal, 1824-1893

287 (above) : Veranda-house, Longmarket St., PMB. c 1870.

288
House, Pinetown. (R.B. Lewcock.)

289
Elizabeth Nursing Home, Northdene, (R.B. Lewcock.)

290
House, Bellair, DBN. (R.B. Lewcock.)

291-292
Veranda columns and brackets.

292
House Shepstone, PMB. 1855. (N. MUS.)

288   289
290
292   291

293
House, DBN. 1865.

294
House, Fort Napier. PMB. c 1900.
(R.B. Lewcock.)

295
House, DBN. 1870. (L.H.M.)

296-300
Veranda brackets and balustrades.

297
Dinizulu's house, Vryheid. c 1900. (N. Arc.)

293	294
	295
296	297

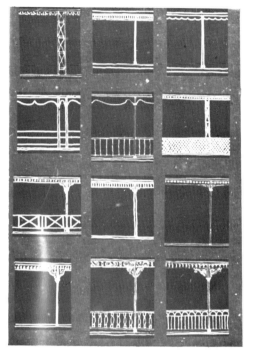

299   300

302   303

301

299 : House, Prince Alfred St., PMB. 1895.   300 : House, Voortrekker St., Newcastle. 1875.   301 : House, Mooi River. 1895.   302 : House, Ridge Rd., DBN. 1903. (Don. Lib.)   303, 306 : Veranda fascias, brackets and balustrades.

304	305
306	307
308	

304   Post Office, Inanda. 1880.

305, 306   Houses, Glenwood, DBN. c
             1885.

307, 313   Verandas; fused fascias and
             brackets.

308   House, Loop St.,PMB. c 1875.

309
Port Captain's House, Point, DBN. 1900.
(L.H.M.)

310
Belgrave Hotel, DBN. (L.H.M.)

311
House, Chelmsford Rd., DBN. 1900.

312
House, Chelmsford Rd., DBN. 1900.

313
Gaoler's House, Newcastle. 1895.

309   310
311   312
313

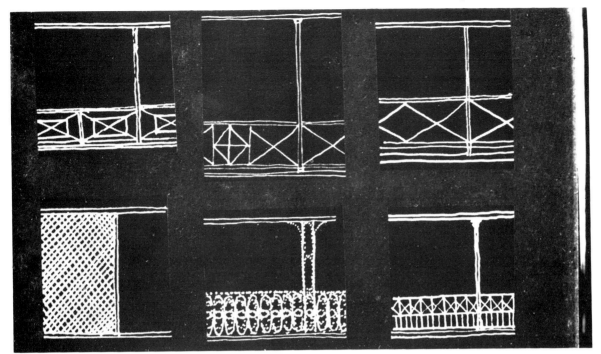

314-318 (above and overleaf)
Balustrades and Trellis.

315 (centre)
House, DBN. 1859. (L.H.M.)

316 (left)
House, Berea, DBN. 1865. (K.C.M.)

317 (top Left) : Mackenzie Nursing Home, Berea, DBN. 1890. (L.H.M.)

318 (top right) : House, Burger St., PMB. 1889.

319 (above)   : House, Bulwer Rd., DBN. 1895.

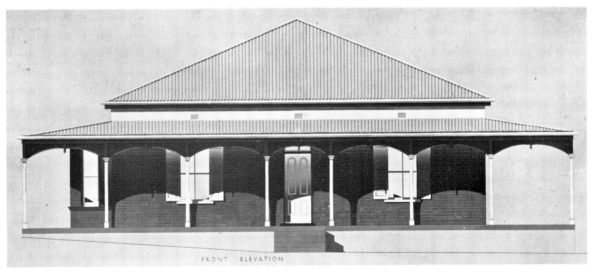

FRONT ELEVATION

320 (top)
Tweedie Hall, Howick. W. Street-Wilson, c 1890.

321 (above)
House North (2), Northdene. 1904. (Dwg. R. Sears.)

322 (left)
Downside, PMB. 1857. (Ogilvie Collection).

323	324
325	326
327	

323
Hindu Temple, Tongaat. 1895. (R.B. Lewcock).

324
"Greystones", near Estcourt. 1873.

325-328
Fretwork patterns - 1890's. Houses, Glenwood, DBN.

326
Veranda, House, Glenwood, DBN.

328 (top left) : Fretwork pattern   330 (top right): Shop, West St., DBN. 1880.

329 (above) : House, Burger St., PMB. 1895.

331, 332 : House Loudon, Ridge Rd., DBN. c 1895.

332	333
334	335
336	

332
Living Room, House Loudon.

333
Fireplace, House O'Brien, Burger St., PMB.
c 1900.

334
Encaustic tile pattern. 'Eastlake, Hints on
Household Taste'.

335,336
Wallpaper designs. 'Eastlake, Hints On
Household Taste'.

337

338

339

337
Plan, House, 10th Ave., Greyville, DBN. c 1900.
(Dwg. L. Chapson.)

338
Veranda-house, Hillary. DBN. 1885. (R.B. Lewcock).

339
House with veranda, New England Rd., PMB.

340 (above left)
Rear garden, Warrington House, PMB. 1855.

341 (above right)
House, Longmarket St., PMB. c 1875.

342 (left)
House, Pietermaritz St., PMB. 1885.

343 (below)
House, Loop St., PMB. 1885.

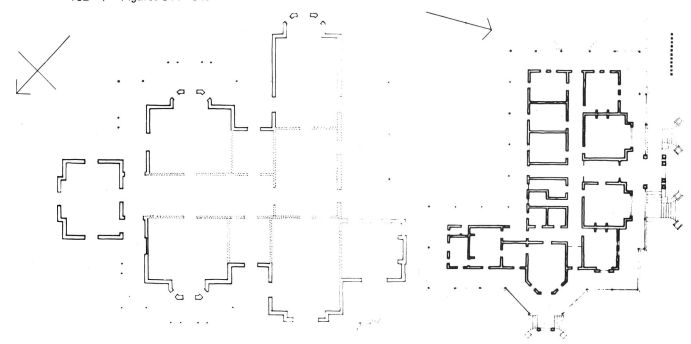

344 (top left) : Plan, House Overpark, Loop St., PMB. 1884. (Meas. Dwg. M. Loveridge.)   345 (above) : Overpark, Loop St., PMB. 1884.   346 (top right) : Sans Soucci, Trelawney Rd., PMB. 1883. A. Halder. (Meas. Dwg. A. Wilson.)

347 (top)
Sans Soucci, 1883. 'Twentieth Century Impressions Of Natal'.

348 (above)
Sans Soucci, 1883. (P.C. Newmarch).

349 (top) : Sans Soucci, 1883 (P.C. Newmarch).   350 : (above left) :
Sans Soucci, 1883 (P.C. Newmarch).   351 (above right) : Trading
stores, Umzinkulu. c. 1905.

352 (top)   : W. Sink's store, Richmond. 1870. (N. MUS.)

354 (above left) : House with veranda-room, Seaview, DBN. 1890.

355 (above right) : Gazebo-roof. Malvern, DBN. c 1885. (R.B. Lewcock).

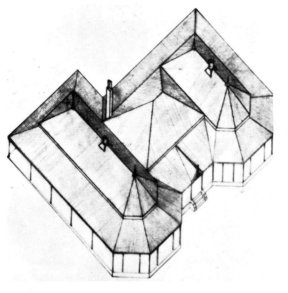

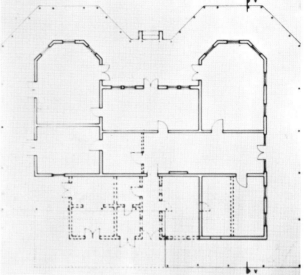

356 (top left)   : Axonometric of Trevean, Bellair. R.S. Upton. 1882. (Dwg. P. Pretorius).

357 (top right)   : Plan, Trevean. (Dwg. P. Pretorius.)

358 (above), 359, 360: Trevean, Bellair. 1882. R.S. Upton. (R.B. Lewcock.)

359 (top)
Trevean, Bellair.

360 (centre)
Trevean, Bellair.

361
Billiard Room, Trevean.
c 1895. (Dwg. M.J. Truscott.)

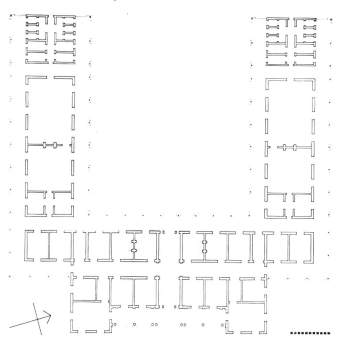

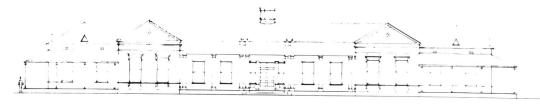

362, 363 : Plan and elevation of Addington Hospital, DBN. R.S. Upton
and P.M. Dudgeon. 1877 (RECONSTRUCTION BY THE
AUTHOR.)

364   : Addington Hospital, DBN. 1877. (L.H.M.)

365   : Entrance, Addington Hospital.

362   365

363

364

366 (left)
Kitchen block, Addington Hospital,
P.M. Dudgeon. 1877.

367 (below)
Additions to Addington Hospital, 1892.
W. Street-Wilson. (L.H.M.)

368 (top) : Alexandra Hotel, Point Rd., DBN. 1879.
P.M. Dudgeon. (L.H.M.)   369 (centre) : Ulundi
Court, Royal Hotel, Smith St., DBN. 1890. (L.H.M.)
370 (left) : Warehouse and offices, James and Hitchens,
Bamboo Square, Point, DBN. P.M. Dudgeon. 1881.
(L.H.M.)

371 (top)
Sutton Flack and Co., Commercial Rd.,
DBN. 1881. (L.H.M.)

372 (centre)
Plan, Town Hall, Durban. (Now Post Office)
P.M. Dudgeon. 1881-1885 (RECONSTRUC–
TION BY AUTHOR).

373 (left), 374
Town Hall, DBN.

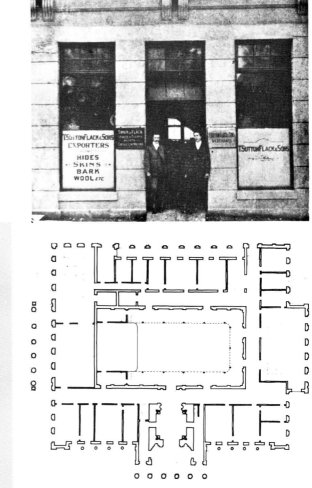

374 : Town Hall, Durban.   375 : Town Hall, Leeds C. Brodrick.
1853.   376 : Town Hall, Portsmouth. W. Hill. 1884.   377. : Rear
elevation, Town Hall, DBN. (L.H.M.)

374   375

376   377

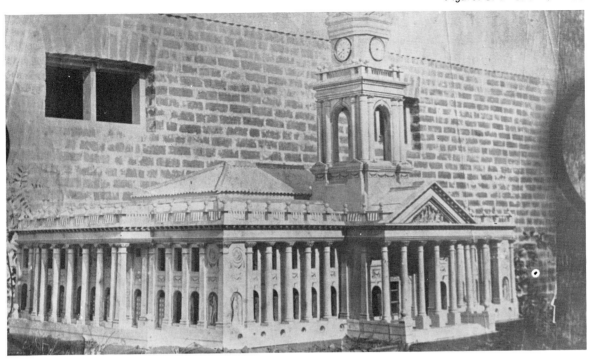

378 (above)
Model of Durban Town Hall. P.M. Dudgeon.
(L.H.M.)

379 (left)
Detail of Elevation, Town Hall, DBN.

380 (above), 381 (below)
Interior, Town Hall. DBN. (L.H.M.)

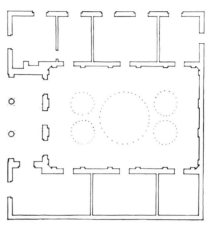

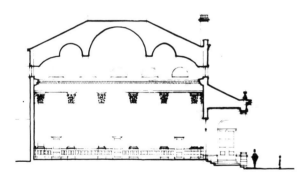

382 : Veranda. Harvey, Greenacre and Co., West St., DBN. P.M. Dudgeon. 1882. (L.H.M.)   383 : Town Offices, Church St., PMB. Upper Floor, P.M. Dudgeon.   384 : Masonic Temple, Kokstad. P.M. Dudgeon. 1882. (L.H.M.)   385 : Plan, Standard Bank, Church St., PMB. P.M. Dudgeon. 1881, 1882.   386 : Section, Standard Bank, PMB. 387 : Standard Bank, PMB.

382	383
384	385
386	
387	

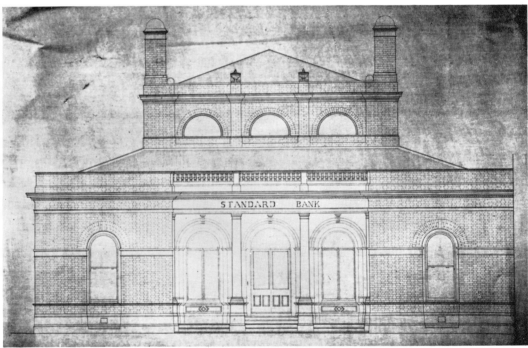

388 (top left) : Cast Iron Railings, Standard Bank, PMB. 389 (above)
Church Street elevation, Standard Bank, PMB. 390 (top right) ; Interior, Standard Bank. PMB.

391 (above)
Standard Bank, PMB.
(R.B. Lewcock).

392 (left)
Chimney, Standard Bank,
PMB.

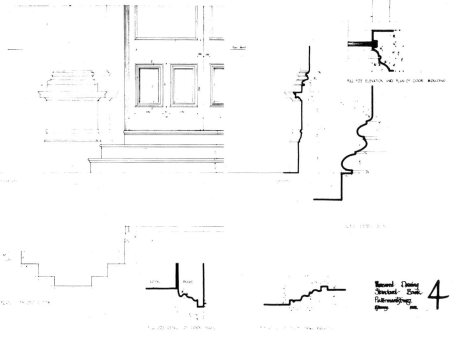

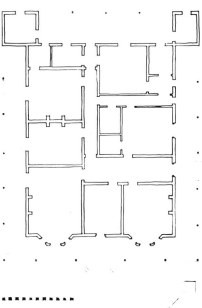

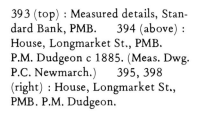

393 (top) : Measured details, Standard Bank, PMB.   394 (above) : House, Longmarket St., PMB. P.M. Dudgeon c 1885. (Meas. Dwg. P.C. Newmarch.)   395, 398 (right) : House, Longmarket St., PMB. P.M. Dudgeon.

396-398 (above & right)
House, Longmarket St. Pmb. P.M. Dudgeon.

399 (below)
Clark House, Pietermaritzburg College.
P.M. Dudgeon, 1885-86. (meas. Dwg.
P.J. Englebrecht).

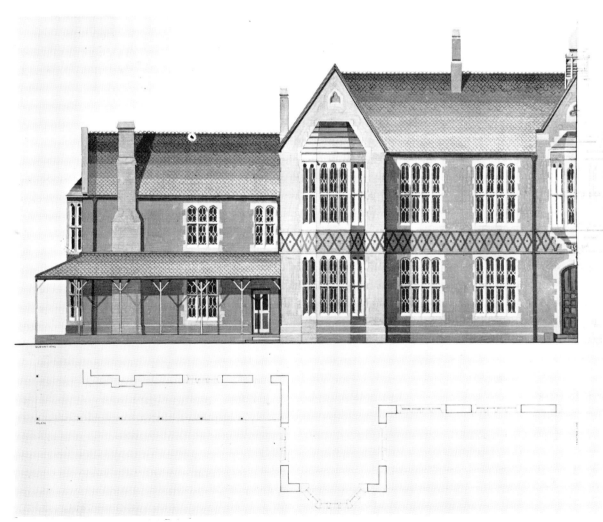

400, 401 : Pietermaritzburg College. The Victoria Hall on the left of
400 dates from 1895. (Ogilvie Collection).

402	403
404	405
406	

402   Norwegian Church, Marburg. 1882.

403, 404   Marianhill, the Village (Marianhill)

405   Monastery tower, Marianhill.

406   Abbott's house, Marianhill.

407 (top left), 408 (top right) : Monastery gateway, Marianhill. 409
(above), 410 : Cathedral, Marianhill.

410 (top)
Cathedral, Marianhill.

411 (above left)
Doorway, Cathedral, Marianhill.

412 (above right)
Convent, Marianhill. (The part of the building
on the left was built after 1920).

413 : Marianhill Mission church, Ixopo   414 : Veranda-house, Marianhill Mission, Ixopo.   415 : St. Dominic's Academy, Newcastle. 1892. 'Natal Mercury Pictorial', 1903.   416 : Chapel, St. Dominic's Academy, Newcastle. 1892.   417 : Oakford Priory. 1885. 'Natal Mercury Pictorial 1903'.

413	414
415	416
417	

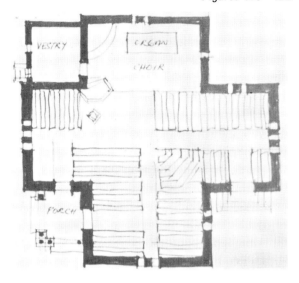

418	419
420	421
422	

418
Cathedral, Memorial crypt, DBN. 1886.

419
Plan, Berea Presbyterian Chruch, W.E. Robarts. 1884.

420, 421
St. Andrew's Presbyterian Church, Commercial Rd., DBN. 1892.

422
Dutch Reformed Church, Vryheid. 1893.
(N. MUS.)

423

424   425

426

423, 424 : Dutch Reformed
Church, Vryheid, 1893. (N. Mus);
425 : Side entrance, Dutch Reformed
Church, Vryheid, 1893.   426 :
Dutch Reformed church, Utrecht,
1893.

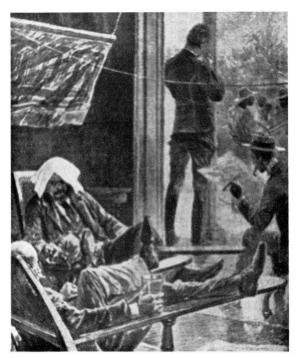

427   428

429   430

431

427
Athenium, Chapel St., PMB. (Ogilvie Collection).

428
Fence, Athenium, Chapel St., PMB.

429
Entrance doorway, Athenium, Chapel St, PMB.

430
Prince Alfred Lodge, PMB. 1885. (N.MUS.)

431
Lounge, Durban Club. 1880's. (Dwg. L.H.M.)

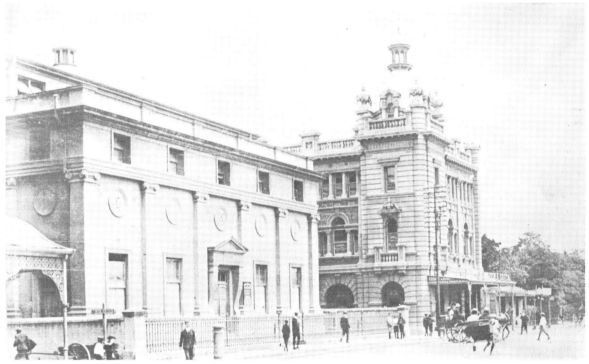

432 (top)   : Theatre Royal, West Street, DBN. 1882. (L.H.M.)

433 (above), 434 : Port Natal Masonic Lodge, Smith St., DBN. 1893.
                   (L.H.M.)

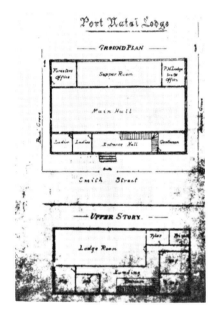

434 (top)   : Port Natal Masonic Lodge, Smith St., DBN. (L.H.M.)

435 (above left) : Plan, Port Natal Masonic Hall, Smith St., DBN.
                           1893 (MASONIC ARCHIVES).

436 (above right) : Commercial buildings, DBN. c. 1890. (L.H.M.)

437   438

439

440

437
Design for a Civil Service Club. G.H. Rodwell. 1889. (N.ARC.)

438
A gabled, commercial building, DBN. Early 1890's. (L.H.M.)

439
Commercial buildings, Smith St., DBN. (L.H.M.)

440
Tower, Bamboo Square, Point, Durban. W. Street-Wilson. (L.H.M.)

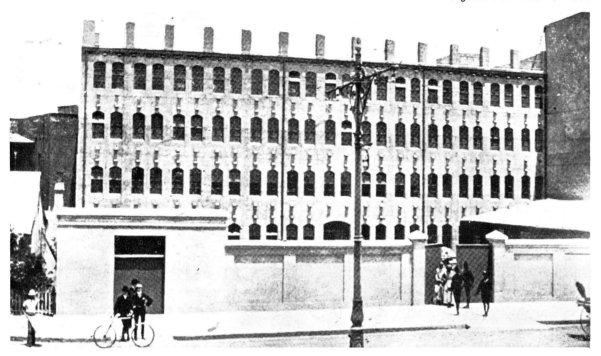

441 (above)
Barracks, African Boating Co., DBN.
'Twentieth Century Impressions Of Natal'.

442 (left)
Masonic Hotel, West St., DBN. (L.H.M.)

443 (below)
Humphrey's Hotel, Amamzintoti. 1895.
(L.H.M.)

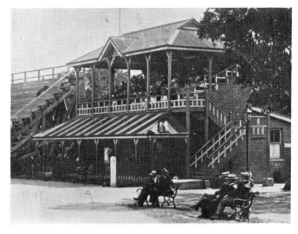

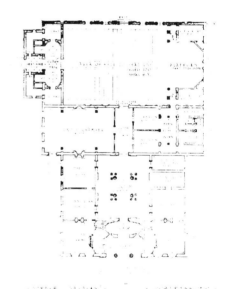

444	445
446	447
448	449

444 : Public Baths, West St., DBN. W.H. Powell. 1891. (L.H.M.)   445
Albert Park Pavilion, 1889. (L.H.M.)   446 : Market Hall, Market
Square, PMB. J.S. Brunskill 1884. (N. MUS.)   447, 448 : Ladysmith
Town Hall, R. Walker. 1894. (N. MUS.)

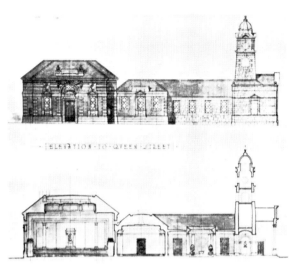

449 (previous page), 450 (top left)
Plan, Elevation and Section of additions to Ladysmith Town Hall. Cock and Ralston. 1917. 'Journal of Transvaal Architects, 1917'.

451 (top right), 452 (left)
Town Hall, Newcastle. W. Lucas. 1898.

453 (overleaf)

454 (below)
Town Hall, PMB. 1893.

453 : Perspective, Town Hall, PMB. W. Street-Wilson and P. Barr. 1893.
(N. MUS.)

455 (above)
Interior, Town Hall, PMB. 1893. (L.H.M.)

456 (left)
Tower, Town Hall, PMB. 1899.

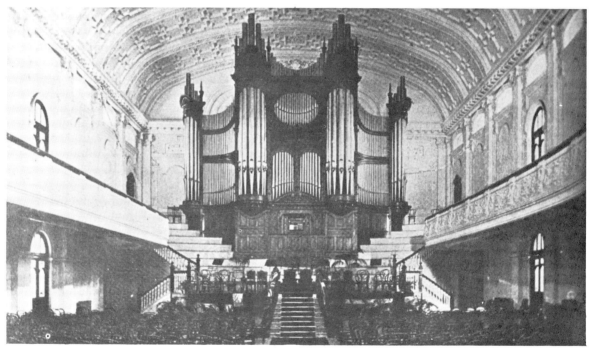

456a (top)   : Town Hall. PMB, from Commercial Rd. (N.MUS.)

457 (above) : Interior, Town Hall, PMB. 1899.

458 (left)
Town Hall, PMB. 1899.

459 (below)
Ground floor plan, Town Hall, PMB.
(RECONSTRUCTION BY THE AUTHOR
FROM DWGS. CITY ENGINEER PMB.)

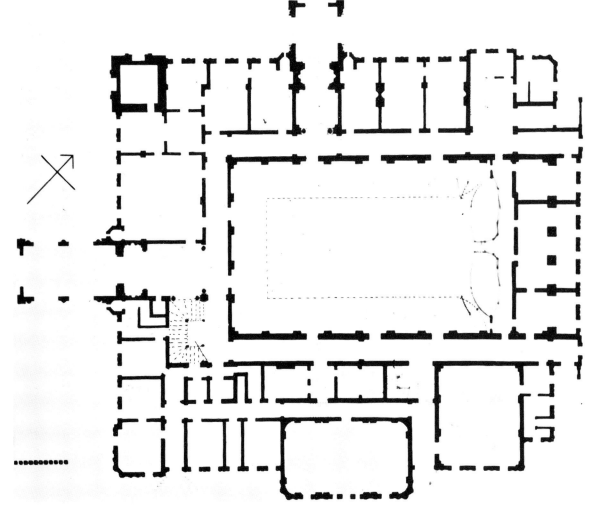

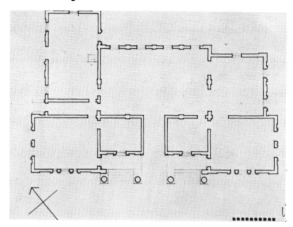

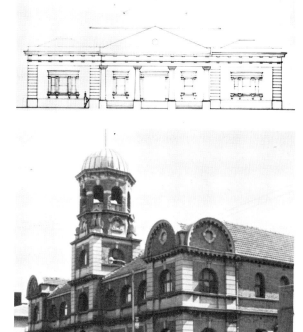

460, 461 : Plan and elevation of Custom's House, Point, DBN. C. Jenkyn. 1884. (Meas. Dwg. Author.)   462 : Custom's House, DBN. 1884. (Roof originally of slate.)   463 : Water Police Station, Point Rd., DBN. 1884. C. Jenkyn.   464 : Boy's Preparatory School, Pietermaritz St., PMB. A. Singleton. (N. MUS.)

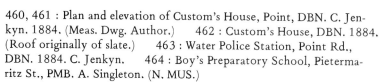

460   461
464   463
462

465   466

467   469

468

465 : Courthouse, Estcourt. A. Singleton.
1887.   466 : Courthouse, Dundee. A. Sin-
gleton. 1888.   467 : Tollhouse, Colenso.
A. Singleton. (1879) (by courtesy of
J. Clarke).   468, 469 : Asylum, Town Hill,
PMB. Colonial Engineer. 1876 and 1889.

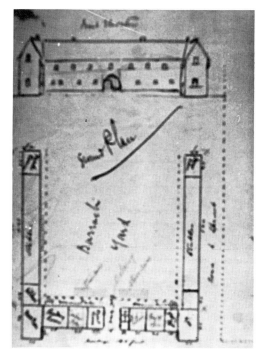

470 (top left) : Entrance Portico, Asylum, PMB. 1889.

471 (top right) : Sketchplan, Mounted Police Barracks. A. Hyme. 1878.
(N. Arc.)

472 (above) : Mounted Police Barracks, Alexandra Rd., PMB. 1876-
1890.

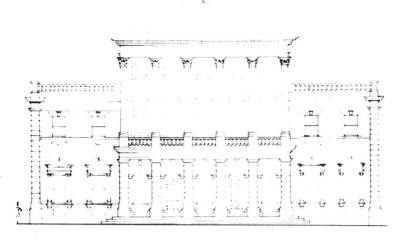

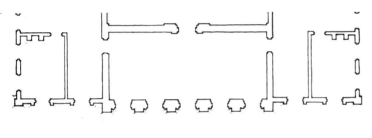

473   474

475

476

473
Part plan and elevation, Legislative Assembly building, Longmarket St., PMB. J. Tibbit. 1886.

474
Details, Entrance Portico, Legislative Assembly building, PMB.

475
Design for the Clark Hall, Paisley, Scotland. W.H. Lynn. 1875.

476
Cast Iron fence and gate, Legislative Assembly building, PMB.

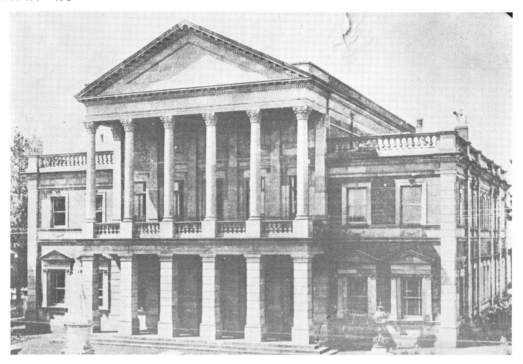

477 (top)   : Legislative Assembly building, PMB. 1886 (N.MUS.)

478 (above left) : Legislative Assembly building, PMB. 1901.

479 (above right) : An Edwardian Town house, Berea Rd., DBN. 1904.
                    (Dwg. C. Borges de Costa.)

480 (top)   : Penshurst, Essenwood Rd., DBN. W. Street-Wilson. 1904.
              (Dwg. D Rosswatt).

481 (above) : House Bunting, Pietermaritz St., PMB. 1897. (Dwg.
              P. Englebrecht.)

482 (top)
Emmanuel Cathedral, DBN. W. Street-Wilson
and A. Fyfe. 1901.

483 (left)
Presbyterian Church , Howick, 1897.

484 (above)
Design for the Inchanga hotel, W. Street-
Wilson. 1901.

485 (top left)   : St. Peter's Anglican Church, Vryheid. Baker and
                    Fleming. 1911.

486 (top right) : Club Arcade, Smith St., DBN. H.G. Veale. 1901.
                    (L.H.M.)

487 (above)   : Pietermaritzburg. 1853. (N. MUS.)

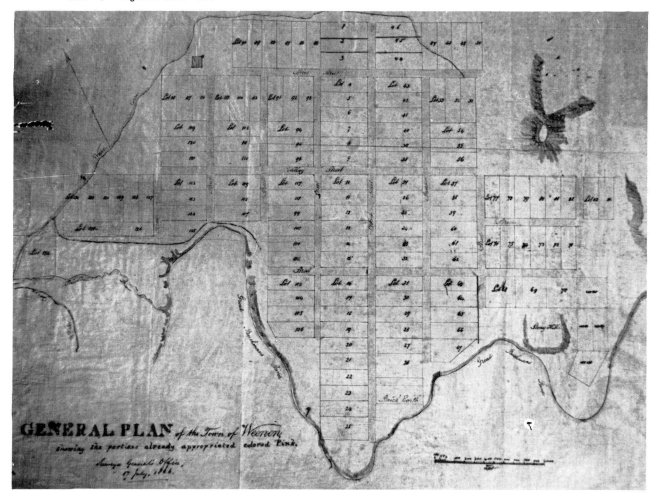

487a (above)
Plan of Weenen. S.G.O. 1866. (Laid out 1839) (N. Arc.)

488 (left)
Utrecht, 1880's (K.C.M.)

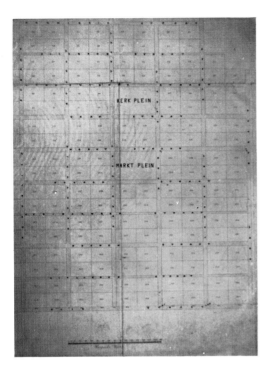

489 (left)
Plan of Paulpietersberg, 1896. (N. Arc).

490 (below)
Plan of Richmond, J. Moreland. 1850.
(N. Arc.)

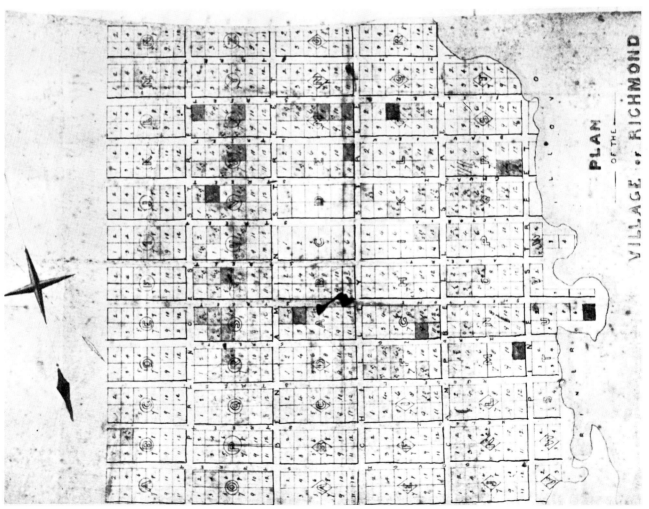

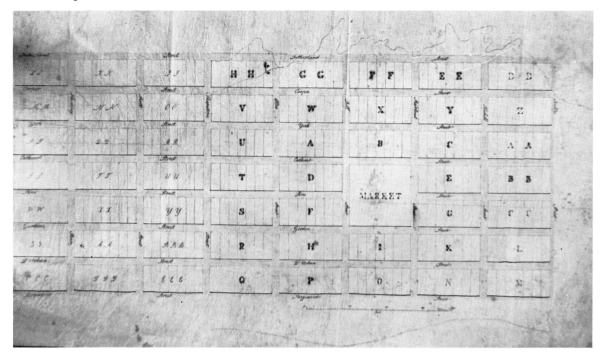

491 (above) : Plan of Greytown, 1850. T. Oakes. (N. Arc.)

492 (below) : Plan of Ladysmith, J.Bird. 1850. (N. Arc.)

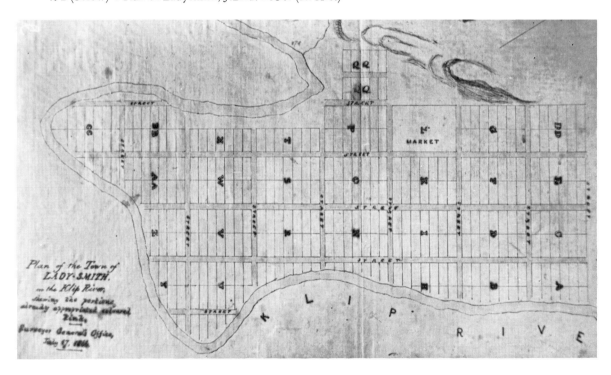

493 (above)
Town allotments. PMB. (N. Arc.)

493a (left)
Sluits, Longmarket St., PMB. 1860's.

PLAN OF THE TOWN OF D'URBAN.

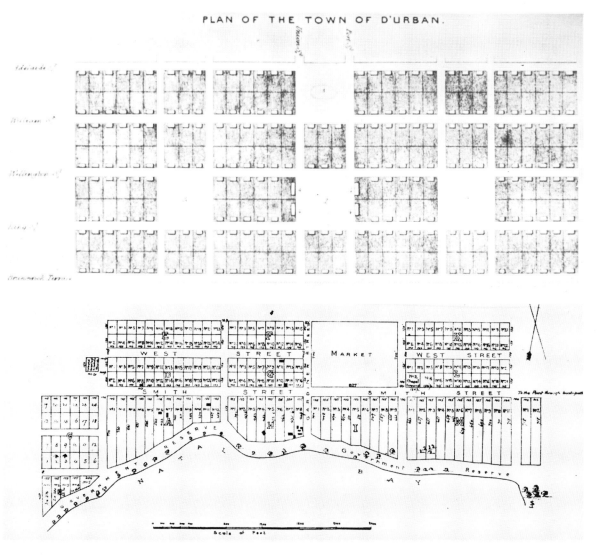

494 : Market day, Market Square, PMB. 1860's (N. Arc.)   495 :
Gardiner's Plan of Durban. 1835. ('A Journey to the Zoolu Country').
496 : Cato's Plan of Durban. 1840. 'Russell., The History Of Old Durban'.   497 : The Umgeni River, DBN. 1851. (Watercolour, K.C.M.)

494   497

495

496

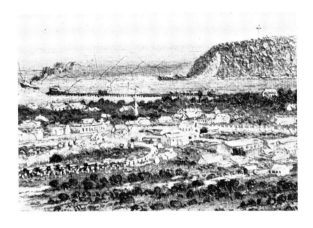

498 (top left)   : Durban from the Berea. 1870. 'Oil Painting', Thomas Baines (O.H.M.)

499 (top right) : Suburban House, Bellair, DBN. 1885. (R.B. Lewcock.)

500 (above)   : A late 19th Century Town house, Chapel St., PMB. (R.B. Lewcock.)

501 (top)   : Pietermaritzburg, 1890. (Ogilvie Collection).

502 (above) : West St., DBN. 1852. (L.H.M.)

503 : Entrance gateway, house, Bulwer Rd., DBN. c 1895.

504 (top)
House, Bulwer Rd., DBN.

505 (above)
Church Street, PMB. 1850 Watercolour by
S. Lloyd. (AFRICANA MUSEUM).

506 (left)
Church Street, PMB. c 1895. (N. MUS.)

507 : Church St., PMB. 1875. (N. MUS.)

508 (above) : Burger St., PMB. 1865.
 (N. MUS.)

509 (below) : West St., DBN. 1878. (Dwg.
 L.H.M.)

509A (above right) : West St., DBN. 1908-9 (Ogilvie Collection).   510
(top) : House North (2), Northdene 1904. (R.B. Lewcock.)

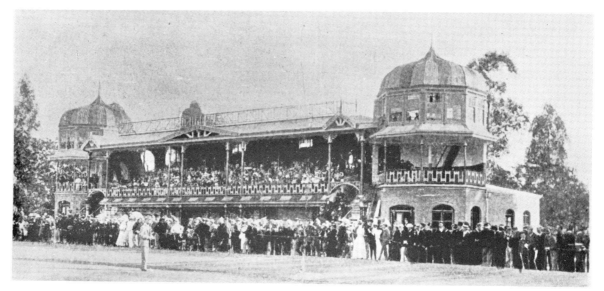

511 (top)   : Town Gardens, DBN. c 1900.

512 (above) : Oval and Jubilee Pavilion, PMB. W. Lucas. 1897.

513 (top left) : Bridge over the Umzinduzi River, Alexandra Park, PMB.

514 (top right) : Fountain, Town Gardens, Ladysmith. (L.H.M.)

515 (above)   : Street, Vryheid.

516 (top left) : Commercial precinct with verandas, Vryheid.   517
(above) : Market Hall, Pine St., DBN. 1901. W. Street-Wilson. Bandstand in the foreground. (L.H.M.)   518 (top right) : Lane between
Longmarket and Church St., PMB.

519   521

522

520

519 : Madressa Arcade, Dbn. c 1910.   520
Rickshas at the intersection of the Victoria
Embankment and Gardiner St., DBN. 1904.
'Twentieth Century Impressions Of Natal'.
521 : Internal wall of reed laths, Warrington
House, Church St., PMB. 1850. (N. MUS).
522 : Stone Church, Dundee. 1903. (Don.
Lib.)

523	524
525	526
527	

523   Wire-cut bricks. House O'Brien, Burger St., PMB. 1895.

524   Facebricks. Thorpe-Lodge, Berea, DBN. c 1905. (L.H.M.)

525   Brick mouldings. Stock Exchange, Timber St., PMB. 1884.

526   Macrorie House, PMB.

527   Colonial makeshift. Stables, House Shepstone, Pine St., PMB.

528   529

530   531

528 : Carved door and etched glass fan and sidelights, Athenium,
Chapel St., PMB. (R.B. Lewcock).   529 : Door, Customs House,
Point, DBN. 1884.   530 : Sliding sash window, House North, Northdene, DBN. 1860. (R.B. Lewcock.)   531, 532. : Sliding Sash windows.
houses Newcastle and PMB.

532
Sliding sash windows, House Newcastle

533.
Stained glass lights to entrance doorway and encaustic tiles to hall floor. House O'Brien, Burger St., PMB.

534
Stained Glass, House Shepstone, PMB. c 1900.

535
Stained glass panel, House O'Brien, Burger St., PMB.

536.
Pan tiled roof, House Loop st., PMB. 1865.

532	533
534	535
	536

537 (top left)   : Tile hung wall, House Burger St., PMB. 1900.

538 (top right) : Corrugated iron sheets and cast-iron tiles, House North,
                       Northdene, 1860 (R.B. Lewcock.)

539 (above)   : Morewood's Sugar Farm at Verulam, c 1852. 'History
                       Of Natal, by W.C. Holden'.

540 : Cast-iron gateway, Overpark, PMB. 1884.

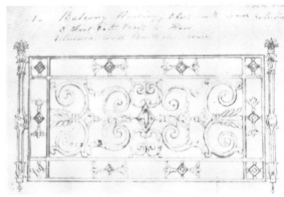

541   542

543   544

545

541, 542
Design for cast-iron balcony panel and
bracket. C.J. Cato. 1862. (L.H.M.)

543
Cast-iron veranda, Talana chemical works,
Dundee. 1890.

544. Jubilee Bandstand, Alexandra Park,
PMB. W. Lucas. 1897. (from Macfarlane's)

545, 547
Vasco da Gama, Memorial clock, Point DBN.
1897.

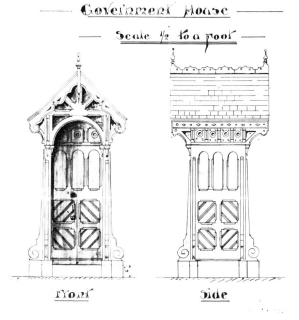

Proposed Sentry Box

Government House

Scale ½ to a foot

front   side

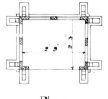

— Plan —

546 (top left) : Cast-iron work, Palmdene, Loop St., PMB. 547 (opposite) : Vasco da Gama Memorial clock. 548 (top right) : Detail of the Standard Bank, PMB, 1881-1882 by P.M. Dudgeon. F.R.I.B.A. 549 (above left) : Detail, Standard Bank, PMB. 1882. P.M. Dudgeon. 550 (above right) : Drawing of a Proposed Sentry Box for Government House, PMB. c 1890. 'Natal Provincial Building Services'.

Index

Figures refer to page numbers in the book; except those with an asterisk, which refer to figure or illustration numbers. Durban has been contracted to Dbn; and Pietermaritzburg to Pmb.